Barbara Morris

Inspiration for Design

THE INFLUENCE OF THE VICTORIA

AND ALBERT MUSEUM

VICTORIA AND ALBERT MUSEUM

Published by the Victoria and Albert Museum, London 1986
Text © 1986 Trustees of the Victoria and Albert Museum
Illustrations © Trustees of the Victoria and Albert Museum
or as acknowledged
All rights reserved

ISBN 0 948107 39 1

Produced by the South Leigh Press Ltd,
The Studio, Chilcroft Road, Kingsley Green, Haslemere, Surrey GU27 3LS

Designed by Peter Campbell

Distributed by Trefoil/V & A Bookservices,
13 St. John's Hill, London SW11

Typeset by AKM Associates (UK) Ltd,
Ajmal House, Hayes Road, Southall, London

Printed in Great Britain by R.J. Acford
Chichester, Sussex

Contents

Acknowledgements

My grateful thanks are due to many of my former colleagues in the Victoria and Albert Museum for their help and advice and for generously passing on information. I am particularly indebted to Anthony Burton for making his notes on the foundation of European museums available to me; to John Physick, whose pioneering work on the history of the Museum buildings has been invaluable, and to Jennifer Opie for her suggestions concerning ceramics. Betty Elzea undertook research for me in the United States and alerted me to a number of useful sources. I must also thank Mr Widar Halen of Norway for generously making available parts of his yet unpublished thesis on Dr Christopher Dresser and the influence of Japan.

My heartfelt thanks also go to David Bowman for patiently typing and re-typing a considerable portion of my original manuscript.

BARBARA MORRIS

Introduction

The influence of the Victoria and Albert Museum on design, from its inception as the Museum of Manufactures at Marlborough House in 1852, is inestimable, and the present volume can only aspire to touch on aspects of it. It is an influence that ranges from the broad conspectus of raising public taste to the specific direct influence of individual objects, or groups of objects in the collections. It is not only an influence confined to this country but one that was to have a profound effect abroad on the development of museums both in Europe and the United States, for in the second half of the 19th century the South Kensington Museum was seen as the model for many museums of the applied arts.

The closely linked South Kensington Museum and School of Art were often described as the 'South Kensington System'. As such they inspired many generations of art students and designers, and, together with the touring exhibitions of objects from the Museum's collections, spread the influence of the Museum far beyond the metropolitan area.

There can hardly be any artist, craftsman or designer working in this country who has not been influenced to some extent by the Museum's collections. Almost any autobiography or volume of reminiscences written by an artist or designer pays tribute to the formative influence of the Museum. The list is almost endless and those I have quoted represent a somewhat arbitrary personal choice.

To attempt to cover the whole field would be virtually impossible and I have therefore chosen to concentrate on aspects that can be fairly precisely documented, either by written or visual evidence. Inevitably there will be important omissions and it is hoped that this volume will at least stimulate further research on this fascinating and never ending subject.

The Precursors

I. THE GOVERNMENT SCHOOLS OF DESIGN

The Victoria and Albert Museum has, since its inception, been concerned with promoting good design; indeed it was conceived for that very purpose, to provide inspiration to designers and manufacturers and to elevate the taste of the general public. In the early 19th century the industrial revolution, with increasing mechanization and new technology replacing the old, traditional methods of handcraftmanship, had led to declining standards in both design and execution. England was facing increasing competition from abroad, especially from France where the Government had been intimately concerned with the design of manufactures since the late 18th century.

In 1835 a Select Committee on Arts and Manufactures was appointed by Parliament 'to enquire into the best means of extending a knowledge of the Arts and of the Principles of Design among the people (especially the manufacturing population) of the country'. One of the committee's recommendations was that 'the opening of public galleries for the people should, as much as possible, be encouraged'.

The British Museum, opened to the public in 1759, was primarily a museum of antiquities, and the National Gallery, started in 1824, was concerned only with paintings. Most provincial museums in existence at that time could perhaps best be described as 'Cabinets of curiosities' which did little to contribute to raising the design consciousness of the population as a whole or to provide inspiration for the designer or artisan.

A further Select Committee in 1836 proposed the introduction of Government Schools of Design, both in London and the provinces, particularly in the centres of manufacture, as were already established in France, Switzerland and Germany. A few firms, among them the Birmingham firm of Jennens and Bettridge, the leading producers of papier-mâché, had their own training schools, and the Birmingham Society of Arts had a collection of casts, but artisans had to pay a guinea subscription to study it. Most artisans had to rely on illustrated periodicals like the *Mechanics Magazine* to obtain more knowledge of their trade or craft. What art schools existed were there to train painters and sculptors, not designers for industry. The report also advocated art training in State-aided elementary schools so that the future artisan, designer or craftsman could be indoctrinated at an early age.

The first Government School of Design was set up by the Board of Trade in 1837 at

Somerset House, in premises recently vacated by the Royal Academy, with John Buonorotti Papworth (1775-1847) as Director.

The School had its own collection of plaster casts and the nucleus of an art library. In 1838, £1,500 was spent on buying examples of contemporary applied art from Paris, and each year further examples were added, including a number of items from the Paris Exhibition of 1844. Copies of Raphael's arabesques in the Vatican, purchased at the sale of John Nash's property, were to prove particularly influential. It was these collections, assembled by the School of Design both for use by students at Somerset House and for circulation to the provinces, that formed the nucleus of the collections of the Victoria and Albert Museum.

The students of the School of Design were initially all male, but in 1842 it was decided to set up a female School of Design 'partly to enable young women of the middle class to obtain an honourable and profitable employment, and partly to improve ornamental design in manufactures'. The first principal of the female school was Mrs Fanny McIan, who steered her students more towards the study of nature than towards plaster casts and secured commissions for them from the goldsmiths Storr and Mortimer, from Apsley Pellatt, the leading London glass manufacturer, from Ackermann and others. She also sold some of her students' designs for the decoration of porcelain, and the annual exhibitions of student work, both male and female, were often to provide suitable designs for manufacturers.

In 1849 a Select Committee was set up to investigate the School of Design and one of its members was Sir Henry Cole (1808-82) whose activities are more fully described in the next chapter. In 1852 Cole was appointed as General Superintendent of the School of Design and he brought about a radical transformation by instituting special technical classes including instruction for moulding and casting in plaster, and enamelling and painting on porcelain. The great German architect and design theoretician, Gottfried Semper (1803-79) was appointed Professor of metalwork, pottery and furniture, a post he held until 1855. Evening classes in architectural detail and construction were arranged under C. J. Richardson, the Elizabethan revivalist. As part of this reorganization, the Female School was moved to Gower Street and renamed the Metropolitan School of Ornament for Females. When the Museum of Ornamental Art was set up at Marlborough House in 1852 (see Chapter III), Cole established a special course for women wishing to study the art of chromolithography in order to illustrate the objects in the collections. Female students were later to play an important part in the decoration of the new museum buildings after the move to South Kensington in 1857. Cole was also successful in winning important public commissions for his students, including the funeral carriage of the Duke of Wellington, the Department of Science and Art post-box, and the decoration of the Prince's Chamber of the House of Lords.

The School of Design had become the Central Training School when it was removed to

Marlborough House in 1852 and was renamed the National Art Training School in 1863. It was reconstituted as the Royal College of Art in 1896, and enjoyed close proximity to the Museum until it was moved into new buildings in Kensington Gore in 1962. The Museum and the art school were always closely linked and in the second half of the 19th century were often referred to jointly as 'South Kensington'. The setting up of an MA Design History Course in 1982, run jointly by the Royal College of Art and the Victoria and Albert Museum with tuition by the staff of both institutions, has re-established this close relationship.

The first provincial School of Design opened at Manchester in 1838 and was recognised for grant in 1842. Between 1842 and 1884 over 200 provincial schools, or classes attached to other institutions were founded throughout England, and to a lesser extent in Scotland and Ireland, together with a number of important London schools such as Lambeth (1854), and Chelsea and Hornsey, both founded in 1882. Until 1889, all these schools followed the Course of Instruction for Government Schools of Art set up by Henry Cole in 1852. National Graded Examinations in Art and Annual National Competitions were also organized and, to ensure the complete uniformity of the courses, thousands of prints and plaster casts had to be produced. Thus not only the National Art Training Schools but also the provincial schools maintained, even if somewhat indirectly, close links with the Museum; after the move of the Museum to South Kensington, the 'South Kensington System' became the main means of training not only painters and sculptors but also designers. To list all the prominent artists and designers who received their training on the South Kensington System would need a book to itself, but among the early pupils were Christopher Dresser (1834-1904), who entered the School of Design in 1847, and Kate Greenaway (1840-1901) who entered the National Art Training School ten years later in 1857.[1] Such was the system's reputation that the great French jeweller and glass artist René Lalique (1860-1945) completed his training at Sydenham School of Art from 1878 to 1880.

II. SIR HENRY COLE

Sir Henry Cole (knighted in 1875) was the most energetic figure in the design reform movement of the 1840s and 1850s and was to become in effect the first director of the Victoria and Albert Museum, being the founder of its ancestor, the Museum of Ornamental Art, an institution he referred to as his 'child'.

Cole came from a modest background, and left Christ's Hospital at the age of fifteen, having won a silver medal for writing which enabled him to get employment as a clerk to Sir Francis Palgrave, a sub-commissioner of the Record Office. Here Cole spent nine years, transcribing ancient documents and preparing them for publication. From 1832 to 1835 he worked directly under the secretary of the Record Commission but was dismissed after a quarrel with his superior. Three years later, in 1838 he was re-instated as an assistant keeper

The 'Hop Story' beer jug designed by J. H. Townsend for Felix Summerly's Art-Manufactures and registered by Minton's in 1847.

at the newly constituted Public Record Office, a post he held until 1852 when he transferred to the Board of Trade.

Here we are only concerned with his career as far as it affected matters of design; other aspects of his public career and his many unofficial activities are fully described elsewhere.[2] Cole's interest in the decorative arts had arisen partly through his official work, which included a handbook on Hampton Court, and his involvement with the Society of Arts. Founded in 1753, the Society of Arts had always been concerned with design, and this interest increased when Prince Albert, himself an amateur designer, became its President in 1843. Cole had first met Prince Albert in 1842, but his involvement with the Society of Arts came about largely through his introduction to John Scott Russell (1808–82) who was then Secretary of the Society. Russell was a marine engineer and later the designer, with Isambard Kingdom Brunel, of the first steamship, the *Great Eastern*. Exact contemporaries, Cole and Russell were kindred spirits and were both railway enthusiasts.

In 1843, having found no suitable picture books for his two daughters, Cole embarked on a series of children's books, entitled *The Home Treasury*, and published under his *nom de plume* of Felix Summerly, the name he was to use for all his non-official activities.

He had commissioned the illustrations from leading painters of the day, including Mulready, whom he had met in connection with the design of pre-paid envelopes in December 1839.

The Society of Arts had held small exhibitions of manufactured goods in 1844 and 1845, and in the latter year offered prizes for a tea-set and beer-jugs to be exhibited at their premises the following year. Cole, with his usual entrepreneurial zeal, persuaded Herbert Minton, the head of the Stoke-on-Trent ceramic factory, whom he had met at a dinner party in 1842, to enter the competition for the beer-jug, at the same time deciding to have a go at the tea-set himself. Cole's first step was to go to the British Museum and look at Greek earthenware for inspiration on shapes, followed by a three-day visit to Minton's factory in April 1846 to supervise the execution of his design. It was a simple design in the then fashionable 'Etruscan' manner, with a lion spout to the tea-pot and a ram's head on the lid.

Tea set designed by Henry Cole and made by Minton's. Awarded a Society of Arts prize in 1846.

The cup was deep so that the tea would not cool quickly and the jug was three-lipped so that it would be easily poured right or left-handed.

Both Cole's tea-set and Minton's beer-jug won the prizes. The tea-set was a great success: Prince Albert particularly admired the jug, which was made also in silver, and had the set adopted as a breakfast service at Balmoral. The service kept several workmen busy at Minton's for many years and it was still being made in 1875, being widely exported. Strangely, few examples seem to have survived. Cole regarded the tea-set as of great significance. He presented an example to the Museum 'which I hope may be kept and always exhibited there as a link in the chain of circumstances leading to that Great Exhibition, which sowed the seed for the beginning of the South Kensington Museum'.

Neither Cole nor his circle recognized the division of the arts into the fine and the decorative or applied arts, the latter being generally considered the poor relation of the former. In 1847 Richard Redgrave appeared before a committee of the Council of the Government School of Design and was questioned by Mr Cockerell, R A, on the differences between fine and applied art, defined by him as 'Poetical Art' and 'Prose Art'. Redgrave having affirmed that in his view architects were as much concerned with making a poetical impression on the mind as painters, Cockerell pressed him on the decorative arts: 'Would you say the same of design as applied to manufactures, to chintzes, to jewellery, to vases, to calico-printing and china painting?' Redgrave replied: 'Even there I conceive that the power of making an impression upon the mind may be exerted as well as in the painter's art. If the poetry of invention does not enter into these designs, we shall never have proper designs.'

It was perhaps not surprising, therefore, that Cole should feel that the way to improve the appearance of manufactured objects was to have them designed by leading painters and sculptors of the day. Accordingly, in 1847, encouraged by the success of his tea-set, Cole set up his Felix Summerly Art Manufactures. The preface to the first catalogue set the tone: 'Francesco Francia was a goldsmith as well as a painter. Designs for crockery are attributed to Raffaello. Leonardo Da Vinci invented necklaces. In the Gallery of Buckingham Palace is a painting by Teniers to ornament a harpiscord, and in the National Gallery there is one by Nicolo Poussin for a similar purpose. Holbein designed brooches and salt cellars, Albert Dürer himself sculptured ornaments of all kinds. At Windsor is ironwork by Quintin Matsys. Beato Angelico and a host of great artists decorated books, and in fact there was scarcely a great mediaeval artist, when art was really catholic, who did not essay to decorate the objects of everyday life. Beauty of form and colour and poetic invention were associated with everything. So it ought still to be, and we will say shall be again.'

With these lofty precedents, Cole gathered together a team of prominent artists (including John Absolom; John Bell, sculptor; T. Creswick ARA; William Dyce RA, master of the School of Design; J. R. Herbert RA; J. C. Horsley, master of the School of Design; Daniel Maclise RA; William Mulready RA; Richard Redgrave ARA, H. J. Townsend ARA, master of the School of Design; and Sir Richard Westmacott RA, a member of the Council of the School of Design), and enlisted the services of most of the leading firms to execute their designs for both useful and purely ornamental categories of household goods. Each article, according to Cole, was to be of 'superior utility which is not to be sacrificed to ornament: to select pure forms: to decorate each article with appropriate details relating to its use, and to obtain these details as directly as possible from nature.' It would not be appropriate here to describe all the items listed in the catalogue, which was more in the nature of a prospectus, as it is likely that some of the more outlandish articles may not even have been put into production. Many of the objects were in the illustrative, narrative style, even 'imitative naturalism', a style which was to feature prominently in the Great Exhibition of 1851, only to be condemned one year later in the 'False Principles' display at Marlborough House.

Nearly a hundred of the Felix Summerly Art Manufactures were exhibited at the Royal Society of Arts in 1848, and some were again shown in 1851, but surprisingly few seem to have survived. A number are in the collections at the Victoria and Albert Museum, mostly not acquired until after the move to South Kensington, or when the Jermyn Street collection was transferred in 1901. The most popular items were probably produced in fairly large quantities and had a considerable influence on public taste. Among these was a wooden bread platter, designed by John Bell, ornamented with carvings of wheat, rye, barley and oats which was to become the standard British breadboard until the advent of sliced, wrapped, supermarket bread. With the recent revival of 'real bread', the Summerly-inspired bread boards have now become collectors items and feature in all the shops specializing in kitchen antiques. One of the most successful items was a christening mug with figures of guardian angels, designed by Redgrave in 1848, first made by the Royal Goldsmiths, Hunt and Roskell, and later by Harry Emmanuel. Redgrave's 'Well Spring' water carafe, made by John Fell Christy of Lambeth and registered on 25 October 1847, with its appropriate design of water plants encircling the body, was much admired by the *Spectator* as being 'among the most beautiful designs, the materials conducing to an effect at once modestly sober and gay, cool and sparkling'. It was probably this carafe that inspired Richardson's of Stourbridge to produce, in 1848, a whole range of water jugs, carafes and goblets similarly enamelled with water lilies, irises, or sea weeds and coral.

Richardson's also produced a number of items of glass for the Felix Summerly Art Manufactures, items which anticipated the fashion for the more thinly blown, delicately engraved or gilded glass which by 1860 ousted the heavy cut glass of the previous decade. These included the 'Bubbles Bursting' champagne and soda water glasses, engraved or gilded with naked putti disporting themselves among cascades of bubbling liquid, designed by Townsend; the 'Flask' decanter with gilt enamel or Parian stoppers and matching glasses, and the 'Tendril' wine glass and finger bowl designed by Redgrave. A finger bowl with a waved pattern designed by John Bell anticipated that designed by Philip Webb for William Morris in 1860. His flower tazza, made in opal or frosted glass with a gilded snake

Clear glass jug painted in enamel colours. Made by Richardson's and registered in 1848.

The 'Well Spring' jug designed by Richard Redgrave for Henry Cole's Felix Summerly's Art-Manufactures. Made by J.F. Christy, Lambeth and registered in 1847.

'Comic Art-Manufactures' by Luke Limner satirising the Felix Summerly Art-Manufactures, c. 1851. Above: the title page and, below, a satire of the 'Hop-Story' jug.

entwining the stem, was in the manner of the current French opalines, except that the gilded mesh cover fitting on to the bowl with gilt claws anticipated the popular rose bowls of the Edwardian period; and a wine glass and tumbler with applied blobs of glass foreshadowed the Art Nouveau glass of the turn of the century.

Most of the items however were more or less in tune with current taste. These included Parian figures by Minton and the Shakespeare clock, made in Parian by Minton, or in bronze, and the 'Two Drivers' and 'Hop Picking' jugs by H. J. Townsend.

More influential than the Felix Summerly production was the *Journal of Design and Manufactures*, which Cole, with the backing of Chapman and Hall, initiated in 1849, as a vehicle for setting out his ideas and those of his circle on a wide variety of topics, promoting those objects of which he approved, including the Summerly productions, and subjecting the others to fierce criticism. *The Journal of Design* exercised a considerable amount of influence, particularly on designers and manufacturers during the three years of its existence.

The visual puns and illustrative character of many of the Felix Summerly designs were satirized in a pamphlet entitled 'Comic Art Manufactures', with sixty four designs collected by 'Luke Limner Esq'.[3] The pamphlet cost one shilling. Some of the satirical drawings and punning captions were pure inventions, bearing little relation except in spirit to the actual Summerly designs, but others, such as the 'Milk Jug' was an exact parody of Townsend's 'Hop Jug', substituting milk for beer. The pamphlet, typical of the humour of the time, at least serves to emphasize that the Summerly Art Manufactures made a considerable impact on the public.

The exhibitions of manufactured goods at the Society of Arts became increasingly popular and on 3 January 1848, Cole wrote to Prince Albert's secretary, Colonel Phipps, suggesting that there should be a national exhibition of British manufactures. Exhibitions of French manufactures had been held in France since the late 18th century and when Cole visited the exhibition of French industry in Paris in

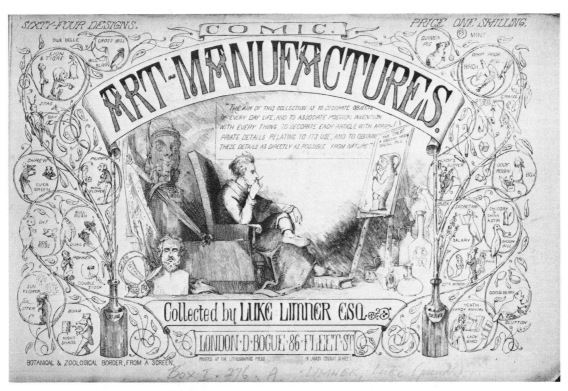

Marlborough House in 1857 showing part of the Soulages Collection. Watercolour by W. L. Casey.

1849, it gave him the idea that the national exhibition planned for 1851 should be an international one, an idea keenly approved of by the Prince Consort. The story of the Great Exhibition, of which Cole and the Prince Consort were the real initiators is well known; here we are concerned only with its aftermath.

III. THE MUSEUM OF ORNAMENTAL ART

The Great Exhibition of 1851 closed in a blaze of glory on 15 October with a ceremony attended by Prince Albert. It had attracted over six million visitors, mostly paying one shilling entrance fees. When all the bills had finally been settled, it was found that the exhibition had made a profit of £186,000 which passed to the Commissioners of the 1851 Exhibition of which Prince Albert was the President. He, with his ally, Henry Cole, had ambitious plans for spending the money on bringing together the existing learned and artistic societies on one site south of Hyde Park, which 'would serve to increase the means of Industrial Education, and extend the influence of Science and Art upon Productive Industry.'

In 1848 a Select Committee, of which Cole was a member, was set up to enquire into the School of Design, which it was felt had not lived up to its expectations. Cole was too busy with the Great Exhibition to play much part at the beginning but once the exhibition was over he took over as General Superintendent in 1852, and his first act was to institute new, more practical classes. The School premises were cramped, the plaster casts were stored in the basement and Cole approached Prince Albert about accommodation. The Prince offered Marlborough House with the idea that the School should be rehoused with a new Museum of Manufactures, soon to be called the Museum of Ornamental Art, which opened initially for two months in May 1852 and then on a more permanent basis in September. Although the plaster casts moved earlier, the School of Design did not move into Marlborough House until 1853, being accommodated in two wooden huts built in the courtyard.

Marlborough House. The sixth room painted by C. Armytage in 1857.

The introduction to the first catalogue of the Museum of Ornamental Art stated its three-fold aims: 'Some specimens are included which . . . are intended to illustrate the history of various manufactures, some for extreme skill of manufacture or workmanship, whilst others are intended to present to the manufacturers and the public choice examples of what science and art have accomplished in manufactures of all kinds, and this not so much with a view to the works being copied or imitated, as to show that perfection and beauty *in art* are not matters of caprice or dependent on the fancy of the beholder any more than perfection and beauty in nature.'

The catalogue continued with a section on the *General Principles of Decorative Art* as laid down by Redgrave, Cole and Owen Jones, and the public were requested 'not to look at the articles in the Museum as mere objects of 'vertu' or curiosity, but to examine their beauties or defects with reference to the principles laid down'. From the onset Cole stressed the importance of the educational value of the museum: 'Unless museums and galleries are made subservient to purposes of education, they dwindle into very sleepy affairs.'

To the collection of plaster casts and objects bought for the School of Design, were added a number of items acquired from the Great Exhibition with a sum of £5,000 allocated for the purpose by the Treasury. The select committee included Cole, Redgrave, A. W. N. Pugin, who had been in charge of the mediaeval court at the exhibition, and Owen Jones. The purchases from the Exhibition included Pugin's great 'Mediaeval press' or cabinet, some of his candlesticks and chalices executed by Hardman, electro-plate by Elkington, a huge silver pilgrim flask by Lambert and Rawlings, and a number of pieces of French silver, metalwork and jewellery, mostly in the Renaissance style, chosen for the excellence of the workmanship. There was also a strong emphasis on Eastern manufactures, the purchases being supplemented by a loan of Indian and Chinese silver bracelets from Cole's own collection, and the textiles were largely of Eastern manufacture. Some manufacturers lent specimens of their productions (carpets by Messrs Lapworths, silk from Jackson and Graham), while Queen Victoria herself lent extensively from the Royal Collection of Sèvres porcelain, and also some of her Meissen and Oriental porcelain.

Each specimen, the catalogue stated, 'has been selected for its merit in exemplifying some right principle of construction or ornament, or some feature of workmanship to which it appeared desirable that the attention of our students and manufacturers should be directed', and the *Art Journal* somewhat grudgingly admitted that the committee had on the whole acquitted themselves satisfactorily.[4]

Students had free admission to the Museum at all times and the public on Mondays, Tuesdays and during Easter and Christmas; but on Wednesdays, Thursdays and Fridays anyone except a student had to pay 6d. Students of the Department of Science and Art could examine and copy any article which could be removed from the case or portfolio for purposes of study, free of charge, but the public had to pay 6d for each object or 1/- for any number of examples in one portfolio. In order to encourage manufacturers to use the collection, an annual subscription of one guinea purchased a season ticket which was transferable to any member of their firm, or any person in their employ.

In 1853 John Charles Robinson (1824–1913), who had been an art teacher at the School of Design at Hanley, was appointed curator of the Museum. Robinson was born collector, a fine scholar and connoisseur, with a particular interest in the Italian Renaissance. It is to him that the V & A owes the foundation of its exceptional holdings of mediaeval and Renaissance art. Outstanding purchases consisted of pottery and porcelain from the Bandinel Collection in 1852–3, and of pottery, porcelain, majolica and glass from the collection of Ralph Bernal, MP, in 1854.[5] The influence of these collections on English manufactures is of great significance and is dealt with in subsequent chapters. The fact that some of Robinson's purchases have subsequently been proved fakes, should not detract from our admiration of his taste and discrimination, bearing in mind the general state of knowledge at the time. Another outstanding purchase brought to Cole's notice by Herbert Minton was the Soulages collection which opened at Marlborough House on 30 October 1856.

One of the most interesting and influential aspects of the Museum of Ornamental Art at Marlborough House was the display of objects to illustrate 'False Principles in Design', an idea that foreshadowed the Council of Industrial Design's 'cautionary designs' of nearly a century later, and was set up primarily to demonstrate to the public what was bad taste.

The introduction to the catalogue of the 'False Principles' display, written by Richard Redgrave, stated that 'the chief vice in the decoration common to Europe in the present day is the tendency towards *direct imitation of nature*, in this natural or merely imitative style'. He cited metal imitations of plants and flowers, a class of objects featuring prominently in the 1851 Exhibition, and fostered by the recently invented process of electrotyping the natural object. Even worse were specimens where ormolu stems and leaves bore porcelain flowers, illustrated in the display by a gas burner where the gas flamed from the petals of a convolvolus.

Other examples of imitative naturalism included a flower pot in earthenware of reeds, painted blue, bound with a yellow ribbon, and scissors in the form of a stork, the beak opening the reverse way and the body of the bird made to open in the direction of its length.

This imitative naturalism was manifest in furniture where 'enormous wreaths of flowers, fish, game and fruits etc., imitated *à merveille*, dangle round sideboards, beds, and picture frames'. Redgrave elaborated on sideboards with garlands of imitative flowers projecting so far from the slab as to need a 'long arm' to reach over it, and 'cabinets, bookcases so bristling with walnut-wood flowers and oak-wood leaves as to put use out of the question'. To such objects Redgrave gave the name 'hollybush' style, which he considered made it as dangerous for a lady to walk in the room as it would be to walk in a real wood.

Carpets sinned in all directions, and the nine specimens included in the 'False Principles' display were criticised for imitative floral designs with flowers out of scale, imitation architectural mouldings and scrolls, imitation of pierced Gothic panelling, even representations of landscapes, and cornucopias filled with flowers, resting upon nothing. Such carpets figured prominently in the 1851 Exhibition, but an examination of the catalogue of the 1862 Exhibition shows few such examples. The same sin of imitative naturalism applied to chintzes. Redgrave felt that as a light summer fabric chintz should have light-weight patterns, simple designs of floral ornament, flat geometrical all-over patterns or stripes; whereas the prevailing taste was for large, coarse flowers such as dahlias, hollyhocks, full-blown roses and hydrangeas – as in the hollyhock chintz which won a prize at the 1851 Exhibition, and was included a year later in the 'False Principles' display. One century later the same chintz appeared in *Design Magazine* as a superb example of a traditional British chintz – such is the cycle of taste.

Even worse horrors were included in the paper-hangings or wallpapers section – perspective representations of a railway station and of the Crystal Palace and the Serpentine; horses, water and ground floating in the air; representations of battles; imitations of ribbons in festoons etc. Dress fabrics and handkerchiefs came in for similar criticism. Four patterns for trousers with 'geometrical forms totally unfit for the garment for which they are intended, interfering with the form of the wearer' made a deep impression on a fictional Mr Crumpet, residing at Crump Lodge, Brixton. In the story, entitled *A House Full of Horrors*, published in Charles Dickens' *Household Words* of 4 December 1852, Henry Morley graphically describes Mr Crumpet's reaction to the display. Mr Crumpet relates how, when he came home from the City, his wife was in the habit of remarking that his 'cheerfulness was like a bird at tea . . . But . . . for the last five weeks I have been haunted by the most horrid shapes . . . my whole house is full of horrors . . . The matter is this: I have acquired some Correct Principles of Taste. Five weeks ago, I went to the Department of Practical Art in Marlborough House to look over the museum of ornamental art. I had heard of a Chamber of Horrors there established, and I found it . . . It was a gloomy chamber, hung round with frightful objects in curtains, carpets, clothes, lamps, and what not . . . I could have cried, sir. I was ashamed of the pattern of my own trowsers [sic] for I saw a piece of

Bread platter, polychrome transfer-printed by F. and R. Pratt of Fenton, and included in the 'False Principles in Design' display at Marlborough House.

them hung up there as a horror. I dared not pull out my pocket handkerchief while any one was by, lest I should be seen dabbing the perspiration from my forehead with a wreath of coral. I saw it all; when I went home I found that I had been living among horrors up to that hour. The paper in my parlour contains four kinds of birds of paradise, besides bridges and pagodas . . . finishing my cup of tea just at that time, I dropped my cup and saucer – with a cry of agony 'Butter-fly – inside my cup! Horr-horr-horr-i-ble!'

In the field of pottery and porcelain, dinner and dessert plates were criticized for having pictures of flowers or landscapes in the centre of the plate which must necessarily be covered when the plate was used. Simple ornamental borders, such as those designed by Pugin for Mintons, were preferred. A bread platter by Pratt of Fenton, with polychrome transfer-printed decoration of Christ walking through a cornfield (after a painting by S. Warren, the copper-plates engraved by Jesse Owen) was singled out on two grounds. Firstly, the whole surface being covered was considered objectionable, while the religious picture, especially the quotation from St. Matthew which surrounded it, was considered out of place on a bread plate and very inappropriate to the intended use. It seems that Messrs Pratt of Fenton, who had received high praise for their wares in 1851, took some notice of the criticism for they later dropped the religious text from the design.

The popular moulded jugs also came in for criticism. 'A water jug, general form ungraceful and broken by ornament consisting of grapes, leaves and infant Bacchanals' – although a similar jug by Charles Meigh had won a Society of Arts medal in 1848, and also one which was 'a rude imitation, in blue earthenware, of a trunk of a tree, on which are applied figures, vine leaves and grapes'. This was probably the 'Babes in the Wood' jug, which was said to be 'one of most popular ever manufactured'.

Glass offended on several counts, where the brilliancy of the surface and transparency was obscured by grinding, or by the application of colour. Heavy cutting which destroyed the outline of the object was also condemned. Redgrave's principles on glass, quoted below, coincided with the opinions of John Ruskin, who dismissed all cut glass as barbarous, and foreshadowed the principles of Eastlake and Morris, and the Arts and Crafts movement

generally, all of whom advocated the exploitation of the essential qualities of the material. Thus Redgrave wrote: 'The more simple mode of manufacturing glass is productive not only of the most beautiful shapes, but of its best qualities; and blown glass unites thinness, translucency, and pure surface, to forms which combine the greatest symmetry with varied curves, that is, the sphere, resulting from the circular motion of the workman's instrument, elongated by the breadth and weight into the ellipse and its combinations'.

The criticism was effective as far as glass was concerned, as once again a comparison between the exhibits at the 1851 and 1862 Exhibitions will show. Gone were the 'prickly monstrosities'; instead we find thinly blown glass, decorated with engraved ornament, as shown in the decanter from the service made by Apsley Pellatt for the Prince of Wales.

The reformers were perhaps most persuasive in the field of surface decoration, where flat patterns of geometric ornament or conventionalized flowers superseded the imitative naturalism and direct representation of nature. However, as E. J. Poynter pointed out in his lecture on *Decorative Art*, first given at University College, London, in 1869 (and published in his *Lectures on Art*, first edition 1873), 'the determined insistence upon the necessity of a purely flat kind of decoration has produced, as a result, a kind of work quite as unfortunate, if not more so, than the vulgar rococo ornament which it has superseded'. He went on to point out that it was as difficult to design a good flat diaper as any other sort of pattern, and that such flat patterns gave opportunities for violent juxtapositions of colour, whereas the shaded scrolls and flowers had at least forced designers, to a certain extent, to break up these tints. He cited, in wallpapers especially, violent blues opposed to raw red, or orange and magenta patterns on arsenic green grounds in what people supposed to be the 'Gothic' taste. It was against this sort of background that William Morris designed his first wallpaper in 1862 (not issued until 1864), not in revolt against 'the direct imitation of nature' of some ten years earlier.

Dickens again refers to the 'False Principles' laid down by Cole and his colleagues in *Hard Times*. Chapter XI of his manuscript bears the names 'Gradgrind, Cole, Sissy and Bitzer' and the words 'Marlborough House Doctrine'.[6] *Hard Times* was serialized in *Household Words* in the summer of 1854 and Cole was satirized as a school inspector, 'a mighty man at cutting and drying'. Having asked a class of children if they would paper a room with horses, or use a carpet with flowers on it, and not having received the resounding negative answer he hoped for, he expounded at length on taste: 'You are not to have, in any object of use or ornament, what would be a contradiction in fact. You don't find that foreign birds and butterflies come and perch on your crockery. You never meet the quadrupeds going up and down the walls . . . you must use, for all purposes, combinations and modifications (in primary colours) of mathematical figures which are susceptible of proof and demonstration. This is the new discovery. This is fact. This is taste. What is called taste is another name for fact.'

Although undoubtedly the 'False Principles' display had a far-reaching influence on designers, manufacturers and public taste, there was a considerable outcry against the stigma officially placed on goods in the display, especially on the part of manufacturers whose wares were singled out for this treatment. So incensed were some people that in 1853 a three-volume pamphlet, running to some hundred pages, was written under the pseudonym of Argus and published by Houlston and Stoneman of 65 Paternoster Row, London. Addressed 'To Manufacturers, Decorators, Designers, and the Public general' under the title of 'A Mild Remonstrance Against The Taste – Censorship at Marlborough House In Reference to Manufacturing Ornamentation and Decorative Design', the three volumes delivered fierce attacks on Richard Redgrave, Owen Jones and Henry Cole, describing them as the 'Triumvirate of Taste – the Great Trinity!'

The pamphlet opened satirically with the words: 'Englishmen know nothing of Taste. The saying is as trite as any proverb. Frenchmen, Italians, Arabs, Indians, Chinese, Tartars, and even Savages are all in the secret. Benighted Britons – always renowned for Tin – know nothing of Beauty, nothing of Refinement, nothing of Fine Art, nothing of Taste. Of course, there are a few exalted spirits in this island of rain, and fog, and demi-darkness – a travelled few – who have become conscious, we may almost say proudly conscious, of the fact.' Redgrave possibly came in for the most abuse for his *Principles of Design*. The writer suspected Owen Jones to be 'Half a Moor, and more than half a Mussulman . . . in his mode of thinking on taste', referring to his *Plans, Elevations, Sections and Details of the Alhambra* published in 1842. The Museum was attacked for the money it spent on modern foreign objects from the 1851 Exhibition, for example: '£200 for a knife – a modern French knife!' Referring to Redgrave's views of glass, particularly 'the false and bad taste of grinding and colouring glass', the writer suggested that he should follow his advocacy of transparency, '*to see through things*', notably through 'the fallacies of that book of yours . . . "Redgrave on Design".' Argus also reminded Redgrave and Cole of the Felix Summerly Art Manufactures, which in many cases violated their own principles in the matter of 'naturalism'.

All the 'Principles' as laid down in the appendix to the Marlborough House catalogue were queried one by one, and the prominence given to Indian objects in the collection, with their laudatory catalogue entries, came in for vehement attack.

The third volume concluded with the writer's own principles: 'Ultimate Principle – Human Progress and Enlightment. This demands Art, and deprecates Conventionalism. Immediate Principle – Commerce. This demands the Complex in Ornamentation in preference to the simple'.

Each volume cost 6d, but 'with a view to gratuitous distribution by manufacturers amongst their correspondents and customers', the price was reduced to 40 shillings for a hundred copies. How many were printed and distributed is not known. The 'False Principles in Design' display was withdrawn, because it was realized that the singling out of individual manufacturer's products for public criticism was to some extent self-defeating, as it antagonized some who might well have mended their ways with the more gentle persuasion

Printed Tussore silk with a design taken from a Persian pattern book in the collection of the Museum of Ornamental Art, illustrated in Owen Jones' Grammar of Ornament. *Printed by Thomas Wardle for Liberty's and shown in the British India Pavilion at the Paris Exhibition of 1878.*

of letting the fine objects in the Museum speak for themselves. The general public also often misunderstood the 'False Principles' display, for they thought that everything exhibited in a museum was to be admired. The 'Triumvirate', however, stuck to their principles and Redgrave's *Principles of Design* (1853), together with selections from his other writings, formed the basis of the *Manual of Design*, edited by his son Gilbert R. Redgrave, published as one of the official South Kensington Art Handbooks in 1876.

The reaction against the 'imitative naturalism' so prominent at the 1851 Exhibition caused the Museum to develop somewhat of a bias towards Indian and Islamic art, particularly as far as flat pattern was concerned. Both Owen Jones and Redgrave expressed a preference for those styles, and Cole went along with them. Writing of the 1851 Exhibition[7], Jones remarked that among the general disorder everywhere the works not only of India but of all the contributing Mohammedan countries – Tunisia, Egypt, and Turkey – showed 'so much unity of design, so much skill and judgement in its application with so much elegance and refinement in the execution' that they 'excited a degree of attention from artists, manufacturers, and the public which has not been without its fruits'. Redgrave admired the Indian patterns for their extreme simplicity and felt that, although the individual motifs might sometimes be ill-drawn and commonplace, 'the due attention paid to the just ornamentation of the fabric . . . the choice of tints . . . the ornamental forms . . . will give many lessons to our designers and manufacturers'.

Similarly, in the *Grammar of Ornament*, Owen Jones remarked that 'the Indian collection at South Kensington Museum should be visited and studied by all in any way connected with the production of woven fabrics. In this collection will be found the most brilliant colours perfectly harmonised – it is impossible to find a discord. All the examples show the nicest adjustment of the massing of the ornament to the colour of the ground; every colour and tint, from the palest and most delicate to the deepest and richest shades, receiving just the amount of ornament that it is adapted to bear.'

The Moorish or Alhambresque style, popularized by Owen Jones' and Jules Goury's *Plans, Elevations, Sections and Details of the Alhambra*, published in 1842, was also a style

A German (Bavarian) woven silk of 1874 showing the influence of Owen Jones.

favoured by the Museum. The oriental galleries, comprising Indian, Chinese and Japanese courts with decorations designed by Owen Jones in 1863, included tilework and a painted plaster tracery in the Moorish style, with a stained glass window en suite. Unfortunately only Jones' original designs survive.

The casts of the relief ornament of the Alhambra, made by Jones on site either in plaster or unsized paper, passed into the hands of a modeller, Henry Alonzo Smith. In 1880 James Wild (1842–92) himself an Islamic enthusiast, wrote to the Director suggesting that they were worthy of a place in the South Kensington Museum, as they might be of use to students. The plaster casts and some 200 paper impressions were acquired and these were duly circulated throughout the country. During the present century one cast and all the paper impressions were destroyed, but fortunately four casts remain.

Even before this a French vase based on the 'Alhambra' vase had been bought from the Paris Exhibition of 1844 for the Government School of Design, passing into the Museum collection, and other pieces of ceramics in the 'Moorish' and Islamic styles were added in the 1850s.

But it was in the applications of flat pattern that the 'Moorish or 'Alhambresque' style was most apparent, on textiles, wallpapers and tiles. Sometimes the whole ornament would be more or less faithfully copied, at other times the characteristic 'feathering' or treatment of the leaf form would be picked up, as in some designs by Owen Jones himself and those by Christopher Dresser.

Although by the 1860s the Museum was concentrating more on the Renaissance, the 'oriental' influence of the collections continued to grow and Matthew Digby Wyatt, writing on *Orientalism in European Industry* in 1870[8] remarked that 'we work now in almost all departments of production, especially in carpets, rugs, tiles, floor-cloth, mural decoration, paper-hangings, shawls, and to some extent in jewellery and mosaics, in the spirit, if not in the forms of oriental art. Its influence is a growing one and, as I believe, a highly beneficial one.' He was right and the

'Stanhope' silk designed by Owen Jones and woven by Benjamin Warner, Spitalfields, about 1870.

The 'Brompton Boilers' about 1863.

'oriental' influence, the term by that time embracing most of the Near and Far East, was to be a major factor in the evolution of the aesthetic movement to which the Museum collections were to make a significant contribution.

Many of the earliest textiles, for example, produced by Liberty's, the firm founded by Arthur Lasenby Liberty in 1875, were produced from fabrics in the Indian section of the Museum, including their Mysore silk, designed for evening robes, and printed in gold 'in rare and conventional designs copied by permission from the originals in the Indian Museum'. Other Liberty designs, including an all-over marigold diaper, printed on their 'tusser' silk by Thomas Wardle of Leek, were copied from a Persian manufacturer's pattern-book in the South Kensington Museum, illustrations from which appeared in *The Treasury of Ornamental Art* (1857) and in the *Grammar of Ornament*. Many of these early Liberty fabrics were exhibited by Thomas Wardle in the British India Pavilion of the Paris Exhibition of 1878 and subsequently acquired for the Animal Products Division of the Museum, then housed at Bethnal Green.

South Kensington

IV. THE SOUTH KENSINGTON MUSEUM

Already by 1854 Cole and Redgrave realized that the space available at Marlborough House was inadequate, and Prince Albert asked Gottfried Semper to prepare plans for a new museum on the 1851 Commissioners' Lands. Semper produced plans and a painted cardboard model but the scheme proved impracticable and too expensive and on 14 June 1855 Prince Albert proposed the erection of an 'iron house' on the Brompton Park Estate. Work began early in 1856 and was well under way by May when the *Builder* (10 May 1856) described the building as 'like a three-fold monster boiler'. The building, thereafter known as the Brompton Boilers, survived until 1866 when it was partially demolished and parts were removed in 1867-8 to form the framework of the Bethnal Green Museum.

Inspite of the ugliness of the building, and the problems of heating and lighting, the Museum prospered. In an introductory address on the functions of the Science and Art Department, delivered on 16 November 1857, Henry Cole waxed lyrical on the value of the Museum to the working class: 'The working man comes to the museum from his one or two dimly lighted rooms, in his fustian jacket, with his shirt collar a little trimmed up, accompanied by his threes, and fours, and fives of little fustian jackets, a wife, in her best bonnet, and a baby, of course under her shawl. The look of surprise and pleasure of the whole party when they observe the brilliant lighting inside the museum show what a new acceptable and wholesome excitement this evening entertainment affords to all of them. Perhaps the evening opening of the Public Museums may furnish a powerful antidote to the gin palace.' The refreshment rooms, constructed in temporary buildings during 1856-7, provided another practical alternative.

Cole also emphasized that he saw the Museum not only as a metropolitan institution but as a storehouse or treasury of science and art for the use of the whole kingdom. Apart from the Circulating Museum (described in chapter VII), the museum sent objects to special exhibitions in the provinces including the important Manchester Art Treasures Exhibition in 1857.

On 14 December 1857, J. C. Robinson, the Curator, gave his lecture on 'The Museum of Ornamental Art', described in the *Art Journal* [9] as being 'earnest and practical', stressing the

Visitors to the South Kensington Museum. Cartoon from Punch, *17th April, 1869, by Sir John Tenniell.*

value of ornament, and the importance of a workman bringing his mind to bear on his productions. The *Art Journal* criticized, however, the contents of the Museum as being almost exclusively devoted to Renaissance objects, a criticism that had been made earlier by Gottfried Semper. These collections were to prove most influential and the Renaissance bias was reflected in a series of illustrations of decorative art objects from the Museum 'suggestive to designers and manufacturers', published in the *Art Journal* in 1857. The concluding remarks accompanying them hoped 'that the increased publicity given . . . by their reproduction in our columns, will induce our traders to pay more frequent visits to the very remarkable collection of which the originals form part', a collection which, the writer felt, was now entitled 'to a first rank among the museums in Europe' and one which was of real importance to both the art student and the manufacturer.

As the *Art Journal* pointed out, the articles were not intended as 'models for literal reproduction', but for the designer and manufacturer 'they will convey an infinity of suggestions, which, when elaborated and worked out, will be no mere copies of preceding types; but on the contrary truly original works, replete with that pure artistic style, which is the invention of no one person alone, but which has been always handed down in the very way here indicated. Viewed in this light, collections such as that at South Kensington are of the highest national importance.'

In 1858 the Museum held a special exhibition of works of art manufacture, including furniture and woodcarving, textiles and carpets, wallpapers, silver and metalwork, jewellery, ceramics and glass, designs for which were produced by artists, either directly or indirectly connected with the Department of Science and Art at South Kensington. Reviewing the exhibition, the *Art Journal* (1858, p. 251-2) pointed out how much the Department had achieved 'by making the public familiar with excellence, cultivating the eye and mind to its appreciation, and inducing a sort of horror of that which is bad or base in design and execution; while assuredly its directors have taught the manufacturer where they might study what is pure and good – in books, in models, in drawings, in ancient produce, in modern productions.'

Many of the leading manufacturers' productions were included in the exhibition and in each case there was seen to be an improvement. To mention a couple of examples cited by the *Art Journal*, the tea-trays of Jennens and Bettridge bore no relation to the papier-mâché of the 1830s and 1840s where 'masses of huge gaudy colours, with unmeaning splashes of gold, were considered essential to make a work look valuable'. Similarly with carpets, there were 'none of the old, huge, abominable bunches of big flowers, scattered among rocks, or temples, or in gigantic vases,' and the carpets by Jackson and Graham, Lapworth and others, designed by pupils of the schools were praised as 'beautiful specimens'. Indeed the *Art Journal* considered that the improvement was apparent in 'every branch of British Art-Manufacture', an improvement due in a great measure to the influence of South Kensington.

Tribute to the value of the Museum was also paid by the architect William Burges (1827–81) in a series of lectures delivered in the 1860s at the Society of Arts, the Architectural Association, and the Museum itself, and published in 1865 under the title of *Art Applied to Industry*. In his introduction Burges remarked that 'a great source of improvement is the excellent Museum at South Kensington'. Comparing its collections with those of the Cluny Museum in Paris he felt that while the latter might have had some richer objects, there were many that were of little use, whereas South Kensington had 'been formed with reference to the special object of instructing the workman and designer, and the consquence is there is no rubbish in it'. He wished, however, that it had been placed in a more central position, such as Charing Cross where, in his opinion, 'it would have had an immense influence in educating the public generally, for people would then run in for half-an-hour when they

*Two tile panels
personifying Art and Nature made
by Maw & Co., Broseley, about
1880, showing the influence of F.
W. Moody's designs for the
Museum buildings. Collection of
H. & R. Johnston-Richards.
Photograph by courtesy of Julian
Barnard.*

were passing, as they do at the National Gallery: and it is precisely those half-hours that are the most precious, for people then confine their attention to one or two things and study them well, knowing that they have no time for the others; whereas when they go to see the Museum as a sight they try to see as much as possible, and nothing gets properly studied. The consequence is that the Museum at South Kensington does only one-half the good it might do, and is visited principally by students, sight-seers, and the inhabitants of the vicinity, whereas it ought to catch all and every condition of life.'

Similar tribute to the value of the Museum, particularly in the training of designers, was given by Matthew Digby Wyatt in a lecture on 'Fine Art Applied to Industry' delivered at Cambridge in 1870 when he was Slade Professor of Fine Art.[10]

Numerous other examples could be cited paying tribute to the beneficial effect of the Museum's collections, which throughout the early years were supplemented by loans, an influence which is discussed in more detail in the chapters on specific industries.

The permanent buildings of the South Kensington Museum were envisaged from the start as a work of art, the idea being that the building itself should be as much an inspiration to designers and craftsmen as the collections it contained. At the same time it was felt that public taste would be elevated by the beauty of the surroundings, being struck with awe and wonder as in a great cathedral, or royal palace. The decoration of the buildings, both inside and out, were to be a veritable encyclopaedia of the arts and sciences, with portraits of eminent painters, sculptors, craftsmen and scientists depicted in mosaic, stained glass and terracotta, or at least their names enshrined in Renaissance-style cartouches on the walls and staircases.

At the same time as the temporary buildings were going up, Captain Francis Fowke of the Royal Engineers embarked on his plans for the permanent buildings, the first to be completed being the Sheepshanks Gallery, the upper floor being opened in 1857, the gallery below a year later.[11]

The style generally adopted by Captain Fowke was based on that seen 'in the North Italian buildings of the fifteenth century', red brick with fawn-coloured and red terracotta being chiefly used. The modelled ornaments were mainly designed by Godfrey Sykes (1825-66), or, after his death, by Reuben Townroe (1835-1911) and James Gamble (1835-1911) all pupils of Alfred Stevens, and by Francis Wallastan Moody (1824-86), assisted by students of the school of art. Other artists involved in the decoration were William Bell Scott (1811-90), and Sir Edward Poynter (1836-1919).

Captain Fowke's designs for the new museum buildings were exhibited in the Architecture Section at the Paris Exhibition of 1867 and were awarded a gold medal by the jury. Not only perspective views, elevations and sections but actual parts of the building were erected in the Champ de Mars as part of the exhibition. These included two of the terracotta columns modelled by Sykes for the lecture theatre façade, the quadrangle door panels, parts of the brickwork and four mosaics (See Chapter on Ceramics and Glass) were exhibited in Class II of the British Section.

The style of these buildings became a model for a number of European museums and no doubt popularized the use of moulded terracotta as a building material, which became the speciality of Doulton and a number of other firms in the last quarter of the 19th century. Internally, the most influential aspects of the museum buildings were the decorations of the three refreshment rooms. Hermann Muthesius, the German architect, was sent to England in 1896 and began to study English progress in art and design, to see how it was that England had achieved her pre-eminence in the decorative arts. He stated in his monumental work *Der Englische Haus* published in 1904, that 'the refreshment rooms at South Kensington furnish the best examples of the aims of interior design at the end of the 1860s. The central area was designed by the South Kensington School, in the most elaborate renaissance forms applied in an entirely academic manner.' This, the main refreshment room, known as the Gamble room since its reopening in 1976, was the work of the Museum's own design team of three pupils of Alfred Stevens,

35

The Grill Room or Dutch Kitchen at the South Kensington Museum, designed by E.J. Poynter, 1868–71.

Godfrey Sykes, Rueben Townroe and James Gamble. Soon after work had begun on the room, Godfrey Sykes died, and most of the detail, the majolica columns, the frieze of *amorini*, the lunettes and mirror frames, the enamelled iron ceiling and stained glass were designed by James Gamble, but the ceramic alphabet was by Godfrey Sykes. The majolica work in the Renaissance style, much influenced by the work of the della Robbias, was carried out by Minton, Hollins and Co. in 1867, and in commissioning it Cole was no doubt inspired by the Prince Consort's dairy at Frogmore, executed by Mintons in 1858. The idea was that ceramic cladding was extremely hygenic for a restaurant, as it could easily be kept clean, and although not as influential as Henry Cole had hoped, it undoubtedly led to a number of interiors in a similar style, notably the Criterion complex in Piccadilly designed by Thomas Verity in 1870-74 and executed by W. B. Simpson of the Strand. A number of impressive restaurant and hotel interiors with moulded ceramic decoration were carried out by Doulton, including decorations in coloured faience at the Holborn restaurant in 1883-85, designed by T. E. Collcutt, the architect of the Imperial Institute, and the Smoking Room at the Hotel Cecil in the Strand designed by W. P. Rix in Indian style in 1896, now both unfortunately destroyed. Cole was particularly proud of the enamelled iron ceiling, which like the majolica wall cladding was easy to keep clean. He exhibited examples of his enamelled iron ceilings at the Paris Exhibition of 1867, the catalogue entry stating that 'these ceilings were invented to answer the requirements of the South Kensington Museum where much gaslight is used, and where precautions against fire are necessary'.

The enamelled iron ceiling had been inspired by the enamelled advertisements on station platforms, for Cole was a great railway enthusiast, but in 1916 it was suggested that the process should be reversed. The November issue of the Journal of the Design and Industries Association, in an article entitled *A Lesson to Shopkeepers*, took an imaginary shopkeeper round the Design in Industry exhibition at Burlington House. The writer suggested that artists such as Phoebe and Harold Stabler might be employed to 'design and superintend the making of pictorial enamelled signs for the store - our railways proclaim loudly enough

Interior of the 'Brompton Boilers' showing the textile collection, about 1863.

the need for the employment of an artist in this trade, and it is now more than half a century since the refreshment room at the South Kensington Museum should have taught the possibilities of this material.'

The East Refreshment Room, sometimes called the Dutch Kitchen or more generally the Grill Room was designed by Edward Poynter (1836-1919) in about 1866. Poynter was to become Slade Professor at the University College of London in 1871 and from 1876-81 director for Art at South Kensington. He directed the National Gallery from 1894-1905, became president of the Royal Academy in 1896 and was knighted in the same year.

The *Standard*, which had been critical of some of the Museum decorations, remarked that 'there is a comfortable, home look about it . . . The style adopted is that of the old fashioned blue Dutch tile, set in panelling . . . The panels are in plain dark walnut, the tiles being the work of the pupils in the art schools of the museum . . . First, just above the floor, a course of alternate fruits and flowers; then one of land and seascapes; then fruits and flowers again; then one of groups of figures, chiefly mythical; and finally a third of fruit and flowers.'

Above these were large figure panels, representing the seasons and the months dressed in typical reformed 'aesthetic dress', the type generally called 'Greek', such as that favoured by the Morris circle, and similar to the costumes designed by Godwin and Walter Crane. The ornamental details, however, were in the Renaissance style with garlanded columns, and swags of fruit and flowers.

This decoration no doubt set a fashion for blue and white tiles, and many of the architects, including Philip Webb and Richard Norman Shaw, used old Dutch tiles in their fireplaces, or contemporary blue and white tiles, such as those produced by Morris & Company. It was also one of the earliest schemes of interior decoration to revive the use of pictorial tile panels and thus set a fashion for the numerous tile panels that decorated restaurants, public houses, butcher's shops and children's wards in hospitals, notably St. Thomas's, which became the speciality of Doulton, Minton and other Staffordshire firms of the latter part of the 19th century. The tiles were painted on Minton blanks by seven female students from the South Kensington Museum painting class between 1867 and 1871. An

Study at the South Kensington Museum

article in the *Graphic* of 26 February 1870 congratulates the Museum on having found a new and worthwhile occupation for young women. The success of this enterprise led to the establishment of the Minton Art Pottery Studio in Kensington Gore and generally made painting on pottery and porcelain a popular pastime, particularly for women. It was no doubt instrumental in bringing about the annual competitions for painting on porcelain, organized by Howell and James of Regent Street, London, during the 1870s and 1880s. The craze soon spread to the United States and numerous 'how to do it' books were devoted to the subject.

The moulded plaster frieze, also designed by Poynter, had a row of peacocks around the cornice. Peacocks, and peacock feathers, like the sunflower, were to become the dominant motifs of the aesthetic movement, and it is probable that the frieze of Walter Crane's 'Peacock and Amorini' wallpaper, registered in 1878, was inspired by this.

The huge cast iron fireplace and grill, which gives its name to the room, is signed and dated 'E. J. P. 1866'. On either side of the grill were two 'hot chambers', the doors of which were embellished with burning braziers and Tudor roses, with magnificent brass hinges in the form of eagle's heads. Above was an open brass grill with sunburst designs. In his *Hints on Household Taste* (second edition, London, 1869), Charles Lock Eastlake complains of the black ugliness in a modern kitchen range, but sees no reason 'if the material by which it is made is properly treated why it should not be as picturesque an object as any in the house', and cites 'the cooking apparatus of the grill room . . . of the South Kensington Museum' as 'an admirable instance of such treatment'. This, like Alfred Stevens' stoves, evidently helped to improve the standard of design of stoves and fireplaces, as witness the superb series of fireplace surrounds, with similarly treated ironwork, albeit with a strong Japanese influence, designed by Thomas Jeckyll for Barnard, Bishop and Barnard of Norwich in the late 1870s.

The decorations of both the Grill Room and the Central Restaurant room were in keeping with those of the rest of the Museum, but the third, the so-called Green Dining Room, is very different: it was to have the greatest influence on public taste and made an important contribution to the 'aesthetic' style of interior decoration. Late in 1865, somewhat

Sketching in the South Kensington Museum. Painting by A. J. Sherman. Photograph: Sotheby's.

surprisingly, Cole, Redgrave, and Fowke approached the firm of Morris, Marshall, Faulkner and Co., established less than five years before on 11 April 1861, to prepare designs and estimates for the Western Refreshment Room. The Museum authorities had no doubt been impressed by the firm's exhibit at the 1862 Exhibition and had purchased stained glass made by the firm, designed by William Morris and Burne-Jones, in 1864. Although Morris himself undoubtedly supervised the whole scheme, most of the actual designs were by Philip Webb (1831-1915). The Room was more or less complete by the end of 1868. The lower portion of the Room was panelled in oak, stained green (now somewhat unsatisfactorily re-decorated with modern, flat green paint during the 1978 restorations). Above this is a series of painted panels of figures of the months, or the twelve signs of the Zodiac, with the two extra panels of the sun and the moon designed by Burne-Jones, alternating with panels of foliage and fruit on gilded grounds. The upper portion of the walls was covered with moulded plaster panels of olive branches and blossom, surmounted by a frieze of dogs chasing hares, designed by Webb, and inspired by the decoration on the font in Newcastle Cathedral. The ceiling was divided into panels with leaf decoration in yellow, with small diaper borders, originally pricked into the wet plaster, in the mediaeval tradition, as at Morris's Red House at Bexley Heath.

The stained glass windows have figure panels designed by Burne-Jones with small roundels above and below with charming naive designs of rabbits, a whale, and simple mediaeval flowers designed by Webb.

The division of the wall surface into three areas of dado, filling and frieze was to set the pattern for all the 'artistic' houses of the 1870s and 1880s, a treatment recommended in the numerous books on interior decoration aimed at the professional and middle classes, of which the Macmillan *Art at Home* series provides excellent examples. The treatment varied according to taste and means. The dado might be panelled wood, leather, paper, or, for the avant-garde, Japanese or Indian rush matting; the filling, wallpaper or damask; the frieze moulded, painted or stencilled. Most of the wallpapers of the 1870s and 1880s followed the same trend with three harmonizing patterns designed to be *en suite* as dado, filling and frieze.

The Prince Consort Gallery at the South Kensington Museum. Drawing by John Watkins c. 1876.

The general colour scheme of the room, with its bluish-green and olive tints, also set the fashion for the subdued tones of the aesthetic movement, the 'greenery-yallery' satirized by Gilbert and Sullivan.

Equally influential were the painted panels of foliage, described by Lethaby as 'vegetation like herbal drawings'.[12] Similar panels of foliage, fruit, and blossom became the hallmark of the ebonized 'art furniture' of the aesthetic period, on sideboards, cabinets and corner cupboards. The stencilled, diapered backgrounds, showing an early example of Japanese influence, were also much copied. At Castell Coch, the mock mediaeval castle built near Cardiff by William Burges for the Marquis of Bute, the drawing room has panels of foliage and flowers which are clearly modelled on those of the Green Dining Room.

The decoration of the Green Dining Room together with that of the Armoury at St. James's Palace, commissioned in 1866, represented the first important secular work by Morris, Marshall, Faulkner & Co. and was instrumental in putting the firm on the map, so that by the 1870s anyone who had pretensions to artistic taste had to have at least a Morris wallpaper, even if they could afford no more, for Morris's exacting standards meant that his products were inevitably expensive.

The Green Dining Room soon became an important meeting place for artistic circles. The painter Thomas Armstrong (1832–1911) who became Director of the Art Division of the Museum in 1881, had met Morris in the early 1860s and greatly admired him. Armstrong[13] spoke of how the Green Dining Room took the place of Gréliches and the Progrès of his earlier days in Paris for reunions with his artist friends – Poynter, Lamont, Whistler and Du Maurier. It also provided a congenial rendezvous for meetings between the heads of the Museum complex, Prof. Huxley, Dean of the College of Science, General Festing, Director of the Science Museum, John Hungerford Pollen, special editor of the Department, and J. C. Sparkes, Principal of the Art Training School, 'Armstrong's genial personality being a passport to friendship among them'. Moncure Conway, in his *Travels in South Kensington* (1882), described the Green Dining Room and remarked that 'one may dine at the South Kensington amid one of the pleasantest little picture galleries in existence'.

The Photographic Exhibition held in the Museum in 1858, photographed by Charles Thurston Thompson.

V. PUBLICATIONS AND PHOTOGRAPHY

Cole and his colleagues realized the importance of well-illustrated publications in spreading knowledge of the collections to those who could not visit the Museum for themselves. One of the first of such publications was the *Treasury of Ornamental Art* [14] published in 1857 with descriptive notes by J. C. Robinson, the curator of the Museum.

The 46 plates, as the preface stated, were examples of 'ornamental' or 'decorative' art, and were selected 'on the widest possible basis, in order to respond to every phase of connoisseurship, antiquarian interest, and practical utility to the art student, in short a complete "museographic" work has been projected'.

The illustrations included objects bought from the 1851 exhibition, mediaeval and Renaissance works of art, including objects from the Bernal Collection, purchased in 1855, with a considerable quota of Indian and Near Eastern examples, plus a few examples from other sources such as an ivory diptych from the British Museum.

The Museum also embarked on a policy of definitive catalogues, one of the first being J. C. Robinson's *Catalogue of the Soulages Collection* (1856). Outstanding among the catalogues were those of *Majolica, Hispano – Moresque, Persian, Damascus and Rhodian Ware* by C.D.E. Fortnum, FSA (1856); *Indian Art* by Major H. Cole, Henry Cole's eldest son (1874); *Ancient and Modern Furniture and Woodwork*, by John Hungerford Pollen (1875) and *Glass Vessels* by Alexander Nesbitt (1878). The policy of producing definitive catalogues naturally continued but as the collections grew, the task became increasingly difficult and since the 1930s the Museum has concentrated more on picture books, with some notable exceptions such as Sir John Pope-Hennessy's *Catalogue of Italian Sculpture* (1964) and more recently the catalogues of *British Watercolours* (1980) and *Wallpapers* (1981).

In 1875 the Museum embarked on a series of handbooks published by Chapman and Hall under the editorship of William Maskell. As a note in each volume stated, these handbooks 'were reprints of the dissertations prefixed to the large catalogues of the chief divisions of works of art in the museum . . . arranged and so far abridged as to bring each in a portable shape'. It was hoped they would be useful 'not alone for the collections at South Kensington

43

but for other collections by enabling the public at a trifling cost to understand something of the history of the subjects treated.'

The first volumes, published in 1875, covered tapestries and textiles, ivories, furniture and woodwork, majolica, and musical instruments, and volumes devoted to Japanese pottery, English earthenware and porcelain, French pottery, precious stones, bronzes (which included champlevé enamels), College and Corporation plate, Persian art, Russian art, and the industrial arts of India, Scandinavia and Denmark, were added during the late 1870s and 1880s. Many of the volumes went into several editions and were widely distributed; they were frequently given as prizes in the schools of art throughout the country. Produced either in paperback or with a characteristic dark green binding with embossed gold lettering and the crown and V. R. in black, many examples can still be found in antiquarian and second-hand bookshops throughout the country.

Probably one of the most influential of the Art Handbooks was Richard Redgrave's *Manual of Design* compiled by Gilbert Redgrave in 1876 from his father's earlier writings and addresses. The first section dealt with the general principles of ornament, the second with the application of those principles to various manufacturers, and the third with the teaching of ornament and the education of the designer. This book, as did many of the other handbooks, remained in print for many years, and was widely regarded as a standard textbook for designers in many fields.

The more detailed and specialized information contained in the Museum's catalogues and handbooks devoted to specific subjects was summarized and brought together in one volume entitled *The Industrial Arts*[15], first published in 1876 with a preface by William Maskell.

The preface pointed out that the Museum, from the time the collections were first exhibited at Marlborough House, had now been open for nearly a quarter of a century, and that 'it is scarcely possible to estimate the amount of influence for good which has been exercised over the art productions of English workmen: and this has been widely owned, not only at home but abroad . . . Many a man, ignorant of what is in him, may be strolling through the museum simply to fill up a vacant half-hour; and his eye falling on some object of particular importance to himself he will have reason to look back to the accidental visit. A thought may strike him in the way of some improvement in a mechanical process, or of some application of artistic decoration not yet attempted, – and new ideas may be roused, or energy given to dormant powers, of the nature of which he was perhaps not even aware. The main benefit to be expected from the public exhibition as that of South Kensington is a higher average of knowledge among people generally.'

The handbook was intended to give general information on the various 'art industries from furniture to lace', for those who had little knowledge of the subject and could not afford to buy the more expensive books, and, as the preface stated, 'this book is not meant for learned people, the object of it is to give the "commonest information" . . . that which is most widely wanted and very seldom at hand'.

Whereas the main catalogues had some coloured plates, the handbooks had only black and white woodblock illustrations, but in 1881 the Museum embarked on an ambitious series of *Portfolios of Industrial Art*, consisting of photo-chromo-lithographic reproductions of objects in the collections. As the preface to each portfolio stated, 'the process adopted, that of Mr. William Griggs, enables not only the form and details to be reproduced but also the colours to be delineated and thus furnishes, at a very moderate cost, a far more accurate and effective representation than would otherwise be obtained'. It was believed that the work would 'prove of value and interest not only to the students in schools of art . . . but also to many others engaged in various branches of industrial art, and to the general public'.

The portfolios, published in six volumes between 1881 and 1898, covered English, French, German, Spanish, Flemish, Italian, Sicilian, Swedish, Oriental, Persian, Saracenic, Russian, Chinese, Indian and Egyptian art. Particularly valuable were the reproductions of two-dimensional objects, such as textiles and embroideries, which were often given with the motifs in full size and were greatly welcomed by design studios. Some of the individual plates, mounted on green cards, were still being sent to art schools after the Second World War.

One of the most important sources of design in the 19th century – and later – was Owen Jones's *Grammar of Ornament*, first published in 1856. As Michael Darby has pointed out[16] it was almost certainly at Cole's suggestion that the volume came into being, for although not officially a member of the department Owen Jones worked closely with Cole and Redgrave. Owen Jones (1809–74) was a pupil of the architect Lewis Vulliamy and after travelling in Europe and the near East from 1830 to 1833 he set up practice in London. Most of his buildings and schemes of interior decoration have now been demolished and his fame rests largely on his published work and his designs for flat patterns for wallpaper and textiles. He was appointed by Cole as Superintendent of Works of the Great Exhibition of 1851 and in 1852 joint director of decoration of the Crystal Palace, being responsible for designing the Egyptian, Greek, Roman and Alhambra Courts.

When the Museum of Ornamental Art was set up in 1852, Cole offered Jones a professorship, an offer which was turned down; but in June of that year Jones gave four lectures 'On the True and False in Decorative Arts', which were subsequently published by the Department of Science and Art as their official doctrine, and were to become the guiding force for a whole generation of students of design. The idea of the *Grammar of Ornament*, which covered every style from the primitive to the Renaissance, appears to have been conceived as a means of making the ideas of the Museum more generally available, particularly to the students of design in the provincial schools who had no easy access to the metropolis.

The complete set of thirty seven principles, described as 'General Principles in the Arrangement of Form and Colour, in Architecture and the Decorative Arts', were set out at the beginning of the volume, the final proposition being that 'no improvement can take place in the Art of the Present Generation until all classes, artists, manufacturers, and the public are better educated in art, and the existence of the general principles is more fully recognised.' The volume consisted of 112 colour lithography plates accompanied by an explanatory text which was first published in 1856, and reprinted in 1910 and 1928 (and in 1972 by Van Nostrand Reinhold Company of New York). It rapidly became an indispensable source book for designers, particularly for designers of flat pattern, and no design studio could be without their copy. It has remained so even to the present day, a constant source of inspiration – if stuck for an idea, a glance through the *Grammar* will bring something to mind. Even William Morris, whose designs were usually regarded as the antithesis of those of Owen Jones, had his own personal copy.

From the beginning the Museum's influence was also spread widely through the reproduction and sale of photographs of museum objects.

At Henry Cole's suggestion a department of photography was established in the buildings in 1856, with Charles Thurston Thompson (1816–68) as superintendent.[17] Thompson was initially a wood-engraver but during the 1840s took up the recently discovered process of photography.

Thompson's first studio was set up in the new lecture theatre building, and soldiers, from the detachment of sappers garrisoned in the buildings to act as firemen and carry out other tasks, were recruited as his assistants.

Thompson's department fulfilled a number of functions firstly in producing an invaluable photographic record of the early development of the Museum, the earliest record of its kind in the world. But, as Cole explained to a Select Committee of the House of Commons in 1860, 'the photographic Department of the South Kensington Museum has arisen from a desire expressed by the various schools of art throughout the country to obtain specimens of the highest objects of art at the cheapest possible rate'. Not only the Museum's own collections but those of other museums including the Louvre, and objects in private collections were photographed by the department and prints were sold to the schools of art as well as to the general public. When commercial photographers objected to the competition Cole pointed out that the risk to the objects would have been too great for owners to give permission to a trade photographer to do the work.

One of the major achievements of the studio was the taking of the first photographs of Raphael's cartoons in 1858, then at Hampton Court, being lent to the Museum ten years later. As well as the cartoons, Raphael's drawings from Windsor Castle and Oxford University were sent to South Kensington to be photographed by Thompson and with the Prince Consort's permission prints were circulated to the art schools.

In November 1858, Cole had a visitors' room set up where all the Museum's photographs, as well as plaster casts and Elkington's electrotypes were displayed, with a photographic sales section. In 1889, photographs were sold to the public from the catalogue stall; since 1952, by which time the number of photographs for sale had increased

On preceding page: Interior of the Casts Court showing Trajan's Column. Restored in March, 1982.

I Wood-block printed chintz included in the 'False Principles' display at Marlborough House: 'No. 11 Direct Imitation of Nature'.

enormously, a special photographic sales room has been provided.

The Art Library, established in 1852, included photographs as well as books and the purpose of the collection was educational, intended to supplement the illustrations and books. The collection included photographs of architecture and of works of fine and decorative art in the museums and galleries throughout Europe. Already by 1868, when an index of the collection was published, there were some 24,000 items, which included what are now regarded as masterpieces of Victorian photography, such as portraits by Julia Margaret Cameron, views by Roger Fenton and photographs of Egypt and the Holy Land by Francis Bedford. The collection was such that in 1939, when the Museum held an exhibition devoted to Victorian photography to celebrate its centenary, the items on show were drawn almost entirely from the Museum's own resources.

There is little doubt that the Museum's interest in photography did much to promote the art in early years, and has subsequently helped to make early photographs valuable collectors' items.

In 1977 the Museum's collection of photographs was transferred to the Department of Prints and Drawings, where it has continued to grow, its emphasis being placed on the aesthetics of the medium from its beginnings until the present day. The new galleries devoted to photography in the Henry Cole building, opened in March 1983, mean that some of the collection is always on display in a series of changing exhibitions, further stimulating the use of photography as an artistic creative medium, and providing inspiration for the professional and amateur alike.

VI. THE CASTS COURTS AND THE SCULPTURE COLLECTIONS

A collection of plaster casts 'of ornamental art and all periods' was begun in 1841 at the Government School of Design and by the time the school moved to Marlborough House in 1852 some 1550 examples had been assembled. The collection was catalogued by

R. N. Wornum and published in 1854, with illustrations by Cole's 'female class for wood-engraving'. The casts continued to be used by the students and were also sent out on loan to the provincial schools of design.

When the Museum moved to South Kensington in 1857 the casts were joined by the collection of the Architectural Museum in Cannon Row, founded by Gilbert Scott and others, which was particularly strong in Gothic examples. This alliance was short-lived for in 1869 the collection was moved to the new Architectural Museum in Tufton Street, returning again to the Victoria and Albert in 1916. However, in 1861 some 3000 plaster casts of Gothic architectural details, made as models for stonemasons working on the new Houses of Parliament in the 1830s, were added to the collection.

From then on, the Museum set about acquiring casts in a more systematic manner, with emphasis on mediaeval and Renaissance examples, paralleling the acquisition of original works of art.[18]

The cast collection was particularly valuable in providing references for architectural detail and there is little doubt that much of the carved stone and stucco decoration of Victorian houses, and of gravestones and monuments, owes its inspiration to it. As the *Art Journal* pointed out in 1860,[19] 'the stone cutter who passes through the West gallery of the South Kensington Museum is extremely likely to gather a few hints which may be of great value to him for he sees there not only the best examples of Gothic carvings, from the study of which he may be enabled to throw more feeling into his works, but he also finds there casts of leaves of our common plants, casts of whole branches . . . in which the leaves are displayed, also casts of leaves that have been grouped together into fixed disposition, by which he becomes awakened to the fact that the finest examples of Gothic foliage are those that are the mere adaptions of the common plants which surround us everywhere . . . that a lesson thus learned is impressed on his mind in a manner much more lasting than when gathered from reading a book, is a truth which is daily becoming more manifest.'

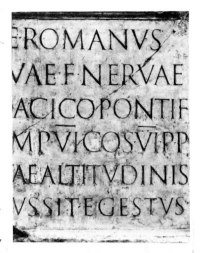

Detail of the Roman lettering on the plaster cast of Trajan's column.

II
Design for the Lecture Theatre façade of the South Kensington Museum by Francis Fowke. Exhibited at the Paris Exhibition of 1867.

III
The central refreshment room designed by Godfrey Sykes and James Gamble, with majolica tilework by Minton and Minton Hollins, 1866-68.

49

Many of the casts were made by the London firm of Brucciani and others were purchased from firms in France and Germany, but a considerable number were acquired by exchange with other museums, a project fostered by Henry Cole.

As J. C. Robinson remarked,[20] 'one of the objects of the museum was to obtain casts and other reproductions of the most notable treasures of continental museums, galleries, of monuments *in situ* in churches, palaces etc., and in general to secure the best possible representations of those great masterpieces of art, the originals of which, or their like, can never be acquired.'

The collection soon grew to such an extent that it had to be dispersed in various parts of the Museum, until in 1870 Major-General Henry Scott drew up plans for two splendid architectural courts which were opened in 1873. The impact of concentrating the collection can hardly be exaggerated.

Since comparatively few people were able to make the journey to Italy, France, Germany, or Spain, let alone India, to see the originals for themselves, the advantages to education were enormous, as the items provided a sense of scale, and a three-dimensional quality, that no photograph or drawing could possibly equal.

After the First World War, with the growth of the Modern Movement, and a less academic approach to art education, the casts courts went out of fashion, but the revival of interest in the 19th century that came about after the Second World War has called for a reassessment and the splendidly refurbished western casts court is now regarded as a monument to Victorian enterprise, while the quality of the casts themselves is seen as a superb technical achievement. In some cases the original has been destroyed, or a detail lost through pollution or bad restoration, and were it not for the enterprise of Cole and his successors no record would remain.

One of the most impressive objects of the casts courts was the Trajan's Column, so large that even in two parts it towered above the gallery of the Court. But it was not the bas-reliefs on the column, rather the inscription on the base that was to have such a dramatic influence on letter forms about the turn of the century, an influence fully described by James Mosley, the librarian of St. Bride's Institute, in an article in *Alphabet*.[21]

The Trajan inscription had models of nineteen letters of a large size, beautifully proportioned and superbly executed. One of the first architects and designers to appreciate its importance was W. R. Lethaby (1857–1913), the first principal of the L. C. C. Central School of Arts and Crafts, founded in 1894. Six years later Lethaby became the first Professor of Design at the Royal College of Art, and one of his first undertakings was to have casts made and placed in the college so that students could study and draw the letter forms. The Museum also had casts made for sending out to art schools throughout the country, together with mounted photographs of the inscription, a practice that continued until the closing of the Circulation Department.

By the turn of the century almost every book on lettering contained photographs of the Museum casts, including Edward Johnston's *Writing, Illumination and Lettering*, first

Lamentation over the dead Christ. A Paduan marble relief by Bartolomeo Bellano dating from 1470–75 acquired by the Museum in 1878. This and other pieces of sculpture seem to have had a profound influence on Eric Gill when he studied mediaeval sculpture in the Museum to provide inspiration for his 'Stations of the Cross' in Westminster Cathedral, executed between 1913 and 1917.

A pair of bronze fire dogs by Alfred Stevens executed by Hoole of Sheffield and shown at the Paris Exhibition of 1855. Photograph: The Fine Art Society Ltd.

'Art'. A bronze figure by Alfred Drury, R.A. which shows the influence of Alfred Stevens. Photograph: The Fine Art Society Ltd.

published in 1906, and, after some twenty or more reprints, still regarded as a standard text book. The British Institute of Industrial Art, in the pamphlet *The Art of Lettering and its use in Diverse Crafts and Trades*, published in 1931, described it as 'by common consent the finest example of Roman lettering extant' and the inscription was issued as a guide to signwriters under contract to the Ministry of Works.

The sculptor Eric Gill (1882–1940), who, with Edward Johnston, did so much to promote fine lettering in the 20th century, attributed his interest in letter forms to the name-plates on railway engines that he saw in his childhood at Brighton. Gill certainly knew the Trajan inscription and redrew it for the sheets of *Manuscript and Inscription Letters* (1909) which he prepared with Edward Johnston, but he remarked that 'in inscription carving, while we remember Trajan lovingly in the museum, we must forget about it in the workshop'.[22] Gill admitted that he studied Roman inscriptions as a student, in the Victoria and Albert and elsewhere, but he felt that one should not go back to the old models, but take the lettering of one's own time and improve on it. However, James Mosley has linked a tombstone of 1907, designed by Gill, to the Marchese Malaspina monument (191–1887), a North Italian sculpture of the second quarter of the 15th century; Gill's distinctive form of the letter R has clearly been copied from the Italian inscription.

The influence of Roman letter forms often came via the Italian Renaissance rather than directly from classical art. As James Mosley pointed out in the article already cited, the Roman capitals of the Florentine *Quattrocento*, found among the sculpture and casts at the Museum, provided inspiration to many designers, specific examples being found in the drawings of Walter Crane and the inscriptions on the harpsichords of Arnold Dolmetsch (1858–1940).

The sculpture collected by the Museum from the earliest days was always represented in a two-fold aspect, both as a 'fine art' and as a 'decorative art or industry', and seen as a source of inspiration not only for sculptors, but for wood carvers and other craftsmen. In the 1850s and 1860s J. C. Robinson laid the foundation for what is undoubtedly the finest collection of Italian Renaissance sculpture outside Italy, with outstanding examples by

A bust of St. Cecilia attributed to Donatello which anticipates the style of the late 19th-century school of 'New Sculpture'. Acquired by the Museum in 1861.

Donatello, Rossellino and Arnolfo di Cambio, described by Robinson himself in his *Italian Sculpture of the Middle Ages and the Period of the Revival of Art* (London 1862). In the 1860s examples of fine Byzantine and mediaeval ivories and Gothic sculpture in wood were added. Many of the finest Renaissance bronzes and reliefs, medals, 14th and 15th-century ivories and sculpture in wood, stone and terracotta came with the Salting Bequest in 1910, many of the pieces having been on loan to the Museum since 1874.

The Museum's sculpture collections, particulary the Italian Renaissance pieces, together with the direct and indirect impact of Alfred Stevens (1817–75), were to have a formative influence on the development of the 'New Sculpture'[23], a movement which freed British sculpture, both in the round and as an architectural decoration, from the stranglehold of Neo-Classicism. Many of the exponents of the 'New Sculpture' were trained at the National Art Training School at South Kensington, or at the Lambeth School of Art and the associated South London Technical Art School established in 1879 under Francis Wallaston Moody (1824–86), Jules Dalou (1838–1902) and Edward Lanteri (1848–1917). They were consequently familiar with the work of Alfred Stevens and with the Museum's collections, although it must be admitted that the influence of contemporary French Romantic-Realist sculpture was also important.

Stevens himself had spent nine years travelling in Italy absorbing the Renaissance spirit, and had returned to England in 1842. For a brief period in 1845 Stevens taught architecture, perspective and modelling at the Government School of Design at Somerset House, a task which led to his appointment in 1850 as chief designer to the firm of Hoole of Sheffield. The stoves and grates he designed for them were exhibited at the 1851 Exhibition, at Paris in 1855, and in London in 1862, and several examples were purchased for the Museum's collections. Stevens became the idol and 'master' of three students at the Sheffield School of Art (Godfrey Sykes, James Gamble, Reuben Townroe) and of F. W. Moody, instructor in Decorative Art, all of whom were to become closely involved with South Kensington and the Museum.

Thus the influence of Stevens was spread not only through his own work but also through that of his followers.

The Royal College of Art Students Magazine for 1912 (quoted by Susan Beattie) contains recollections by former students which give a fascinating insight into the teaching methods and the impact of the Museum's collections. The painter George Clausen, a student at South Kensington in 1871, wrote that 'the Museum was our best teacher. The Italian Court with the fine sculptures and terracottas we got to know very well . . . Contemporary Sculpture was non-existent as far as our knowledge and interest went, except for the work and influence of Stevens, whose tradition was being carried on in the decoration of the museum.' Clausen also related that it was Moody, more than any of the other masters, who encouraged the students to study and draw in the Museum, particularly the Italian Renaissance sculpture. Moody worked in the same manner as Stevens, urging a simplicity and breadth of treatment far removed from the laborious finished drawings of the previous era and this new approach was strengthened when E. J. Poynter was appointed to succeed Redgrave in 1875. It was Poynter who persuaded Alphonse Legros to set up an etching class at South Kensington. Legros was a great admirer of Stevens but his most important contribution was to persuade the French sculptor Jules Dalou, who had trained under Carpeaux, to give demonstrations of clay modelling. His realistic modelling shown to perfection in his terracotta groups, was to have a profound influence on the new English sculptors. In 1880 Edward Lanteri, who had been Dalou's pupil in France, was appointed to succeed him at South Kensington, carrying on Dalou's methods.

Some of the exponents of the 'New Sculpture' were trained at South Kensington. Alfred Drury (1856-1944) won a scholarship to South Kensington and was taught by Dalou and Lanteri, winning gold medals in the national competitions of 1879, 1880 and 1881. He took a keen interest in the work of Alfred Stevens, and his reliefs and niche figures for the main façade of the Victoria and Albert Museum, executed in 1905-7, show Stevens's influence.

'Beatrice'. Marble relief by Edward Lanteri (1848-1917) showing the influence of Florentine sculpture.

55

Others who studied under Lanteri included Albert Toft (1862-1949), Reginald Fairfax Wells (1871-1951), Alfred Gilbert (1854-1934) and George Frampton (1860-1928)

The low relief sculptures of Donatello, acquired by the Museum in the 1860s, were to have a profound influence on the development of sculpture in both stone and bronze. Although Eric Gill was inclined to deny he was a learned antiquarian, he is known to have studied the mediaeval and early Renaissance sculpture in the Museum. The 12th-century relief panels of scenes from the life of Christ in Chichester Cathedral seem to have provided Gill with inspiration for his *Stations of the Cross* in Westminster Cathedral,[24] but there seems little doubt that the Paduan relief of the *Lamentation of the Dead Christ* by Bartolomeo Bellano, acquired by the Museum in 1878, also had a profound influence, particularly on the treatment of the drapery and stances of the figures.

Indeed, there can be few 20th-century sculptors who have not been influenced by the Museum's sculpture collections which gradually became fully representative of all periods, including the 19th century with the superb collection of Rodin works, now on view at the entrance of the Henry Cole wing. The collection also includes some fine Gaudier Brzeskas, presented by Sir Eric Maclagan, who was also responsible for acquiring pieces by Modigliani and Ivan Mestrovic (1883-1962). The sculptor Sir Charles Wheeler (b. 1892), in his autobiography *High Relief* (Country Life, London 1968), writes of the great Ivan Mestrovic as 'one of the true geniuses of the 20th century - a revelation of style, strength and profundity, new and exciting. I was very greatly affected.'

The 20th-century sculpture collections include pieces by Leon Underwood, Eric Gill, Maurice Lambert and others, and some small pieces by Henry Moore and other living sculptors, acquired by the Circulation Department, but generally speaking the acquisition of contemporary sculpture is now regarded as the province of the Tate Gallery.

VII. THE CIRCULATION DEPARTMENT

In 1853, one year after the establishment of the Museum at Marlborough House, the Lords of the Committee of Privy Council for the Board of Trade were 'desirous of encouraging the formation of local museums of art, and enabling the students of the local branch schools, who cannot visit London, to inspect such of the works of ornamental art belonging to the Museum at Marlborough House, as may be likely to have a useful influence on the special manufactures of their respective localities.' They proposed that these objects should be lent to the provinces for two months, from 15 July to 15 September, applications to be made by the prospective borrowers on or before 1 July. The Chairman, Treasurer and Secretary of the local School of Ornamental Art had to undertake responsibility for the presentation and safety of the objects and to pay for any damage or loss according to the value stated in the individual catalogue. In addition the local schools were given the opportunity of purchasing any duplicated or superfluous exhibits at half the

*Far left:
Standing
Girl.
Terracotta
by Jules
Dalou
(1838–
1902)*

*Left:
'Charity'.
Bronze by
Alfred
Gilbert,
1900. A
cast of one
of four
figures
commis-
sioned for
the Lord
Arthur
Russell
Memorial
in 1892.*

A travelling 'C' case set up by the Circulation Department with a selection of English ceramics including Wedgwood, Poole, and Grays Pottery. About 1937.

original cost to the Department. As the 1853 report of the Department of Practical Art stated 'by these means the whole country is made to participate in the advantages and prosperity of the central Museum, and its benefits are not limited to the residents of the Metropolis'.

The categories of objects of loan included glass, ceramics, metalwork, ivory carvings, textiles and wallpapers, supplemented by photographs and drawings of rare exhibits. It was decreed that the objects should be available to both students and the public, both during the day and in the evening. Students were admitted free but the public had to pay a moderate fee, higher in the mornings than in the evenings and 'to enable the citizens and others employed in the daytime to share in the benefits derived from the collection, the fee on three evenings a week should not exceed one penny'.

The funds raised from the entrance fees were to be applied to the cost of transport and other expenses, after which a quarter of the remaining sum went towards the art master's fees, a quarter to the General Fund of the school and one half to purchase objects for a permanent museum.

By 1855 the growth of the Museum's collection enabled a more complete and systematic selection to be made which travelled under the title of the Circulating Museum. The introduction of the catalogue described the setting up of the Circulating Museum as 'the adoption of a measure always contemplated as one of the most important objects – it is that, for the first time perhaps in the history of museums, of rendering moveable the treasures acquired, and of bringing home to the millions of the land opportunities for the study of the beautiful in art which have hitherto . . . been the privilege only of dwellers in the metropolitan cities . . . It is thought that the bringing home to the students and the general public in the provinces of even such a collection as is now put in circulation will have a result more than proportionate to the actual extent of the undertaking; at any rate, the opportunity for the leisurely and repeated examination of a series of selected specimens will be more than equivalent to rare and hurried holiday visits to even the greatest Metropolitan museums, when the mind of the student, excited by novelty and the multiplicity of

Selecting examples for the German showcase in a Circulation Department travelling exhibition of Gothic Art in 1949.

attractions too often abandons itself to the merely pleasureable excitement of the moment.'

The writer also hoped that the travelling museum would stimulate local endeavour in setting up their own art museums and also encourage the authorities to seek supplementary loans from local collectors. It was also suggested that in each town where the collection was exhibited the chefs d'oeuvre of the day might be shown with a due record of designers, manufacturers and even the skilled workmen associated with their production, another step which might help to improve both design and public taste.

The Circulating Museum consisted initially of abour four hundred items, representing each section, including some Sèvres porcelain lent by the Queen. The collection was housed in five glazed cases which fitted together to form a stand intended to occupy a 12ft by 6ft space in the centre of a room, elevated on a platform formed of square boxes ingeniously fitted out to provide the packing cases for the objects. In addition there were seventy glazed frames containing specimens of textiles, lace, photographs, and drawings which hung on nine portable wooden stands. A carriage or truck specially constructed was transported by rail and an officer of the Department of Science and Art accompanied the collection, remaining with it during the exhibition period in each locality.

In its first year it visited Birmingham, Nottingham, Macclesfield, and Norwich, attracting over 55,000 visitors. Additional collections were added specifically for the benefit of certain industries.

The Circulating Museum collection was initally sent only to those places which had schools of art and the benefits derived from it depended partly on the arrangements made by the localities. In 1856, at Hanley, in the Potteries, it was visited by over 20,000 people, but in Newcastle-on-Tyne, where the collection did not relate so closely to the local industries (which were 'heavy' rather than 'art') only just over 1,000 people bothered to visit it. Indeed the intention as far as possible was to send the collection to towns engaged in 'aesthetic' and artistic manufactures. In 1857 it was lent to Stourbridge (then, as now, an important centre of glass manufacture), to Worcester, Liverpool, Glasgow, Paisley and Dundee, the Scottish towns being important centres of textile production. Although it was realized that the

'English Chintz'. A Circulation Department travelling exhibition at the Swansea Art Gallery in January, 1957. Photograph: Colquhoun Ltd, Swansea.

temporary withdrawal of objects from the Museum's collections might cause some inconvenience, it was felt that the advantages to the provinces were so great and so appreciated as to more than counterbalance the drawbacks. The 7th Annual Report (1860) was happy to state that during the previous three years the collection had been sent to twenty six places and visited by 306,387 people, whose admission fees benefitted the art schools by upwards of £6,000. It was also recorded that 'although the most fragile articles, such as the Sèvres porcelain and glass, have been transmitted at least 3,690 miles by railway etc. and been packed and unpacked 56 times, no specimens have been broken or damaged.'

By 1862 the collection had doubled and consisted of some 820 objects; during this year, at the time of the London International Exhibition, the Circulating Collection was shown in London and the system was said to have excited great interest among the foreign visitors.

In the 1860s, additional encouragement to the provinces was given by special loans, free of charge, to exhibitions of industrial and fine art which were organized in various localities, commencing with pictures and electrotypes being lent to a show at Alton Towers in 1864, for the benefit of the Wedgwood Institute, which was to house the Burslem School of Art. Similar loans were made to local art and industrial exhibitions including the North London Working Men's Industrial Exhibition at Islington.

The purpose of such events was to raise funds for establishing museums in the localities and a particularly successful one was the Wakefield Industrial and Fine Art Exhibition, held in the Corn Exchange in 1868: it made a profit of £3,000 which was expended in the purchase and erection of buildings for an Industrial and Fine Art Institution including both a School and a Museum of Art.

Another move to encourage the setting up of permanent local museum and art school collections was the willingness of the Museum to make objects available for reproduction by electrotyping, gelatine moulding, plaster casting, and photography, as 'offering facilities for the acquisition of correct copies of the most admirable specimens at a comparatively nominal cost'. The 1860 Annual Report recommended that the Circulating Collection be extended and in that year the acquisition of the Sheepshanks Gift made it possible to add

'British Studio Pottery'. An exhibition mounted by the Circulation Department in the 1960s.

pictures to the scheme which, by this time, included twenty two different categories:-

1 Engravings of the English School;
2 Wood engravings, ancient and modern;
3 Drawings and engravings illustrative of wall decoration;
4 Illustrations of the history of painted glass;
5 Textile fabrics, mediaeval and oriental;
6 Ancient and modern pottery;
7 Ancient and modern glassware;
8 Works in metal;
9 Furniture carvings in wood, illustrated in addition by photographs and drawings;
10 Watercolour drawings and sketches;
11 Oil paintings by ancient masters;
12 Oil paintings by modern masters;
13 Engravings and etchings, ancient and modern;
14 Modern continental contemporary art manufactures, bronze, pottery jewellery, etc;
15 Reproductions of works in metal, fictile ivory etc;
16 A selection of the publications of the Arundel Society;
17 British Museum photographs;
18 Photographs of Raffaello's cartoons;
19 Photographs from the drawings of ancient masters;
20 Photographs of objects of decorative art, chiefly in the foreign museums and private collections (several series);
21 Photographs of paintings, wall decorations etc., and drawings of the same;
22 Architectural photographs and drawings.

From the above list it will be seen that the range provided an almost inexhaustible source of inspiration for art students, designers and manufacturers and brought to the notice of the public, who were encouraged to visit the displays, objects or replicas of objects that they would otherwise not have been aware of, let alone actually seen.

In 1864, some of the local officials of the Department felt that rather than one general collection, specialized collections, relating to the various industries of the localities, might be more helpful, ceramics to Stoke-on-Trent, metalwork to Sheffield, lace to Nottingham etc., and it was agreed that all objects which could be removed from the central museum should be available for loan.

In 1868 the objects were classified into seventeen divisions, with some additional items, such as clocks, watches, basketwork, and bookbinding. Works could only be borrowed from two divisions at a time, plus some framed examples. The Department provided glass cases to house the loans. The objects were normally lent for weekly periods and there was also a circulating library from which books could be borrowed – limited to two folio, four quarto, and eight octavo at any one time, but no book costing less than 10 shillings was circulated as it was reckoned that schools could buy inexpensive books themselves.

The pattern continued much the same throughout the 1870s – in 1873 some 10,000 objects were circulated. The loans had the desired effect in causing privincial museums to be set up and already by 1878, Nottingham Museum and Birmingham Corporation Art Galleries received deposit loans and by the following year the permanent museum borrowers had increased to nine.

In 1869 the Museum purchased 374 duplicate items of modern Italian jewellery from Alessandro Castellani (1824–83) and Augusto Castellani (1829-1914), the noted Italian goldsmiths, silversmiths and antiquarians, specially for circulation to the provinces. The Castellanis were famed for their reproductions of Etruscan and other classical gold jewellery and popularized the archeological style that their father, Fortunato Pio Castellani (1793–1865), had pioneered earlier in the century. Eight cases containing the Castellani and other jewellery, electrotypes and silver plates, plus some bronze and iron objects, were sent to the Birmingham School of Art and arranged as an exhibition. Admission was free and the local citizens were said to have displayed great interest in the collection. Certainly many copies or adaptations of the Castellani jewellery were made in Birmingham in the 1870s and 1880s.

In 1880 it was decided to extend the loan scheme to municipality museums, particularly those in the manufacturing areas. To increase the objects available for circulation, textiles and lace were cut into pieces, and pairs of objects split up. The loan of objects to museums, where they were seen by more members of the general public, gradually became increasingly important and by 1900 there were about eighty museums taking advantage of the system.

The earliest loans to museums consisted of fifty to two hundred objects which were individually picked from the collections displayed at South Kensington and lent for a year at a time. Additional collections were set up, appropriate to the industry of a particular area, including very specialized loans such as Tonbridge ware to Tonbridge Wells, 'to endeavour to resuscitate and improve artistically the small local industry . . . which has existed over a hundred years'.

In 1901, the collection of Art Nouveau objects from the Paris Exhibition, largely comprised of the Donaldson Gift, which had caused such a furore when it was exhibited at South Kensington, was lent first to the Polytechnic Exhibition at Bingley Hall, Birmingham, and then to the Museum of Science and Art, Edinburgh. As the Board of Education for 1901 stated, 'in each case a note was sent explaining the object of the collection and the method recommended in studying the various objects'. There is little doubt that, as in London, the collection had a mixed reception, on the one hand provoking a somewhat hostile reaction and on the other providing a welcome inspiration for designers and encouraging the acceptance of new forms and design motifs on the part of the general public.

As the number of borrowers increased, the existing loan scheme became administratively and practicably unworkable and the completion of the new building in 1909 gave the opportunity to reorganize the whole of the Museum's collections, including those available for loan. The Circulation Department was then formally instituted and each of the Museum's departments was instructed to transfer part of their collections to the Circulation Department, to provide a stock of material exclusively for loan to provincial museums, resulting in a collection of some ten thousand items. The objects available to art schools were separate and additional to this collection. The Circulation Department grew by purchase, gifts and bequests and by further transfers from the other departments. Although absolutely unique pieces, or masterpieces of international importance, could not be made available for loan, the collection was by no means second rate. Some extremely rare items, particularly from those fields in which the Museum's collections were exceptionally rich – Coptic, mediaeval and other textiles, early English watercolours and Chinese ceramics – were included. When any major collection was acquired, either by purchase, gift or bequest, such as the Gulland Bequest of Chinese ceramics in 1931, or the Eumorfopoulous Collection in 1938, a proportion of the pieces were set aside for circulation. This practice continued until the Department was closed by the Government in 1976.

The riches of the Museum were thus made available to the whole country, spreading its influence to every corner of the United Kingdom, for Wales, Scotland, and Northern Ireland as well as England were eligible for loans.

The setting up of the Circulation Department with its own purchase grant was extremely important in the fostering of good modern design. Throughout the 19th century the Museum had bought contemporary objects, particularly from international exhibitions, but after the Paris Exhibition of 1900 this practice ceased, and, as Walter Crane pointed out in the foreword to the catalogue of the 9th Arts and Crafts Exhibition of 1910, it was only the Circulation Department that bought the works of living artists, craftsmen and designers.

The purchases of the Circulation Department, supplemented by gifts from manufacturers and others, built up a comprehensive collection of 20th-century applied art, particularly in the fields of textiles, ceramics and glass, both British and foreign, which provided

IV A Minton maiolica candlestick based on a 16th-century Palissy ware candlestick, both objects having been acquired by the Museum in 1859.

inspiration to art students and designers and also did a great deal to promote an appreciation of good modern design among the general public. Under the direction of Sir John Pope-Hennessy, the curatorial departments were encouraged to buy modern objects, but there was a great reluctance to do so on the part of most of them. The situation has improved in recent years as the present Director, Sir Roy Strong, has ensured that a proportion of each department's purchase grants must be expended on post-1914 objects; this is in addition to the exceptionally important 20th-century objects purchased from Central funds.

The Second World War inevitably caused the cessation of the loans to the provinces and it was not until 1948 that the Circulation Department was able to resume its services. Rather than revive the old pre-war system of permanent loans, it was decided to concentrate on complete exhibitions, of both framed and three-dimensional material, to be lent to provincial museums and art galleries. Some of the exhibitions concentrated on particular periods or styles, such as European Gothic Art, or Islamic Art, or on specialist areas such as Chinese ceramics, Meissen porcelain or English watercolours. The inclusion of contemporary material was probably the most important contribution made by the Circulation Department; the items came either from their own purchases, or were borrowed from other organizations. Many important exhibitions were staged by the Department in the Museum itself and often followed by reduced versions which were circulated throughout the country.

VIII. BETHNAL GREEN MUSEUM

In 1865, when the first permanent buildings of the South Kensington Museum were ready, the temporary cast iron and glass structure was offered to the authorities for North, South and East London, for the purpose of setting up local museums. East London was the only area to take up the offer and a committee under the chairmanship of Sir Antonio Brady, the social reformer, was set up to organize a subscription list. A site at Bethnal Green was found

V
An early 15th-century Hispano-Moresque lustre bowl, acquired by the Museum in 1864, which probably provided the inspiration for the galleon designs of William De Morgan.

VI
Ruby lustre dish by William De Morgan. Merton Abbey period, 1882–88.

in the centre of one of the most densely populated manufacturing and labouring districts of London – and one of the poorest. Having purchased the site, the Committee soon realized that they could not afford to staff, equip and run the museum on the scale envisaged and it was handed back to the Department of Science and Art, to become the first branch of the Victoria and Albert.

The title deeds were formally handed over in April 1869 and the temporary cast iron and glass structure given a permanent brick cladding with mosaic tile friezes of art and industry on the north and south exterior walls. The Museum was officially opened, with great pomp and ceremony, by the Prince and Princess of Wales on 24 June 1872, with the collection of Sir Richard Wallace as the main attraction.

Sidney Colvin[25] wrote in an article in the *Fortnightly Review* on 1 October 1872: 'For the first time since the flats between Shoreditch and the Lea were overrun with miles of dwellings and peopled with millions of inhabitants, the sign of a collective or liberal existence has arisen among that monotonous and depressed community . . . the new Branch Museum of the Science and Art Department at Bethnal Green is the first proportionate building ever raised in these parts for the purpose of public rendezvous, circulation and entertainment.'

Colvin went on to point out: 'By a strange hyperbole one rich man has poured out for show, in the heart of a world like this, the concentrated arts and luxuries of worlds how opposite! The excellent and thoroughgoing public spirit of Sir Richard Wallace still more than the noise of the royal opening processions, has given the first year of the new museum just the prominence to attract the most of public regard . . . the show has drawn on the afternoons and evenings of the free days crowds of the populace – men, women and children to throng the turnstiles, to stroll and sit, to gaze, wonder and get refreshed with the vague satisfaction and vague intelligence, were they no more, that must spring from this new participation in things of an aspect newly pleasureable and bright.'

That this statements was justified is fully born out by the contemporary illustrations of the crowds thronging the galleries. The Wallace Collection, now housed at Hertford House, Manchester Square, comprised the finest examples of French 18th-century furniture, Sèvres porcelain, masterpieces of Rembrandt, Watteau, Fragonard, Peter de Hoogh, and others, together with a host of other art treasures. No French furniture comparable to that of the Wallace Collection was exhibited by the parent museum until it received the Jones Bequest in 1882. As well as the Wallace Collection, at the time of the opening the Museum contained the Animal Products Division, which included leather goods, things made from shells, feathers, and hair, carved ivory and scrimshaw-work, and the Food collections.

For a number of years, however, the Bethnal Green Museum had no art collections of its own and relied on loans from outside sources including the Pitt Rivers Anthropological Collection in 1874, the Franks Collection of Oriental and European porcelain in 1875, the

Bank Holiday at the Bethnal Green Museum. From Museums and Art Galleries *by Thomas Greenwood, F.R.C.S., London, 1888.*

The Prince of Wales opening the Bethnal Green Museun on 20 June 1872.

Willett Collection of pottery and porcelain (some 1,700 pieces illustrating popular British history and now at Brighton Museum) in 1892. The Royal interest in the Museum was maintained by the 1876 exhibition of the presents the Prince of Wales received on his visit to India and Queen Victoria's Jubilee presents in 1888.

During the early years the collections seem to have provided both education and entertainment. From its inception the Bethnal Green Museum has had a dual function: as a branch of a national museum displaying selections from the nation's treasures, and as a local museum, providing a service for the community, and, until the establishment of the Geffrye Museum in 1914, it remained the only museum in the area.

As at South Kensington, the policy of exhibiting the finest examples of craftmanship aimed at inspiring not only designers and manufacturers, but also the working man or artisan who actually carried out the work, as well as improving the taste of the general public. The Museum was originally open until 10 pm on Mondays, Tuesdays and Saturdays.

The two local industries were cabinet-making and silk-weaving, although the latter was already dying by the time the Museum was opened. In 1878 a special Loan Exhibition of Furniture[26] mostly drawn from the collections at South Kensington, was shown at Bethnal Green, and thereafter there was usually a sizeable collection of furniture on show, which was of considerable use to the students of the Shoreditch College of Furniture. Similarly a collection of boots and shoes was related to the work of the nearby Cordwainers School.

A costume collection assembled round the Spitalfields silk collection unfortunately had little influence on the sweat-shops of the local 'rag trade'.

In some ways Bethnal Green became a microcosm of South Kensington, with its emphasis shifting from time to time as the policies of the main museum changed. Many of the superb objects bought from the International Exhibitions from 1851 to 1900 found their way into the basements of Bethnal Green, to be resurected as 19th-century Continental Primary Gallery under Sir John Pope-Hennessy is 1965, accompanied by the Rodin sculptures which had been loaned to the Tate. The Rodins are now back at South Kensington to be joined by the objects as soon as space permits.

In 1919 Bethnal Green assumed the responsibility for both the display and acquisition of the toy and doll collections of the Victoria and Albert, and since 1974 it has been designated the Bethnal Green Museum of Childhood, attracting collectors from all over the world; but the local character of the Museum is maintained by close involvement with the community, particularly with the children.

IX. THE INFLUENCE OF THE SOUTH KENSINGTON MUSEUM ON APPLIED ART MUSEUMS IN EUROPE

Many museums on the lines of South Kensington were set up in the British Isles, one of the most important being that which is now the Royal Scottish Museum at Edinburgh,

Display cases for the Kunstgewerbemuseum, Berlin, modelled on those at the South Kensington Museum. Photograph: Kunstgewerbemuseum, Berlin (West).

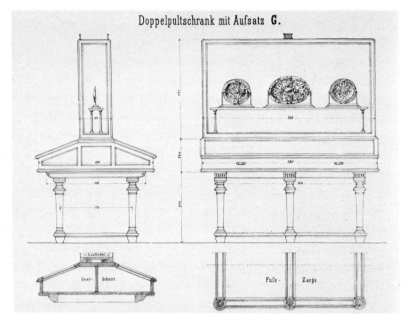

Doppelpultschrank mit Aufsatz **G.**

The Deutsches Gewerbe Museum in the Diorama, showing a similar display to that in the Educational Museum in the 'Brompton Boilers', in 1859. Photograph: Kunstgewerbemuseum, Berlin (West).

inaugurated by the Department of Science and Art as a National Museum of Science and Art in 1860. The building was designed by Captain Francis Fowke and the foundation stone laid by the Prince Consort on 23 October 1861, less than two months before his death on 14 December. The museum was opened by Prince Alfred (who was created Duke of Edinburgh) on 19 May 1866.

The influence of the South Kensington Museum in the setting up of similar museums of applied art throughout Europe is reflected in a report (published in 1875 by the Science and Art Department) of the Committee of the Council of Education at South Kensington, which listed the principal museums in Europe with the character of their collections, their administrations and official publications. In December 1872, Henry Cole sent out a circular letter asking the museums to supply details of their publications so that these could be acquired by the library, either by purchase or exchange with those of the South Kensington Museum. While the list shows that many of the museums' collections were confined to the fine arts or antiquities, by 1875 a number of the museums, particularly those in Germany, in the Austro-Hungarian Empire and in Holland, had collections similar to those at South Kensington.

The first museum in Europe to be organized on the lines of South Kensington was the Austrian Museum for Art and Industry (Angewandte Kunst Museum) in Vienna. The Austrians believed that although they had a natural talent for the arts, lack of training put them at a disadvantage compared to other nations. The idea of a museum devoted to art and industry was considered after the Great Exhibition of 1851, but the political unrest in Europe meant that no positive steps were taken until the 1862 Exhibition, when Rudolf von Eitelberger, professor of history of art at the University of Vienna, was sent to London to report on how the Austrian exhibits compared with those of the rest of the world. His report particularly emphasized the importance of the South Kensington Museum. The Emperor Franz Joseph, impressed with the report, set Eitelberger the task of outlining the scope and the requirements needed to establish a similar museum with the aim of improving the taste of the population. On 7 March 1863 the Emperor authorized the foundation of such a museum. The Emperor himself made available art objects from the imperial collections, from the various imperial castles, the court library, the Schatzkammer and the Arsenal, and authorized the use of the Ballhaus of the Hofburg to house the collections, both on a permanent and rotating basis. He also urged the nobility, private collectors and regional authorities to supplement the Royal loans in forming a representative exhibition, to which, as at South Kensington, would be added contemporary manufactures of a high standard of design and execution. On 31 March 1864 the Imperial Edict announced the foundation of the Austrian Museum for Art and Industry. The foundation committee consisted of various functionaries of the Imperial collections, and the art historians Rudolf von Eitelberger, Dr Gustav Heider, and J. G. Seidl; their aim was the promotion of the applied arts and the general raising of taste by means of the provision of artefacts from both science and the arts. As at South Kensington, the collection was to consist of both originals and copies supplemented by plaster casts and photographs, with published catalogues and explanatory material, lectures and travelling exhibitions which were to spread the message throughout the Austrian provinces.

Rudolf von Eitelberger was appointed the first director, with Jacob von Falke, librarian to the Duchy of Lichtenstein, as his deputy.

The permanent building was begun in 1867 and was completed in 1871. It was very much in the South Kensington manner: red bricks with sandstone details, ornamented with majolica plaques portraying famous artists and craftsmen.

By this time the museum had increased its own rich collections, particularly in the field of textiles, and no longer had to rely on loans. The inaugural exhibition in the new building consisted of contemporary Austrian arts and crafts. The first major report on the museum's activities took the form of a 'festschrift' for the Vienna World Exhibition of 1873, which confidently stated that the aims of its founders had been achieved.

As at South Kensington, a higher school for arts and crafts and applied arts was attached to the museum, a project that had been initiated by the Chamber for Industry and Commerce in Lower Austria in 1867 to train designers for industry, as well as artists, craftsmen, and art teachers. Exhibitions of the students' work was held at the museum every spring and autumn up to the outbreak of the First World War.

The German museums are fully described in Barbara Mundt's volume *Die Deutsche Kunstgewerbemuseen Im 19 Jahrhundert* (Prestel – Verlag, Munchen 1974). The Deutsche Kunstgewerbemuseen in Berlin housed in the Schloss Kopenick since 1967, was founded a century before in 1867, and opened to the public in 1868. The initial impetus for the establishment of the museum came from the Berliner Handwerkerverein, an association of artisans and practitioners of the decorative arts, who campaigned for an institution for the advancement of art allied to industry.

Emulating the interest which her father, the Prince Consort, had taken in the applied arts, in 1866 the Crown Princess Victoria sent Dr Herman Schwabe, as head state-official in Berlin, to investigate the situation in England. His report[27] aroused the interest of the city council and in 1867 a meeting of a private Board urged the setting up of a museum of applied arts. The nucleus of the museum's collections was formed by the German exhibits at the Paris Exhibition of 1867 and a school of design attached to the museum was established the following year.

The museum was at first housed in the 'Gropius'schen Dioramas' and a contemporary illustration shows an assembly of objects that closely resemble the displays in the Museum of Ornamental Art at Marlborough House. In 1873 the collections were transferred to the former Royal porcelain factory until a new permanent building was completed in 1887. The building was designed in Renaissance style by Gropius and Schmieden, with details in terracotta and tilework, and mosaics by Salviati. The terracotta panels bore the names of great artists with emblematic scenes of their work. The interior was grouped around a large central court, intended for loan exhibitions and new acquisitions. It was surrounded by two rows of arcades supported by slender columns, with a majolica frieze in low relief above the upper arcade. Contemporary illustrations show that these splendid courts and galleries were akin to the quadrangle and the north and south courts of the South Kensington Museum, with showcases that were modelled on South Kensington prototypes.

In Hamburg there had been a Society for the Encouragement of the Arts and Crafts since 1765 (Die Hamburger Gesellschaft für Beförderung der Kunst und Hutzlichen Gewerbe); on the occasion of its centenary in 1865, the Society set about creating a decorative arts museum, the Museum für Kunst und Gewerbe. The prime mover was Justus Brinckmanns, a lawyer and scholar, who became the museum's first Director on its foundation in 1869. The museum developed along with a school of architecture and arts and crafts, and in 1877 a new building was erected by the town architect, K. T. Zimmermann, to house both institutions. Brinckmanns was also a follower of Semper and the museum was accordingly arranged in technical categories. From the onset the museum acquired both historical and contemporary objects, including items from International exhibitions, beginning with Vienna in 1873 and including a large collection of Art Nouveau objects from Paris in 1900.[28]

The Stadel Museum at Frankfurt am Main was mainly a gallery of paintings with collections of drawings, and was connected with a school of art; but the Kunstsgewerbe Museum of Frankfurt was not founded until 1877. In Nuremberg, the Bavarian Museum of Industry (Bayerisches Gewerbe Museum) housed objects of art and industry as well as technological collections.

In Stuttgart, the Royal Central Board of Trade and Commerce had set up an industrial collection as early as 1850 under the title of the Würtembergisches Musterlager (known as the Würtembergisches Landmuseum from 1886); it was housed in the barracks until 1896 when the new building was opened.

By the end of the 19th century most of the towns in Germany had their decorative arts museums and the influence of Semper and the South Kensington system was apparent with an emphasis on art applied to industry. Semper's technical classification of the decorative arts, which he outlined in *Der Stil*[29], became the model for all the decorative art museums, including South Kensington, with the collections classified and arranged on the basis of material and technique in the four main divisions of ceramics and glass, metalwork, textiles and furniture, and woodwork. This was a practical and useful arrangement for the training of designers for industry but gradually the museums moved away from this rather restrictive practice and organized the collections in a more flexible way, concentrating on periods rather than materials and techniques.

The Museum of Applied Arts (Iparmüvèszeti Museum) in Budapest, described by Walter

Crane[30] as a sort of 'South Kensington of Hungary', was founded in 1872. The first exhibition of decorative or applied arts had been held in Hungary as early as 1842 but it was the impact of the international exhibitions, particularly London 1862, and Paris 1867 which provided the impetus for setting up a museum. Hungary had participated in both exhibitions and had observed the progress made in British design since the 1851 exhibition. When the Hungarian Parliament accepted the proposal to found a permanent exhibition it met with enthusiastic response and the whole nation contributed gifts to the collection. Under the directorship of György Ráth from 1881 to 1896, and of Jeno Radisics from 1896 to 1917, the museum assembled a collection of distinguished objects, which closely paralleled those of South Kensington, but with a special emphasis on Hungarian items. At the same time the museum encouraged artists and designers, and when, after some seventy years, the collections outgrew the available space a new building, known as the Palace of Applied Arts, was built between 1893 and 1896 to contain both the museum and a school of applied arts on the lines of South Kensington.

Another important East European museum begun on similar lines to South Kensington was the Decorative Arts Museum, Prague (Uměleckoprumyslové Museum) founded in 1885 and temporarily based in the Kunstlerhaus Rudolphinum. The Prague Chamber of Commerce had been working towards an applied arts museum since 1867, following the Paris Exhibition, and indeed a Bohemian Industrial Museum was in existence by 1873. The museum was given its own building in 1900; like so many others, it was in the Renaissance style, adorned with sculptured relief panels of figures engaged in arts and crafts with objects arranged on the Semper plan.

The South Kensington Museum was the main source of inspiration for the Croatian Art Society when its members founded a decorative arts museum in Zagreb, Yugoslavia, in 1880 as 'a collection of samples for master craftsmen and artists who should advance again the production of objects of everyday use and art, undone so much by the onset of the machine and industrial manufacture'.[31]

The initiative came from Dr Iso Kršnjave, Professor of History of Art at Zagreb University. The Croatian Art Society had been appalled at the standard of both industrial and craft exhibits at the numerous international exhibitions since 1851, and the underlying philosophy of the founders was based on the fundamental principles and the theoretical ideas of the Arts and Crafts Movement. In 1882 an Arts and Crafts School was opened in conjunction with the museum. Six years later, in 1888, a new building was erected to house both the museum and the school. The initial collections consisted mainly of gifts supplemented by purchases from important private collections, but acquisitions were gradually made on a more organized basis to build balanced collections of furniture, ceramics, metalwork, and especially textiles. Further objects were acquired through exchange with other museums and purchases from exhibitions at Trieste, Budapest and Vienna. As at the South Kensington Museum, a good art library was gradually assembled.

The Kunstgewerbemuseum, Berlin, in 1898. Photograph: Kunstgewerbemuseum, Berlin (West).

Other museums of art in industry, listed in the 1875 volume, were the Kunst Industries in Amsterdam, and the Museum of Art and Industry at Haarlem, administered by the Netherland Society for the Promotion of Industry.

In Moscow there was a Museum of Art and Industry connected with the Strogonoff School of Technical Drawing; it contained a collection of art objects and antiquities, which seemed, according to their publications, to have a strong national bias indicated by a History of Russian Ornament from the 10th to the 16th century (published 1870) and a manual for designing ornament in the Russian style published the following year.

Strangely enough the Conservatoire des Arts et Metiers (now the Musée National des Techniques, Paris), founded in 1794, which had been acquiring English objects as early as 1820, and, like the South Kensington Museum, combined both science and art, does not appear in the 1875 list, although the museum attached to the Sèvres factory is listed, as is the Museum of Art History at Lyons. The Musée des Arts Decoratifs in Paris, modelled largely on the South Kensington Museum, was not opened until 1877, although France had held exhibitions of applied arts since the 18th century, and the Union Centrale des Beaux Arts, founded in 1864, was extremely active in promoting the decorative arts through exhibitions, periodicals, and publications (in 1882 it changed its name to Union Centrale des Arts Decoratifs).

Other museums that owed their existence to the success of South Kensington, and were founded for the same purpose, could be described, but those detailed above should suffice to prove the influence that the Museum was to have, although perhaps indirectly, on design throughout Europe in the later part of the 19th century and beyond.

The South Kensington Museum was not only the model for many museums in Europe and the United States but also for the Imperial Museum in Tokyo, set up in the mid 1870s. In 1874 the chief Japanese Commissioner, Sano Tsunetami, sought the advice of both the Director of the South Kensington Museum, Philip Cunliffe Owen, and of the Director of the sister museum in Edinburgh, Thomas Archer, on how to organize the new museum in Japan. The designer Christopher Dresser was sent to Japan by Cunliffe Owen to take a collection of English objects donated to the Imperial Museum and was empowered to advise the Japanese on how to exhibit them. The South Kensington Museum was to play an important part in strengthening the ties between the West and Japan.

X. THE SOUTH KENSINGTON MUSEUM AND THE UNITED STATES

Moncure Conway recalls how 'in walking through the School at South Kensington once, I met a young lady who had passed several years in the schools at Philadelphia and the Cooper Institute, but had never found what she required for her training until she came here . . . The school at Philadelphia she said was the best she had known of any in the United States, but when she was there it lacked trained teachers. The teachers were artists in all but the art of teaching. She believed however that the Philadelphia school if associated with a good collection, would turn out well . . . This lady's experience has been several times confirmed by American artists with whom I have walked through the South Kensington Museum. One of the most eminent of them said: What a revolution it would cause in American art to have some such Museum as this in each large city. It would in each case draw around it an art community and send out widening waves of taste and love of beauty throughout the country'.[32]

Moncure Conway points out that these remarks applied to some ten years or so before his volume was published and even in the 1850s Americans had become aware of the need for improved art education for the craftsmen and artists, and of the value of museums of industrial art, by visiting or reading the reports of the international exhibitions. The Americans, according to the report of the United States Bureau of Education, published in Washington in 1873, had been particularly impressed by the fact that, after the British success at the 1862 Exhibition, even the French had sent a commission to England to study Cole's system with a view to adopting many features of the South Kensington Museum and the training school for art masters.

As a result they invited Walter Smith (Headmaster of the Leeds, Holbeck and Keighley schools of art, Headmaster of the Drawing Department of Leeds Grammar School, Principal Art Master of Huddersfield College, and superintendent of Drawing in schools for the poor in many parts of Yorkshire), to Massachusetts, to a post as Director of Drawing for the Boston schools and State Director of Art Education.

In 1863 Walter Smith had visited an exhibition of works by pupils of the French Schools of Design, and, although critical of some aspects of the South Kensington system, particularly the enlargement of the Museum's collections to what he considered to be the deprivation of the Provinces, he recognized 'that art in England is making tremendous progress'.[33]

Smith was soon at work in the United States, travelling the country, lecturing, demonstrating and organizing classes. In a speech to a Convention of the House and Senate of the State of Pennsylvania on 'Industrial Art Education considered economically',[34] Walter Smith vividly recalled the setting up of the Museum in 1852: 'I very well remember being in the house in which the Prince of Wales at present lives – Marlborough House – then the

Jacobean embroidery. Study from an embroidered crewelwork curtain (T. 38–1909) made by Alice Few when on the P.A.B. Widener Fellowship in 1925.
Photograph: Will Brown for Moore College, Philadelphia.

headquarters of the Government Department of Science and Art . . . and seeing the future South Kensington Museum drawn into a courtyard in a single wagon. That wagonload of goods has had more influence upon the destinies of the United Kingdom than the existence of her fleet. That wagonload of goods has grown into the present South Kensington Museum. Year by year, the Government has voted grants and purchased the best works of Ancient and Modern Industrial Art to be found in the world, and the collection has so grown that today it is the largest and most important Industrial Art Museum in the world.

This has not been done without opposition from some. Now and then some Member of Parliament whose instincts and talents were devoted especially to a blind economy, who looked upon all such things as Art Museums as if they were toys, because he was incapable of seeing their influence on manufacture and consequently on trade, would rise in the House and protest against the expenditure.'

But as Walter Smith pointed out such opposition was easily overcome and it was soon recognized, to use his words, that 'the investment in that direction has been so profitable for the nation as bearing on the development of her art industries that I verily believe today if you were to seriously propose to England the sale of the South Kensington Museum, you would sooner get the country to sell its fleet, to Russia or to France, than dispose of its Industrial Museum.'

Smith continued his speech by praising the House and Senate for setting up the Pennsylvania Museum and School of Industrial Art on the same lines as South Kensington, that is 'a Museum which shall be for the industries of the country, what the granary is to the husbandsman, containing the seeds of future prosperity'. He welcomed the fact that a parallel school of Industrial Art was linked to the Museum.

Exhibitions of industrial art were held at the museum throughout the 1880s with one of pottery and porcelain in 1888 followed by an extended one which included glass, terracotta, tiles, stained glass and mosaic work in 1889. Both these exhibitions included a competition for American workmen. The museum, which is now the Philadelphia Museum of Art, has maintained its policy of acquiring examples of applied or decorative art, both historic and

Studies from a Persian 'Resht' patchwork portière in the museum made by Edna Leonhardt while on a P.A.B. Widener Fellowship in 1923.
Photograph: Will Brown for Moore College, Philadelphia

modern. Another link between the South Kensington Museum and Philadelphia was the Philadelphia School of Design for women, founded in 1844 by Mrs Sarah Worthington King Peter, when, from her home in Third Street, Philadelphia, she conducted classes in design for 'genteel women'.[35] In 1851 the Franklin Institute took over the School's operations and it was formally chartered in September 1853 with twelve gentlemen serving on the Board of Directors and with twelve Ladies as a subordinate Board of Lady Managers. The school was closely modelled on the Female School of Design in London. In 1873, a Miss Elizabeth Croasdale, a graduate of the South Kensington School, was appointed principal. She instituted a Normal Art Course for training teachers, based on the South Kensington system. On Miss Croasdale's retirement through ill health in 1886 a prominent portrait painter, etcher and engraver, Emily Sartain (1841-1927), who had studied extensively in Europe, was appointed principal, a post which she held until 1919.

It was during Emily Sartain's tenure that the direct link with the Victoria and Albert Museum was established when the Widener Fellowship in Design was initiated, the winner being sent to study in Europe for a year. An important part of this study was conducted at the Victoria and Albert Museum at first under the direction of Lewis F. Day (1845-1910) and from 1905 until 1924 under Lindsay Butterfield (1869-1948).

The Widener Fellowship was the gift of P. A. B. Widener, who was a Director of the Philadelphia School of Design for Women from 1894 to 1915; when he died in 1915 the Fellowship was continued by his son Joseph Widener. The award gave graduate students a year's study abroad, partly under a professional designer, and also practical experience in a design studio. Each of the successful students received three to four months training in design at the Victoria and Albert Museum. The first tutor, Lewis F. Day, was an outstanding designer of textiles and wallpapers and a prolific writer on design and ornament, who himself drew extensively on the Museum's collections for inspiration. The first P. A. B. Widener Fellowship was awarded for achievement in practical design to a Mary Braid from Philadelphia; most students came from the home state, although later they were to come from other places, including Eastern Maryland and Kansas City.

Lewis F. Day taught the first five recipients, but in 1905 he had to give up teaching through illness and Lindsay Butterfield took over the Widener scholarship from him. According to Lindsay Butterfield's own unpublished biography, he supervised sixteen of the Widener scholarship students, whom he described as 'coming from many States and from them I managed to learn a lot about the American home life. They were with one or two exceptions very interesting and delightful students, they worked hard from 3 to 6 months under me in the Victoria and Albert Museum'.

During the First World War, although the Fellowship was awarded, the recipients had to forego their trip to Europe, but in 1919 the tuition at the Victoria and Albert was resumed.

A number of recipients of the P. A. B. Widener Fellowship were to return to the Philadelphia School of Design for Women as tutors. Mary S. Braid became a textile designer, and later, as Mrs Hartman, was put in charge of the Technical and Decorative Design Class A Course. As the Prospectus for 1925–26 pointed out, 'many graduates of this class have become successful designers for manufacturers; some have offices of their own as practical designers, while others have important positions to teach design'.

Two other recipients, who taught the preparatory class on design, were Emma Buckman and Eleanor Graham, who studied at the Victoria and Albert Museum under Lindsay Butterfield in 1911 and 1916.

In 1923 the P. A. B. Widener Fellowship was awarded to Edna Leonhardt, then 19, to study textile design for a year in London and Paris. At the Victoria and Albert Museum she studied under Lindsay Butterfield who selected examples of historic textiles for her to copy and instructed her in their history. An album of her V & A studies is preserved at Moore College and shows that, as well as studying textiles, she also took motifs from ceramics and from illuminated manuscripts. Among the studies are Egyptian and Roman panels of the 3rd to 7th century, and fruit and flowers from an 18th century Brussels tapestry, Greek Island embroideries, Russian brocades, Persian and Bokhara embroideries, motifs taken from Persian tiles and Chinese robes. Edna Leonhardt (later Mrs Acker), to whom I spoke before her death in 1982, recalled regularly having tea with Lindsay Butterfield in his house in Bedford Park, as she and her mother, who accompanied her to Europe, lived nearby. She also spent some time at the King George and Queen Mary Art College in London and later studied in Paris at the Louvre and the Bibliothèque Forney. She was to become a successful freelance textile designer, a fact that she attributed to her training in South Kensington, and the material she gave to Moore college includes not only her own sketches but a collection of photographs of historic textiles in the Museum.

After further travels in Europe, Edna Leonhardt worked for some years as a resident designer in a textile mill and in 1930 set up her own studio in Philadelphia, being described as the only 'woman textile designer in the country to set up her own freelance work as a business' supplying designs to some twenty-seven firms.

The winner of the P. A. B. Widener Fellowship in 1925 was Alice Dorothy Few of West

Chester, Pa. (later Mrs Joseph Francis Sloane), who was to become a successful artist and textile designer. Among her studies preserved at Moore College, were a number of Coptic textiles, Turkish embroideries, details from the celebrated Abigail Pett bed hangings (T. 13 to I-1929) which were on loan to the Museum for some years before being purchased in 1929. She also made bird studies from ceramics in the Museum. She was obviously a talented student, for Lindsay Butterfield was able to sell a number of her designs to leading manufacturers. They included 'The Bird and Wistaria' cretonne, illustrated here, and the 'Chinese Panel' cretonne, both produced by Liberty in 1926, for which she was paid 79 guineas. She also sold several designs to Turnbull and Stockdale, based on traditional English floral chintzes and a paisley motif, and a design for one of the Sicilian range of fabrics, plus several others for Morton Sundour fabrics. Like Edna Leonhardt, she later studied in Paris under Professor René Trolong and exhibited at the Paris Spring Salon. On her return to the United States she continued to design textiles for a number of American firms and for Jacques Marsche of Paris, until the 1960s.

The success of linking the training of designers for industry to the collections of a great museum was recognized by W. H. French in *Arts and Artists in Connecticut* (Boston and New York, 1879). The first important collection of art opened to the public in Connecticut was instituted in 1831 under the control of the Yale College, and thirteen years later, in 1844, the Wadsworth Atheneum was opened. In 1876 a society and museum, the Connecticut Museum of Industrial Art, was founded in New Haven, the plan being described as the same 'on a limited scale, as that upon which the South Kensington is founded. The Kensington Museum was the aftermath of shame on the part of the British people that the artistic grace of their handiwork was so far inferior to that of the productions of France at the Industrial Exhibition [1851]. The result was most favourable. With almost mushroom growth, gracefulness appeared in England and at the next exhibition [1862 London International Exhibition] the energy inspired had even outdone her rival. Beauty had become more common and grace in usefulness more abundant in the manufactures of England then any other nation.'

The fact that the South Kensington School of Art was firmly linked to the Museum was emphasized by Mr French who went so far as to state that, in the words of the founders, the South Kensington Museum was 'established in 1852 for the purpose of training art masters and mistresses for the United Kingdom'. He points out that by 1879 there were 675 art schools in England instructing some 50,000 pupils, many of whom were artisans mainly attending night schools.

The beneficial effects of a fundamental art education for artisans and designers were recognized in the setting up of the Connecticut Industrial Museum. The first floor of the museum was devoted to a permanent display of industrial art by leading American manufacturers and within two or three years of the foundation classes in the decoration of stoneware and pottery designed for household use, on the South Kensington model, and in the manufacture

79

'The Bird and Wisteria Cretonne' designed by Alice Few when on a P.A.B. Widener Fellowship at the Museum and produced by Liberty's in 1925.

of point and macramé lace had been established, as well as more general art classes.

Similar links can be found with the Cincinnati Art Museum, opened to the public on 17 May 1886, founded largely through the efforts of the Women's Art Museum Association of Cincinnati. In 1854, Mrs Sara Worthington King Peter, who had ten years before founded the Philadelphia School of Design for women, founded the Ladies' Academy of the Fine Arts in Cincinnati 'to aid the cultivation of the public taste'. Mrs Peter travelled to Europe to buy good copies of the works of art 'to furnish a source of intellectual recreation and enjoyment to the people by the establishment of Galleries of copies executed in the best manner from masterpieces of painting and sculpture.' The L. A. F. A. Gallery remained in existence until 1864 when the Association was disbanded and the contents donated to the McMicken University resulting in the foundation of a school of design.

The Cincinnati School of Design held an exhibition in the Women's Pavilion at the Philadelphia Centennial Exhibition of 1876, organized by the Women's Centennial Committee which was disbanded on 18 January 1877. Three weeks later the Women's Art Museum Association of Cincinnati was formed. They were as much if not more interested in the decorative arts as the fine arts and naturally looked to the South Kensington Museum as their model; as a member of the Association wrote, 'the accumulated art culture of all Europe can be brought to us for instruction, by means of models, casts, engravings, photographs, careful descriptions by learned students.' To enlist public support the ladies of the W. A. M. A. held a series of lectures and in 1878 held a loan exhibition consisting of bronzes, mosaics, ancient armour, carved ivories, gold, silver, brass work reproductions (Elkington wares), enamelled metal and porcelain, antique furniture, antique and artistic jewellery, artistic embroideries, antique and modern pottery and porcelain, pictures, engravings, statuary, glass, lace, tapestry, textile fabrics, antique fans, lacquer, wood carvings, etc. The exhibition had a phenomenal success attracting over 13,000 visitors in its six weeks run and making a net profit of over a million dollars. The ladies, encouraged by this response, began to buy objects to be held in trust for future museum collections, including plaster casts, fictile ivories, and Elkington electrotypes of silver and gold treasures

purchased from the South Kensington Museum. In November 1879 they established themselves in the Exposition Building where classes were taught in embroidery, drawing, painting and modelling. A lecture on their pet subject, 'The South Kensington Museum', was well attended by the public and by 1880 the existence of a Cincinnati Art Museum was assured by the promise of 150,000 dollars towards an art museum building provided the local citizens equalled that amount. The ladies continued to collect for the future museum, including items by the recently established Rookwood pottery as well as historic examples, and in 1883, through the good offices of Sir Philip Cunliffe Owen, Director of the South Kensington Museum, a collection of lace, and a tapestry, 'The Storming of New Carthage', were obtained, objects which remain on view today.

Another important American establishment that owes its existence to the South Kensington Museum is the Cooper Hewitt Museum of Decorative Arts and Design, New York, now part of the Smithsonian Institution. In 1859 Peter Cooper opened an institution consisting of a free school, a library and a lecture forum. To this educational facility he gave the name of 'The Cooper Union for the Advancement of Science and Art' which was 'available to the respectable needy without regard for race, creed, colour or sex'. It gave opportunities for study and advancement to thousands of men and women, many of them immigrants, who might otherwise be bound to unrewarding employment with little future. The whole enterprise – the building, the administration, the programme – was financed by Peter Cooper. He dearly wanted to create a museum of arts and sciences but it was beyond his means although he set aside the space.

Later in the century, his grand-daughters, Sarah, Eleanor, and Amy Hewitt, decided to establish the museum envisaged by their grandfather. By this time New York had acquired both an art and a natural history museum; inspired by a visit to the South Kensington Museum, the Hewitt sisters decided to found a museum for the Arts of Decoration. With this aim in view, they began to collect and in a few years they had amassed enough objects. The Museum officially opened in 1897 as the Cooper Union Museum for the Arts of Decoration. The gift of three major collections of European textiles by J. Pierpoint Morgan placed the museum on a par with the Victoria and Albert Museum, certainly as far as textiles were concerned, and the museum also houses important architectural drawings and designs for the decorative arts. In June 1968, the museum was taken over by the Smithsonian Institution and the collections transferred to the present building.

In 1974 the reopening of the Cooper Hewitt was appropriately celebrated with a representative exhibition at the Victoria and Albert Museum, regarded as the progenitor.

The influence of South Kensington can no doubt be traced in many of the museums throughout the United States, and close ties have been established with many of them through exhibitions, loans and publications as well as personal contacts by professional staff; a subject that warrants a volume to itself.

The Museum's Influence on Designers

XI. THE MUSEUM IN THE 1870s AND 1880s

In the 1880s, the role that the South Kensington Museum had played in bringing about a revival in the decorative arts was universally recognized and almost any book of the period relating to this subject stresses this beneficial influence.

This was well summed up by Oscar Wilde in a lecture delivered on 17 May 1882 during his tour of the United States under the title *The Practical Application of the Principles of the Aesthetic Theory to Exterior and Interior Home Decoration, with Observations upon Dress and Personal Ornaments* published in 1924.[36]

In his advice as to what was needed in America he stated: 'You must show your workmen specimens of good work so that they come to know what is simple and true and beautiful. To that I would have you have a museum attached to these schools – not one of these dreadful institutions where there is a stuffed and very dusty giraffe, and a case or two of fossils, but a place where there are gathered examples of art decoration from various periods and countries. Such a place is the South Kensington Museum in London, whereon we build greater hopes for the future than on any other thing. There I go every Saturday night, when the Museum is open later than usual, to see the handicraftsman, the woodworker, the glass blower and the worker in metals, and it is here that the man of refinement and culture comes face to face with the workman who ministers to his joy. He comes to know more of the nobility of the workman, and the workman, feeling the appreciation, comes to know more of the nobility of his work.'

Similarly Moncure Conway describes the effect of the Museum on the visitor: 'Vista upon vista! The eye never reaches the furthest end in the past from which humanity has toiled upwards, its steps traced in fair victories over chaos, nor does it alight on any historic epoch not related to itself: the artist, artisan, scholar, each finds himself gathering out of the dust of ages successive chapters of his own spiritual biography. And even as he so lives the past from which he came, over again, he finds, at the converging point of these manifold lines of development, wings for his imagination by which he passes the aerial track of tendency, stretching his hours to ages living already in the golden year. There is no institution in which one hour seems so brief and so long.'[37]

In an article from the *Fortnightly Review*[38] on 'The English Revival of Decorative Art', Walter Crane (whose own work is discussed later), having briefly described the improvement that had taken place since 1851, wrote that 'the quiet influence of the superb collections at the South Kensington Museum, and the opportunities of study, open to all, of the most beautiful specimens of Mediaeval, Renaissance and Oriental design and craftsmanship of all kinds must not be forgotten – an influence which cannot be rated as of too much importance and value, and which has probably been of more far reaching influence in its effect on designers and craftsmen than the more direct efforts of the Department to reach them.'

Walter Crane (1845-1915), the painter, designer and book illustrator, a friend and follower of William Morris and one of the main protagonists of the Arts and Crafts Movement, also wrote enthusiastically of the Museum in his autobiography.[39] His father was a painter and he grew up in an artistic atmosphere; when the family moved to London in 1857, one of the sights which made the most impression on the young Walter Crane was the South Kensington Museum. Describing it in his memoirs he wrote: 'It must have been in quite early days when it was called the "Brompton Boilers" from the round roofed iron sheds painted white and green which then housed the collections . . . near the entrance was a model of the estate with plans of extension and a label with the inscription "Rome was not built in a day" . . . The Museum was full of interest and variety, and had not the gloom and sepulchral feeling of the British Museum. There were numbers of delightful and interesting things one had never seen before – casts of Italian Renascence [sic] sculpture, mediaeval carving, jewellery and glass, armour and weapons, fireplaces, tiles, furniture and tapestry, all jumbled together as a vast curiosity shop, but making the most attractive *ensemble*, and probably in my case, preparing the way for that keen interest in the arts and crafts of design which in later years was to absorb so much of my time and energy . . . A favourite place with me was a certain corridor leading from the museum on the ground floor to the offices. The walls of this corridor were hung with a collection more or less historically complete of wood engravings. Here one got first acquainted with Burgmair's "Triumphs of Maximilien" and

'Ritter, Tod und Teufel'. A wood engraving by Albrecht Dürer which had a profound influence on Walter Crane.

Facing page: 'The Triumph of Labour'. A woodcut by Walter Crane published in 1891 and described by him as 'the largest and most important single design of mine in woodcut'. It clearly shows the influence of Dürer. Photograph: The Fine Art Society Ltd.

met Dürer again in one's old friends "Ritter, Tod and Teufel" and "Meloncolia" and "The Great Horse" . . . . specimens of Linton's work hung here, and Bewick and his school, and the illustrators of the nineteenth century. No doubt I imbibed many ideas here, and from the varied contents of the museum generally.'

Earlier, in a series of articles on 'Needlework as a Mode of artistic expression' published in the *Magazine of Art*,[40] he again stresses the importance of the Museum to design. Thanking the authorities for their co-operation in providing illustrations from 'their magnificent collection of textiles', he went on to state 'that it is impossible to put too high an educational value upon such collections . . . It is, I think, not sufficiently realised by the public at large that a museum such as this is really a reference library of examples to the designer and the craftsman of incalculable importance and value, and as such bears upon the industries of the whole country'.

In the second of his articles, having recommended the collections of Persian Art in the Museum as providing excellent models for the treatment of floral forms, he warns against mere copying. In many of Walter Crane's own works, notably his wallpapers, textiles and book illustrations, we can find evidence of his study of the Museum's collections, and although one can often pinpoint the specific object, or group of objects that was his inspiration, he never resorted to direct imitation.

Among the many other artists who owed a debt to the South Kensington Museum was Sir Frank Brangwyn. Brangwyn was born in Bruges in 1867, his father Curtis Brangwyn being an architect and designer of church furnishings. In 1875, when Frank Brangwyn was eight years old, the family returned to London and his father found employment as chief draughtsman to Sir Horace Jones, the city architect. Frank Brangwyn was a precocious child who received little formal education and left school when only twelve; he spent his time in his father's workshops, being sent on errands, especially to the South Kensington Museum to make drawings of ornaments and tapestries. The young Brangwyn was entranced by the magnificence of the collections and he used his pocket money to buy artists materials, leaving no money for fares and often having to walk from his home in Shepherds Bush. His

Walter Crane as Cimabue, photographed by Emery Walker in 1885. The costume and the pose based on the mosaic designed by Lord Leighton for the South Court of the South Kensington Museum.
Photograph: National Portrait Gallery.

A Milanese marble fireplace surround acquired by the Museum in 1870 which seems to have inspired many of the 'grotesques' of Walter Crane.

'Christ in the Sepulchre'. A marble relief by Donatello acquired by the Museum in 1861 and copied by Frank Brangwyn who described it as 'faultless' and later bought a plaster cast of it.

skill at sketching objects in both the South Kensington Museum and the British Museum was such that visitors would ask him to make copies of furniture and other items for them, and in this way he made some money. Even more important was that he was noticed by Harold Rathbone (1858–1939), a pupil of Ford Madox Brown, who was to found the Della Robbia Pottery in Birkenhead in 1893. Rathbone had a particular interest in the Italian Renaissance and the Florentine masters. He took the young Frank Brangwyn by the arm and led him to Donatello's bas-relief of *Christ in the Sepulchre*, acquired by the Museum in 1861, and told him to copy it. It made a deep and lasting impression on Brangwyn who later bought a plaster cast of the relief which he described as 'faultless'. Rathbone also introduced Brangwyn to the works of Dürer both in the Museum and through his own personal collection. In 1882, through Rathbone, Brangwyn met A. H. Mackmurdo (1851–1942), the founder of the Century Guild. Mackmurdo walked Brangwyn through the galleries at South Kensington, pointing out works of particular merit and generally encouraging the young artist and teaching him to use the Museum in the right way, for, as Mackmurdo wrote, 'we should study not steal our art, passing all through the alembic of our own mind'. Many years later, talking to William de Belleroche[41], Brangwyn said that 'the influence of the masters is found in all serious work. An artist must be influenced by the old. He should study them and try to understand their outlook. They give him an open path to follow.'

Mackmurdo also took the young Brangwyn to his home, Halcyon House, at Enfield, and it was there in the conservatory that Brangwyn first made sketches of exotic plants, and began to use the brilliant colours which were to characterize his later paintings. Mackmurdo introduced him to the artistic circles of the day – to Oscar Wilde, D'Oyley Carte, Ellen Terry – and to William Morris who took him on as an apprentice in 1882. For Morris he made copies of Flemish tapestries, enlarged patterns for carpets and wallpapers and transferred Morris embroidery designs from paper to fabric for the women to work. It was this apprenticeship that led Brangwyn to design carpets and rugs for Bing's *Maison de L'Art Nouveau* in the 1890s and carpets for Templeton's in the 1930s.

Brangwyn was never to forget the inspiration he gained from the Museum. In 1904, when a young American artist from Chicago, Arthur S. Covey, called to see him, Brangwyn took him under his wing, found him a studio, and on Fridays took him to the V & A for a meal, followed by a guided tour of the galleries with Brangwyn making practical comments on the paintings and sculptures and admiring the craftsmanship of the furniture, which considerably inspired his own furniture designs. Brangwyn was later to say that he loved designing furniture and that if he had more time and energy he would have designed a lot more.

Brangwyn was particularly impressed by the Lord Leighton lunettes and in gratitude to the Museum offered gratuitously to paint the rotunda, an offer that unfortunately the authorities did not accept; in spite of this rebuff, Brangwyn presented his collection of oriental ceramics to the Museum.

One of the most important influences on the development of the aesthetic movement in the 1870s and 1880s, and later on Art Nouveau, was exercised by the art of Japan, and here again the Museum's collections played an important part in bringing it to the notice of the designers, manufacturers and the public.

As early as 1852, some examples of Japanese lacquer had been bought by the Museum, and some bamboo baskets two years later. Japanese woodwork, decorated with straw, from the collection of Sir Rutherford Alcock, was exhibited in the 1850s. In 1865, Queen Victoria presented a collection of Japanese objects, including textiles and embroideries. Further examples of Japanese lacquer boxes were bought from the Paris Exhibition of 1867, and in 1875 a more comprehensive collection which included a large number of Japanese bronzes, vases, bottles and incense burners was bought from Samuel Bing who was later to set up the famous *Maison de L'Art Nouveau* in Paris.

Designs for stained glass windows for Samuel Bing's Maison de l'Art Nouveau, *Paris, by Frank Brangwyn, 1897.*
Photographs: The Fine Art Society Ltd.

Christopher Dresser (1834-1904) was one of the first European designers to really understand Japanese art and, as far as we know, the first to visit Japan for himself in 1876 and 1877. In his preface to *Japan, its Architecture, Art and Art Manufactures*, published in 1882, he states that he had been an earnest student of oriental art since he entered the School of Design in 1847 at the early age of thirteen, and he recalled his teachers drawing his attention to the oriental stands (which included some Japanese objects) at the 1851 Exhibition. He would also have seen the Japanese objects at Marlborough House and Sir Rutherford Alcock allowed him to make some eighty drawings of the objects he had brought from Japan for the 1862 London International Exhibition. At the close of the Exhibition, Dresser bought a number of the Japanese exhibits which were to become the basis of a growing private collection. Dresser's enthusiasm for Japanese art is already apparent in his earliest book on design, *The Art of Decorative Design*, published in 1862, an enthusiasm that is repeated in his numerous subsequent writings.

Dresser was always ready to acknowledge his debt to his early training particularly to the influence of Owen Jones, and he continued to keep closely in touch with the Museum. Dresser's first contacts with Japanese officials were probably made when the Iwakura mission visited the South Kensington Museum in 1872 and he was involved with the director, Philip Cunliffe Owen, and Major Scott in arranging a Japanese Exhibition in a pavilion behind the Albert Hall as an adjunct to the Vienna International Exhibition of 1873. The Japanese exhibits from the latter Exhibition were subsequently acquired by Dresser and Cunliffe Owen for the Alexandra Palace Company, where a reconstruction of a Japanese village was set up in 1874.

It was at the instigation of Cunliffe Owen that Dresser was to visit Japan in an official capacity in December 1876, taking with him a collection of English manufactures donated by the Museum for the Imperial Museum in Tokyo. It was only after his visit to Japan that the Japanese influence became clearly apparent in Dresser's superb metalwork designs, an influence which, combined with his dual concern for the function of the object and the techniques of mass production, was to produce some of the most *avant-garde* designs of the 1880s.

Dresser visited the Philadelphia Centennial Exhibition en route for Japan and lectured on 'Art Industries', 'Art Museums' and 'Art Schools', paying tribute to the work and influence of South Kensington. He must have made a considerable impact in Philadelphia for as late as 1909 his booklet *General Principles of Art, Decorative and Pictorial, with Hints on Color* [sic] *its Harmonies and Contrasts* was included in the list of publications of the Pennsylvania Museum, Philadelphia.

When it was heard that the Japanese were planning an extensive exhibit for the Philadelphia Exhibition of 1876, the Museum authorities negotiated with the Japanese to buy a representative collection of ceramics from their pavilion when the exhibition was over, and these were acquired in 1877. Some of these, with their rough finish and often irregular shapes, made an immediate impact on potters such as the Martin Brothers. These items were

Electroplated tea-service, engraved with Japanese badges. Designed by Christopher Dresser for Hukin and Heath and registered with the Patent Office Design Registry on 26 March 1879.
Photograph: Sotheby's.

described by A. W. Franks in *Japanese Pottery*, one of the South Kensington Art Handbooks published in 1880.

In 1876 an extremely important collection of Japanese art was lent for exhibition at Bethnal Green Museum by W. J. Alt. The collection, which covered virtually every category of Japanese art, was assembled by Alt during a twelve-year residence in Japan from 1859 to 1871, the most important items being presents from Princes and officials of the Japanese government. The exhibiton was accompanied by a detailed descriptive catalogue, written by Mr Alt himself and published for the Science and Art Department in 1876. In his introduction Mr Alt pointed out that there was 'no greater testimony to the value of Japanese art . . . than the fact that it is largely influencing our own manufactures'. He specifically mentioned Minton services – 'the dinner and dessert services, exhibiting graceful floral sprays, birds, and insects, dropped carelessly over the surface' – an obvious reference to W. S. Coleman's 'naturist' service, and also the *closisonné* enamel of Elkington and other manufacturers.

This exhibition, together with the objects in the permanent collections, undoubtedly reinforced the Japanese influence, which was to dominate designs, particularly of ceramics, wallpapers, textiles and embroideries, in the late 1870s and 1880s. Although in the hands of talented designers, such as Christopher Dresser, E. W. Godwin, Bruce Talbert, Walter Crane and George Haité, the influence of Japanese art produced some beautiful textiles, wallpapers and ceramics, at a more commercial level it was not always so beneficial. As John Sparkes (then Principal of the Royal College of Art) and Walter Gandy wrote, 'less conventional than the Chinese, less bound by tradition, the Japanese artists display a delightful freshness of idea that has appealed very strongly to and greatly influenced Western designers. Although the ignorant plagiarisms and hideous eccentricities that passed muster ten or twenty years ago as Anglo-Japanese design might also have imperilled our reputation as a people of taste.'[42]

The interest engendered in the decorative arts in the later part of the 19th century promoted the formation of the National Association for the Advancement of Art and Its Application to Industry under the Presidency of Sir Frederick Leighton. The first Congress of the Association was held in Liverpool during the week commencing 3 December 1888. The Vice Presidents were an impressive array of noble Lords, Members of Parliament, Sir John Everett Millais, and a number of prominent artists and designers including Professor Herkomer, A. H. Mackmurdo and E. J. Poynter, who were Presidents and Honorary Secretaries of the various sections. Walter Crane was President of the applied art section and Mervyn Macartney Honorary Secretary. The art history and museums section was headed by Sydney Colvin and Lionel Cust of the British Museum.

Many of the speakers made reference to the value of the South Kensington Museum, although there was a considerable amount of criticism of the training in the art schools. For instance, the artist Francis Bate complained that the 'Government Schools of Art profess to have benefitted the handicrafts, industrial arts and commerce: their students have wandered through public museums and from the collections of more or less beautiful things have gathered and pieced from this and that, here a little, there a little, to make a pattern for a table cover – without having seen a loom – to decorate a wallpaper about the printing of which they know nothing.'

The sculptor Sir Alfred Gilbert, now best known for his statue of Eros in Piccadilly Circus, remarked that 'our having been able to amass such a collection of gems as the South Kensington Museum contains is sufficient proof of the existence ot taste', while John D. Crace, whose firm had executed many of Pugin's designs, stated that 'we have in England the most magnificent collections of applied art ever brought together in one country'.

Perhaps a note of jealousy can be detected in the address given by Lionel Cust of the British Museum in opening the section on art history museums, when he referred to the collections lodged in 'the most revolting, hideous building that mortal man has ever designed or gazed up, known as the South Kensington Museum.' The architect Edwin Seward, however, felt that 'in any reference to South Kensington it would be hard to overestimate the value to the artistic minded of the magnificent collections which have been brought together in the museum rooms, and of a great part of its teachings'.

The criticism generally turned on the point that the training of designers was divorced from industry and that museums tended to foster copying. The architect John D. Sedding, a great admirer of William Morris, made this point by stating that 'Museums are excellent places for cultured people curious to read and mark the history of art, or for designers, if design is from henceforth to be only eclectic and imitative . . . museums are to my mind constant inducements to mere studio designs – to designs conducted apart from the centre of manufacture. Museums curb invention by inciting to copyism; consequently they hinder the initiation of a common vernacular system of device. Museums lead to stylemongering, which makes design a matter of archaeological research; they tend reliance upon stimulant, they introduce a false standard for current art which deters progress; worse than all they suggest that the regeneration of one design shall come by copying works that were produced by the "full orbed art of olden days", rather than working things up from the ground.' In a way, this attack only serves to emphasise the great influence the Museum had on design for the decorative arts.

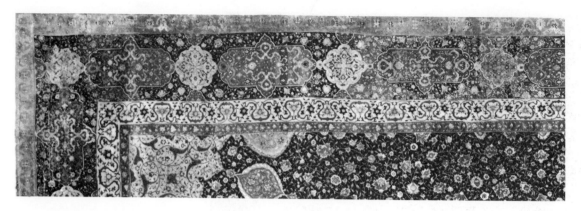

Detail of the 'Ardabil Carpet', one of a matching pair made for the mosque at Ardabil, Persia, and dated 1539-40. Acquired by the Museum in 1893 on the advice of William Morris.

XII. MORRIS AND HIS ASSOCIATES

For more than thirty years William Morris (1834-96) maintained a close relationship with the South Kensington Museum, a relationship that was mutually beneficial.[43] Many of the textiles and wallpapers designed by Morris, which have made his name a household word even unto the present day, owed their inspiration directly to the Museum's collections, a fact that is supported by many of his writings. W. R. Lethaby, in his biography of Philip Webb,[44] recalls Morris saying at a meeting: 'They talk of building museums for the public, but the South Kensington Museum was got together for about six people - I am one, another is a comrade [Philip Webb] in the room'.

When Morris first visited the Museum is not known, but it was probably Philip Webb who introduced him to the collections.

The extent of Morris's dependence on the Museum's collection is perhaps most clearly stated in his evidence to the Royal Commission on Technical Instruction, held at the South Kensington Museum, when he remarked: 'Perhaps I have used it as much as any man living.'[45] Before detailing specific instances of Morris's designs that were based on examples in the Museum's collections, it is perhaps worth quoting some of Morris's views on the value of the collections to the designer, and how they might be best used.

Morris was not in favour of exact copies of historic textiles and stressed that originality was 'desirable in everything in which one applies design to industrial arts'. In his evidence to the Commission[46] on how best to train a designer Morris stated: 'However original a man may be, he cannot afford to disregard the works of art that have been produced in times past when design was flourishing; he is bound to study old examples, but he is also bound to supplement that by a careful study of nature, because if he does not he will certainly fall into a sort of cut and dried conventional method of designing . . . It takes a man of considerable originality to deal with old examples and to get what is good out of them without making a

'Bullerswood' hand-knotted woollen carpet designed by William Morris, 1889.

*An early 17th century Italian silk, brocaded with gold thread, used as the source of J.H. Dearle's
'Rose and Lily' design.*

'Rose and Lily' woven wool and silk compound twill designed by J.H. Dearle for Morris & Company in 1893.

design which lays itself open distinctly to the charge of plagiarism.' Morris went on to
discuss the importance of the collections at the South Kensington Museum and the
desirability of examples being made available to the provinces, although he felt that some
objects were too precious to travel and that it was unwise to break up a great collection: 'I
think to break up a museum which has once been formed is a great mistake. The things have
a certain value in a great collection which they would not have in a small one . . . Here the
things are only wanted for educational purposes and not as commodities. You want types of
good work not a mere multiplication of articles. This typical museum in the metropolis
should contain complete collections in all styles . . . then any superfluity in the metropolitan
museum might be sent to the provinces.'

He then went on to express his reservations about the circulation of objects from the
Museum and expressed the opinion that 'a museum to be of any great use to those who are
studying in it, as artists, or as designers, must be arranged in a permanent manner, so that
one can come day after day and see the same thing; so that a man who is a lecturer can take
his class to a museum and give a lecture on such and such an article, or that a manufacturer
like myself, can take a designer to the museum and say, I want a thing done in such and such
a way; therefore I think it better that the provinces have their own museums.' Morris
approved of the system of copies of the museum objects, which he felt were valuable for the
provinces, but he also felt that duplicates or near duplicates from the Museum's collections
should be sent on permanent loan to the provinces instancing the famous Bock collection of
textiles 'which is one of the best in the world', but which contained many duplicates. He felt
the same criteria applied to the Indian fabrics and also to the ceramic collections,
particularly those of Persian pottery and maiolica.

On the practical side Morris felt that anyone designing for woven textiles should be able
to weave himself, and that he or she should be familiar with all the processes of manufacture,
be it lace, printed fabrics or carpets.

Morris's detailed knowledge of the Museum's textile collections is apparent from his
lecture on *Textile Fabrics*, given on 11 July 1884 in connection with the International Health

A 14th century Sicilian textile acquired by the Museum in 1860 which probably inspired Morris's 'Peacock and Dragon'.

'Peacock and Dragon' hand-loom Jacquard woven wool designed by William Morris in 1878.

Exhibition, which mentions specific fabrics in the Museum including the Sicilian silks, which were 'designed in the heyday of mediaeval art, uniting the wild fantasy and luxurious intricacy of the East with the straight forward story-telling imagination and clear definite drawing of mediaeval Europe, are the very crown of design as applied to weaving'. These silks, as we shall see, provided inspiration for many of his own designs and their importance had been stressed earlier in his lecture *Some Hints On Pattern Designing* delivered at the Working Men's College, London, on 10 December 1881.

The influence of the woven textiles at the South Kensington Museum is strongest after 1876, when Morris himself began to design for woven fabrics, and was thereafter to affect his designs not only for these but also for printed fabrics and wallpapers.[47] His designs before this owe little to historic pattern structures. For example, the design of his 'Daisy' wallpaper, issued in 1864, echoes that of the 'Daisy' embroidered hangings for Red House, the motif based on the illustration in Froissart's *Chronicles*. The 'Trellis' wallpaper, designed the same year, repeats a mediaeval theme occuring in the early paintings of both Rossetti and Burne-Jones. Most of Morris's wallpaper and textile designs between 1872 and 1876 show free flowing patterns, the repeats masked by coiling stems and foliage with a naturalism that does not occur in his later designs.

Relatively few of Morris's designs can be related to specific fabrics in the Museum's collections, for Morris was no mere copyist. The 'Mohair' damask of 1876, however, was clearly based on a 15th-century Rhenish printed linen (subsequently proved to be a fake), and was the inspiration for the two other designs of the same date, the 'Iris' and 'Bluebell' printed cottons, although in all these cases Morris substituted flowers for the rather grotesque birds of the original.

One of the most splendid fabrics, the 'Peacock and Dragon' of 1878, is very clearly related to an Italian 14th-century woven fabric in the Museum, although the motifs are on a far grander scale.

In 1883 the South Kensington Museum acquired an Italian 17th-century art velvet, then thought to be of 15th-century manufacture. The structure of this design, with flowers and

leaves growing out on either side of a diagonal stem, so that their repetition formed a subsidiary longitudinal and vertical grid which gave stability to the motif, was used by Morris in many of his patterns, after 1883, including the 'Wey' chintz (1883), the 'Cray' and 'Wandle' chintzes of 1884 and the 'Norwich' wallpaper of 1889. Several of the textiles illustrated in Peter Floud's articles have now been proved to have been designed by J. H. Dearle,[48] and these will be discussed later.

Morris's carpet designs fall into two distinct categories: those for machine woven carpets, which he regarded as 'make-shifts for cheapness sake', and those for hand knotted rugs and carpets. The first two of Morris's designs for Wilton carpets were registered on 24 December 1875. One has a motif of poppy heads and foliage, the other of acanthus leaves and peonies, and are similar in style to his woven and printed textiles of the same period. They show little evidence of the study of historic carpets which was to be evident when, in 1880, Morris embarked on the weaving of hand-knotted rugs in the coach-house of Kelmscott House on Hammersmith Mall. Although less complex, his designs for Axminster, Brussells and Kidderminster carpets also bear a close relation to his textile designs.

Morris had bought old eastern rugs and carpets even before his marriage and he continued to collect them to furnish all his homes – Red House, Kelmscott Manor and Kelmscott House. His collection was of the highest quality and one of his rugs, a fine Persian vase carpet of the late 16th century (719–1897) which hung in his drawing room at Kelmscott House, was bought for the Museum after his death. It is therefore difficult to assess to what extent Morris's carpet designs are based on those of his own collection as well as those in the Museum.

In 1867, the Lords of the Committee of the Council on Education had appointed a number of Art Referees 'selected from the most competent autorities' to advise them on purchases for the South Kensington Museum. Morris acted in that capacity from 1883 until his death. He was recognized as a foremost authority on both Persian and Turkish carpets, and throughout the 1880s and early 1890s, he was asked to advise on their acquisition,

An Italian silk velvet acquired by the Museum in 1859 and thought to date from the 15th century but now known to be of 17th-century origin. It provided inspiration for the treatment of flowers in many of Morris's textiles and wallpapers.

'Violet and Columbine' wool and mohair textile designed by William Morris in 1883. Photograph: The Fine Art Society Ltd.

giving detailed and scholarly reports on each example set before him. It was largely on Morris's advice that the Ardabil carpet, now acknowledged as one of the Museum's greatest treasures, was purchased in 1893 for the sum of £2,000. This carpet, with its deep blue ground covered with a maze of floral stems, a lobed medallion in the centre, and representations of mosque lamps, was woven in 1540; it is one of the most famous carpets in the world, and certainly the most copied. Reproductions of it on a reduced scale, or carpets with designs incorporating motifs from it, have been the stock in trade of carpet firms since its acquitition by the Museum until the present day, gracing the rooms of anything from mock Tudor to Neo-Georgian, or a typical suburban semi-detached.

Morris himself would have in no way merely copied such a carpet, although he described it in his report as 'far the finest Eastern carpet I have seen'. His aim in embarking on hand-knotted carpets was to 'make England independent of the East for carpets which may claim to be considered as works of art'.[49]

He began with small hand-knotted rugs to be hung on the wall with designs meant to be seen only from one way, including ones with designs of pots of flowers, birds and stylized flowers and leaves. One larger rug, woven at Hammersmith about 1880 and now in the Museum, has a design of Chinese inspiration.

Morris's larger carpets show a variety of patterns including scrolling floral stems as in the Hurstbourne and Holland Park carpets; or more formal designs with medallions and stylized floral motifs more closely based on Persian and Turkish models, and repeating patterns with large motifs and medallions, often cut in half by the border, which recall Turkish velvets and oriental carpets. Some of this most ambitious carpets, such as the 'Bullerswood', were much influenced by Persian vase carpets, with the design running in one direction rather than the more general quartered pattern.

Few of the motifs in Morris's carpets can be linked to specific textiles and carpets in the Museum, for in this field he used the collections more as a general source of inspiration.

Since the inception of the firm in 1861, Morris had dreamed of reviving the art of tapestry weaving on mediaeval lines. He had first come across mediaeval tapestries as an

undergraduate during his trips to France in 1854 and 1855. His first embroidery with flowering trees, birds and his motto 'If I can', completed in 1855 and now at Kelmscott Manor, was clearly intended as a substitute for tapestry, as were the figure embroideries for Red House. In 1879 he wove his first piece, the 'Vine and Acanthus', teaching himself from a French manual of 'Arts et Metiers' and two years later, in 1881, he embarked on tapestry weaving on a commercial scale at Merton Abbey. There is no doubt that the superb collection of early tapestries at the South Kensington Museum provided inspiration not only for Morris himself but for Burne-Jones, who designed most of the figures, and for J. H. Dearle who supplied many of the backgrounds. Morris particularly admired the 'Three Fates' tapestry, acquired by the Museum in 1866, describing it in his lecture on *Textile Fabrics* as 'a representative of a particularly pleasing kind of decoration where figures are introduced on a background of conventional flowers'. This scheme was used for a number of the Merton Abbey tapestries, notably the 'Angeli Ministrantes' and 'Angeli Laudantes' and for the smaller versions of 'Flora' and 'Pomona'.

Many of the finest tapestries acquired by the Museum in the 1880s were bought on Morris's advice and he felt as attached to them as if they had been bought for him personally. The honeysuckle border of the 'Woodpecker' tapestry, woven at Merton Abbey in 1885, is clearly derived from the borders of the Petrarch 'Triumph' tapestries (437, 440, 141–1883), but, as with carpets, Morris would never have resorted to mere copying.

As already stated, it is probable that William Morris was first introduced to the South Kensington Museum by Philip Webb (1831–1915). Webb's sketch-books from 1859 to 1861 (now in the possession of John Brandon-Jones) are full of details of stained glass, tiles, and painted decoration, many of them taken from objects in the Museum's collections. Visits to the Museum, and to the Art Library, where a favourite reference book was the *Vitruvius Britannicus*, seem to have been a feature of his Saturday afternoons, recalled affectionately, but with fading memory, in a letter to his friend and disciple, W. R. Lethaby, written on 8 February 1908. Even late in his life he continued to visit the Museum, mentioning specifically visits in 1899 and 1912, the latter possibly his last for he was then 81.[50]

John Henry Dearle (1860–1932) began his career with Morris & Company in 1878 when he was taken on as an assistant in their Oxford Street shop. Morris was greatly impressed by his talent and chose him to assist in setting up a tapestry loom at the Queen Square workshops; when tapestry looms were installed at Merton Abbey in 1881 he was put in charge. Apart from designing the backgrounds and *verdura* for many of the tapestries, as well as the machine-made and hand-knotted carpets, Dearle was responsible for most of the designs for textiles from the mid 1880s onwards. Recent research by Linda Parry[51] has shown that a number of designs credited to Morris by both May Morris and J. W. Mackail are by Dearle. An analysis of these designs, many of which do indeed show the influence of Morris, demonstrates that Dearle was no mere pale reflection of his master, and that, like Morris, he drew much of his inspiration from the collections of the South Kensington

'Lamentation over the Dead Christ' by Donatello acquired by the Museum in 1863 and one of a number of pieces of sculpture sketched by Edward Burne-Jones.

Museum. He seems, however, to have been attracted to more formal patterns than Morris, particularly Persian and Turkish fabrics, and his designs tend to be flatter and less intricate. A Turkish woven silk (1366-1877), of which a watercolour copy from the Morris Company archives is now in the V & A, was used by Dearle for his 'Rosebud' chintz of 1905, and his 'Eden' chintz of some years later followed the same format. A number of his other fabrics, notably the 'Persian' and the 'New Persian', 'Persian brocatel' and 'Ixia' show a similar near-eastern inspiration. The 'Rose and Lily' silk of 1893, hitherto attributed to Morris, is clearly derived from an Italian 17th-century silk in the Museum. Dearle substituted the original crowns on the design with full blown roses. It is interesting to note that the same design was issued, complete with crowns, as a printed fabric by Thomas Wardle in 1885, and also later printed at Merton Abbey and sold by Morris & Company. In the early 20th century it was no doubt Dearle who was responsible for introducing a range of more or less straightforward reproductions of historic velvets and silks intended mainly for ecclesiastical use. One of them, a woven woollen fabric called the 'Pineapple', was stated to be adapted from a 'XVI-century specimen in the South Kensington Museum' and the other fabrics in the range were no doubt taken from fabrics in the Museum. Another fabric, the 'Millefleurs', was derived from the background of Flemish tapestries in the Museum.

Dearle's designs for carpets, whether machine-made or hand-knotted are much more formal than those of Morris and show the influence of traditional Persian carpets; he is known to have produced at least one design copied from a 17th-century Indian carpet in the Museum.

Morris's life-long friend and collaborator, Edward Burne-Jones (1833-98) was as enthusiastic an admirer of mediaeval tapestries as Morris himself, and he was called in by Thomas Armstrong, the art director of the Museum from 1881-98 to support Morris's recommendation of the purchase of the 'Troy' tapestry in 1887. Burne-Jones' sketchbooks are full of studies made in the Museum, including details from two 15th-century south-German tapestries, the 'Search after Truth' (4025-1856) and 'the Buzzard' (4509-1858). These perhaps relate more closely to his early paintings than to his figures for the Merton Abbey tapestries, which are more strongly influenced by classical, Renaissance, and mannerist works, and particularly the paintings of Sandro Botticelli. His sketchbooks contain numerous studies of Italian Renaissance sculpture in the Museum, including Donatello's *Lamentation over the Dead Christ* (8552-1863), Rossellino's bust of Giovanni Chellini (7671-1861) and the della Robbia roundels of the *Labours of the Month* (7632-7643-1861). His wife Georgiana, in her *Memorials of Edward Burne-Jones* (1904, Vol 2 p. 6), relates how 'sometime after a day in the studio he would go for a change to the South Kensington Museum in the evening, either to draw or to look at books in the reference library'; and in a conversation with his assistant, T. M. Rooke, in May 1897 he confessed to liking the South Kensington Museum much more than the British Museum.[52]

The Museum's Influence on Industry

XIII. THE TEXTILE INDUSTRY

The textile collections of the Victoria and Albert Museum, generally regarded as among the most magnificent and comprehensive in the world, have probably had more influence on design than any other section. As early as 1854, J. C. Robinson, in an introductory lecture on the Museum of Ornamental Art,[53] stated that 'with the division of textile fabrics, including lace and embroidery, museums have literally never concerned themselves, a few tapestries in some of the palaces and ancient show-houses of the nobility being all that has hitherto been available to the public. Indeed, I know of no attempt, except in our own case, to form a textile collection. An inspection of the numerous, beautiful oriental and mediaeval fabrics we have brought together within a few brief months, will nevertheless show how effective and how interesting such a collection may be made.'

The inspiration provided by these historic textiles was soon to bear fruit. One year later at the time of the Paris Exhibition of 1855, the French, to their shame, were forced to admit that English fabrics were preferred to French ones throughout America on account of their superior design.[54]

The 'False Principles' display at Marlborough House had, as we have seen, taught designers and public alike what to avoid, and the lesson had been learned, as a comparison between the British fabrics exhibited in the 1851 Exhibition and those shown at the International Exhibition in 1862 will clearly demonstrate. Gone were the cabbage roses, the exotic hot-house blooms, the shaded architectural details and scrolls, to be replaced largely by flat ornamental designs in various historic styles, simple diapers, or flowers and leaves in Gothic, Medieval or Indian style, some no doubt inspired by Owen Jones' *Grammar of Ornament* (1856). The progress made in textile design in particular was again noted in Chevalier's introduction to the seven-volume report on the 1862 Exhibition written for the French Government.[55]

'Rivals are springing up, and the pre-eminence of France may receive a shock if we do not take care. The upward movement is visible, above all, among the English. The whole world

'The Labours of the Months'. A mid-15th-century tapestry acquired by the Museum in 1867 which inspired a design for a wallpaper frieze by the Silver Studio in 1893.

has been struck with the progress they have made since the last Exhibition [1851] in designs for Stuffs, in the distribution of colours, also in carving and sculpture, and generally in articles of furniture.' Another Frenchman, M Rupert, urged the establishment in Paris of a museum similar to that at South Kensington saying: 'It is impossible to ignore the fact that a serious struggle awaits France from this quarter.' The report from Lyons, whose School of Design was, to a large extent, the model copied by England, said: 'With Great Britain we shall have someday to settle accounts for she has made great progress in art since the Exhibition of 1851.' Moncure Conway emphasises that these statements were even more true in 1882 than in 1862 for 'South Kensington has evidently taken a leading position in Europe. The evidences of this are appearing daily. For example, the firm Messrs Corbière and Sons, which was established in London about twenty-eight years ago as an importing house for French patterns and goods, has now almost changed into an exporting house, sending to France patterns and designs for goods which it obtains from South Kensington. Even this is hardly so grateful to the English as a report, made lately by a large Glasgow firm [possibly Templeton's] that it has for some years been obtaining from this Museum at the annual cost of two hundred pounds designs such as it has been for many years previously securing from Paris and Lyons at the cost of £2,000 per annum. Lyons indeed, after teaching England its art of war has itself lost it. Neither Paris or London will use their newest patterns, one of which . . . represents huntsmen and hounds in full chase after a stag careering all over a drawing room carpet! Taste has for some years been tending to demand richness in substance, vagueness in pattern, quietness in colour, for all stuffs used in rooms. It is greatly to be regretted that the great manufacturers of textile fabrics declined to participate in the Centennial Exhibition [Philadelphia 1876] . . . it would have excited astonishment in America to see what transformation had been wrought in carpets and curtains, and it would at once be recognised that the old fabrics with their fixed scrolls, their glare and glitter, have become barbarous. Messrs Ward of Halifax[56] rolled for me on a floor, side by side, the old patterns and the new, and it was like the eye passing from poppies to passion flowers. "Those blazing ones" said Mr Ward "have gone out of fashion

A late 18th-century French embroidered panel from the 'Silvern Series' of photographs, produced in 1889 from specimens in the Museum. Designs such as this were to contribute to many 'period' designs usually designated as 'Adam style'.
Photograph: Silver Studio Collection, Middlesex Polytechnic.

in this country since the new Schools of Design began, and we never sell a yard of them here." New curtain stuffs have always an unobtrusive, almost dead ground of saffron, or olive, or green, and on it glowing conventional leaves with heraldic form – as daisy, pomegranate, etc. – to supply spots of colour, and the carpets are of much the same character with somewhat larger forms. These exquisite designs are universally recognised as the results of South Kensington.'

One enduring link between the Museum and the textile industry is seen in the work of the Silver Studio from its formation in 1880 until its closure in 1963, which, during these years, produced some 30,000 designs, mostly for textiles and wallpapers, for an enormous range of manufacturers, both at home and abroad reaching all classes of society. It would be impossible and probably fruitless to try and pinpoint exactly how many of these designs owed their inspiration directly to the collections of the Victoria and Albert Museum, but there is enough evidence to show that the influence of the Museum was both considerable and constant. The admirable catalogue of the exhibition of the work of the Silver Studio[57] compiled by Mark Turner in 1980 provides ample evidence and outlines the complete history of the enterprise. Many more precise examples could no doubt be given, but those that I have cited below should be sufficient to make the point.

The Silver Studio was founded in 1880 by Arthur Silver (1853–96). His grandfather had run a cabinet-making business in Reading, and his father James Silver added to this trade that of upholsterer, paper-hanger, estate agent, valuer, undertaker and insurance agent. In 1869 the young Arthur Silver attended the Reading School of Art, established under Sir Henry Cole's regime in 1860, and one of the few remaining products of Arthur's training at Reading is a page in a sketch book dated 1872 with meticulously drawn geometric patterns copied from Owen Jones' *Grammar of Ornament* (1856).

On leaving Reading School of Art in 1872, Arthur Silver was apprenticed to H. W. Batley, a skilled designer of furniture, textiles and wallpapers much influenced by Japanese art in the 1870s, but capable of working in a wide variety of styles which were quickly assimilated by his young apprentice.

Panel of tapestry from the tombs of Upper Egypt dating from the 6th–9th century AD. The bird was the basis of the 'Hedgerow' design by Jane Edgar, the basket being derived from another panel in the Museum.

'Hedgerow'. Screen-printed linen furnishing fabric designed by Jane Edgar for Heal's Wholesale and Export, 1947. The design is based on two textiles from Egyptian burying grounds in the Museum's collection.

In 1878 Arthur Silver married and his eldest son Rex was born the following year. Soon after, Arthur Silver took the bold step of launching out on his own and establishing the Silver Studio from rented premises at 132 Coningham Road, Shepherds Bush, moving to Brook Green, Hammersmith, in 1884.

Like William Morris, whose work he greatly admired, Arthur Silver used the Museum's collections of historic textiles as a frequent source of inspiration for his own designs, an inspiration he decided to make available to those who might not have such an easy access to the originals. In 1889 he decided to publish a series of large scale photographs of what he considered the most significant of these historic textiles, under the title of *The Silvern Series*. A review in the *Berkshire Chronicle* of 24 August 1889 stated that 'a new attempt to widen the usefulness of the splendid designs in South Kensington and other national collections has been conceived and carried out by Mr Arthur Silver, himself a well known art designer. By special permission of the ruling powers, Mr Silver has selected the most suitable objects for reproduction in modern commerce. From these he has produced by the aid of photography, full size working designs, made to the exact size commercially required by the exigencies of looms, blocks and other mechanical restrictions. These practical designs are to be sold to manufacturers, who can then reproduce the original work as accurately as if they had the actual samples before them. This new departure is one likely to influence the applied arts . . . by employing the unerring truth of the concern, the very threads of the warp and woof or the impact of the embossing of the block, can be clearly seen. This enterprise, in no way officially connected with South Kensington, has been the result of years of preparatory work, and the scheme just ready for presentation to the public is likely to raise curiosity both at home and abroad, as the various state departments on the Continent analogous to South Kensington are likely to make large use of it to augment their stock of patterns from our well stocked museum, wherein lie hidden countless treasures practically inaccessible to those more immediately concerned manufacturers whose works are at a distance from them.'

Screen-printed furnishing fabric designed by Frank Ormrod for Liberty's about 1933. The design is based on motifs taken from Caucasian rugs and carpets. (See p.113)

VII Glazed earthenware figure modelled by Phoebe Stabler for Ashtead Potters about 1930 and inspired by a della Robbia putto in the Museum's collections.

The photographs covered a wide variety of subjects from Near Eastern silks with small scale formalized designs to large scale swirling patterns of acanthus scrolls and other classical motifs which were to influence English Art Nouveau of the 1890s. They also included 17th-century Venetian brocades with a pattern of stylized pomegranates and flowers, embossed Spanish leather, English embroidery and a variety of European textiles from the 16th to the 18th century. The photographs sold widely to manufacturers throughout the 1890s, notably to Templetons, the Glasgow carpet manufacturer, to Simpson and Godlee (who had printed textiles for the Century Guild in the 1880s) and to Liberty's. To what extent the *Silvern Series* of photographs sold abroad it is difficult to assess. However Arthur Silver and other designers in the Studio, including John Illingworth Kay (who joined about 1892), Harry Napper (who joined about two years later), and Rex Silver, who took over the management of the Studio on his father's untimely death in 1896, sold their designs widely in France, Belgium, and, particularly from 1914 onwards, in the United States, and their work was frequently illustrated in foreign periodicals.

Arthur Silver did not necessarily intend manufacturers to copy the designs in the *Silvern Series* exactly or make straightforward reproductions. He hoped that through them manufacturers would turn to the Silver Studio to adapt the Museum originals to suit contemporary tastes. He himself rarely produced slavish copies but used the historic prototypes as a source of inspiration. A good example of his use of a Museum piece is the design of a wallpaper frieze in 1893 (bought by Charles Knowles and subsequently printed without the figures) which seems to derive from the German mid-15th century tapestry of the *Labours of the Month* acquired by the Museum in 1867.

The point of inspiration rather than exact reproduction is provided in an interview with Rex Silver, reported in the *Christian Science Monitor* of 4 May 1923 entitled 'The Trend in Design in Modern Fabrics'. Speaking to the reporter, Rex Silver stated: 'We have become less "groovy", and although we are using tradition, it is a much freer way so that we are making things suited to the present broader outlook. The designers also have to watch the modern methods of production and their endeavour is to help to give freshness to old ideas.

VII
Glazed earthenware figure modelled by Phoebe Stabler for Ashstead Potters about 1930 and inspired by a della Robbia putto in the Museum's collections. Photograph: Sally Chappell.

VIII
Glazed earthenware plaque advertising Osman towels, modelled by Reginald Till about 1923 and influenced by della Robbia roundels in the Museum's collections. Photograph: Sally Chappell.

IX
'Oak' Cameo glass vase by Emile Gallé made in the 1890s and showing the influence of Chinese glass and snuff bottles. Photograph: Sotheby's

A Caucasian Soumak carpet acquired by the Museum in 1878.

We specialise in designs for printed linens and cottons based on old silks and embroideries, because we find that people are looking for fabrics suited to rooms decorated in different periods . . . in fact nowadays to be a designer you have to be *au fait* with all the traditional styles. The Victoria and Albert Museum is a great inspiration, but it is no use just copying old pieces because everybody is doing that. If you want to make a design of a particular period you have to get imbued with the spirit of the period and imagine you are a designer of those days and are carrying on their tradition. We also want to keep up our originality and that is what I think we are doing.'

Rex Silver showed the reporter a number of designs, some based on old English chintzes and one of a procession of Chinese dragon boats passing through a series of lakes, broken by clumps of trees. Rex Silver explained that the design 'was based on an old Chinese painting at the Victoria and Albert Museum. It was just a tiny picture and a practical interpretation of it had to be made to suit modern methods of production.' He went on to explain that Chinese designs were very popular because they went with Chippendale furniture and, we might add, not only with 18th-century Chippendale and later reproductions but with the contemporary Chippendale-influenced furniture of Hille and Sons, and modern lacquered Chinoiserie and Japanese-style lacquered furniture.

The importance of the Victoria and Albert Museum to the Silver Studio was emphasised by another of their designers, Winifred Mold (b. 1894), who joined the Studio in 1912, but always worked at home, finally leaving in 1935. She recalled how Rex Silver was continually encouraging his staff to go to the Museum which provided the source of many of the Studio's designs during the years from 1912 to 1920, ranging from Chinoiserie and floral chintzes to neo-Adam and other 18th-century styles. The designers sought inspiration not only in the textile collection but in the wide variety of objects, for example woodcarvings by Grinling Gibbons which inspired a chintz with floral swags and birds.

Lindsay P. Butterfield (1869–1948), a prolific designer of textiles and wallpapers, left school at eighteen and while working at a West Indian Merchant's office in Mark Lane, London, attended evening classes at the Lambeth School of Art from 1887 to 1888, when he was apprenticed to his cousin, the architect Philip Johnstone. One year later, on advice from his godfather, the artist John Belcher, he was sent to the National Art Training School at South Kensington, where he stayed for three years concentrating exclusively on pattern design. It was here he began his close connection with the South Kensington Museum, a constant source of inspiration for the wallpaper and textile designs which were to make his reputation as one of the leading pattern designers of his generation. While at the National Art Training School he won many prizes, including gold and bronze medals. He received his first commission for wallpaper design in 1892 and subsequently designed for most of the leading British fabric and wallpaper firms, at the same time teaching in various art schools (including the Central School of Arts and Crafts and Kingston-on-Thames School of Art) until he retired in 1934 at the age of 65.

In 1909, Lindsay Butterfield was instrumental in forming the Design Club with premises in Newman Street, the aim being to further good design by bringing together designers and manufacturers in one organization. The designer members included Butterfield, Walter Crane, Lewis F. Day, C. F. A. Voysey, Archibald Knox, Ambrose Heal Junior, W. G. Paulson Townsend, G. M. Ellwood, and Rex Silver. On the manufacturing side were Mr Lasenby Liberty, Metford Warner of Jeffrey & Company, Mr Burton from the Pilkington Tile and Pottery Company, with representatives from Alexander Morton & Company, F. & C. Osler, Arthur Sanderson and Sons, Rottmann's and Wedgwood, and a number of other firms. The motto of the Club was 'Hand, Heart and Head', considered the three essentials of good design, with a symbolic badge designed by Voysey. As well as discussions, exhibitions were held. The Club ran for some five years but closed just before the outbreak of the First World War, to be followed by other similar but more ambitious organizations such as the Design and Industry Association and the British Institute of Industrial Art, both of which were to have close associations with the Victoria and Albert Museum.

In his unpublished autobiography, Lindsay Butterfield wrote that the Victoria and Albert Museum was his chief source of inspiration, but he detested mere copying, and he would take from each example just what he wanted and no more. The result of this selective approach was his *Floral Forms in Historic Design* (Batsford, London 1922) with floral motifs selected and drawn by him mainly from objects in the Victoria and Albert Museum, but including examples by William Morris and C. F. A. Voysey, designers whose work had had a great influence on his youth.

The preface to the volume and descriptive notes were written by W. G. Paulson Townsend who stressed the value of the Victoria and Albert Museum to designers. To quote from the preface: 'In the great Museum of Industrial Art at South Kensington a solution to most of the problems in Decorative and Applied Art can be found by the designer and art worker if he has sufficient time for search and study. The magnitude of this wonderful collection – which is always growing – is overwhelming to the student, who, without careful guidance is left bewildered among this accumulation of wealth, with its various appeals and diversity of purpose. The carefully chosen examples of conventional plant forms in this portfolio are produced not merely to save the trouble to those students who have the opportunity of studying the originals in the museum, but lead them into the right channels and help them search for themselves. For those who are working under the worst possible conditions away from all museums and collections . . . of such decorative materials, these reproductions will be of very great assistance.'

The preface stressed the value of studying historic ornament and criticised the excesses of some modern designs 'in which the bonds of association with most of the past are indeed very slender'. At the same time Paulson Townsend warned against mere copying and cited Morris and Voysey as bringing to applied art 'new ideas and new conceptions, each distinctive in style, but exhibiting a thorough knowledge of historic ornament, sound judgement in the selection and interpretation of these decorative elements, combined with their own power of creation, which are the basic qualities of great art'.

The eighteen plates in the volume concentrated on relatively few flowers (the rose, the carnation, almond and peach blossom) drawn from such diverse sources as Rhodian, Turkish and Syrian pottery and tiles, Persian and Indian textiles and carpets, Chinese embroidery and lacquer, Flemish tapestry, Italian and other European brocades and embroideries, English embroidery and Spitalfields silk, with roses drawn from textiles and wallpapers by Morris and Voysey, especially versions of the English 'Tudor' rose, beloved of the English Arts and Crafts movement. The final plate was devoted to roses and carnations from Gerard's *Herbal* which, as the caption stated, had 'appealed very strongly to artists and designers in recent years', among them Morris who was fortunate enough to possess his own copy.

Textiles from all periods in the Museum collections, from those from the Egyptian burial grounds onwards, have continued to provide source material, but here it is only possible to illustrate a few examples. Not only textile firms in this country but firms in the United States, including Boris Kroll Inc. and Brunschwig, have regularly sent over their designers to study and draw inspiration from the Museum collections, as well as seeking out 'documents' for more or less straightforward reproduction (see also the statements of individual designers in the Appendix).

As well as the permanent collections, special exhibitions devoted to textiles have played their part in setting trends. There is little doubt that the exhibition of *Victorian and Edwardian Decorative Arts* in 1952, which was the first post-war exhibition to focus attention on the textiles of William Morris, was responsible for the reprinting of Morris's designs by Sandersons and other firms, textiles that have become – and remain – best sellers with the public at large.

Two exhibitions of English chintz played a vital part in revitalizing the British textile industry: the first was assembled by the Circulation Department of the Museum at the Cotton Board, Manchester, in 1955, and entitled *English Chintz: Two Centuries of Changing Taste* (later circulated in reduced form); the second was the more comprehensive exhibition of *English Chintz* of 1960. Both exhibitions drew a great deal from the researches of Peter Floud, the Keeper of Circulation, who died at the early age of 48 in the midst of preparing the later exhibition. As an article in *The Ambassador*, the leading British export magazine, stated, the first exhibition traced the development of printed furnishing fabrics over two hundred years and stressed the world influence of British designers; the show was 'very closely studied by the industry, its designers, students and general public' and was widely reported throughout the world. The second exhibition included many loan items from museums and collections throughout Europe and the United States. Three leading firms, Heal's, Hull Traders, and Edinburgh Weavers, commissioned new designs from Lucienne Day, John Drummond and Olive Sullivan, to link up with this exhibition and show how traditional English designs could provide inspiration for patterns that were entirely new.

XIV. EMBROIDERY

The revival of the art of embroidery that came about in the second half of the 19th century owed a great deal to the influence of the South Kensington Museum with its magnificent collections of both ecclesiastical and secular historic embroideries.

The revolt against the stultifying influence of the ubiquitous Berlin woolwork came first from ecclesiastical quarters in the 1840s with a plea for the revival of mediaeval styles of church embroidery.[58] Pugin's *Glossary of Ecclesiastical Ornament* (1844) provided suitable motifs for church works of all kinds, and his views on embroidery are clearly set out in his book *On the Present State of Ecclesiastical Embroidery* (1843). Equally influential was the Ecclesiological Society's (formerly the Cambridge Camden Society) *Ecclesiastical Embroidery* (1848), twelve plates of working patterns of flowers, drawn full size from mediaeval vestments and furnishing, made by Miss Agnes Blencowe, a friend of the Gothic revival architect George Edmund Street. A set of these plates is now in the print room of the Victoria and Albert Museum.

From the 1860s superb examples of mediaeval embroidery were available for study in the South Kensington Museum, the most important being the celebrated 'Syon' cope, the finest surviving example of *opus anglicanum*, dating from 1300–20. It was acquired by the Museum in 1864, having previously been shown in the Museum's exhibition of art treasures from private collections in 1862; it became the foundation piece of the collection of early English church embroidery and was to provide inspiration for generations of needlewomen, an influence that, according to the architect John Dando Sedding, led to servile copying. Sedding himself was a distinguished designer of altar frontals and church furnishings and although he regarded museums as 'excellent places for cultured people to read and mark the history of art', he felt that they could be a trap for designers. In his contribution to *Arts and Crafts Essays* (1893) he makes specific reference to the Syon cope: 'The flowers we embroider were not plucked from the field and garden but from the camphor-scented preserves at Kensington [i.e. the South Kensington Museum]. No more museum-inspired work! No more scruples about styles! No more loathly Persian tile quilts! No more awful 'Zoomorphic' table cloths! No more cast-iron looking saints, or Syon cope angels, or stumpy Norfolk-screen saints.' This attack only serves to emphasise the extent of the influence of the collections; even Sedding must have realized the value of the Museum for in his praise of William Morris he speaks of him as 'a very giant of design, cultured at the feet of antiquity, leaned in the history of art'. He must have been aware of the beneficial influence the Museum had on Morris's designs, but he, like Morris, believed that historicism must be combined with a direct observation of nature.

It was with the works of William Morris and his associates that the revival of embroidery for domestic as well as church purposes may be said to have begun.

Mooris's first attempt at embroidery was made in 1856 when he was working in G. E.

Panel from a three-fold screen, the embroidered silk panel designed by May Morris. Made by Morris & Company for the drawing room at 'Bullerswood', Chislehurst, Kent, 1889.
Photograph: Sotheby's.

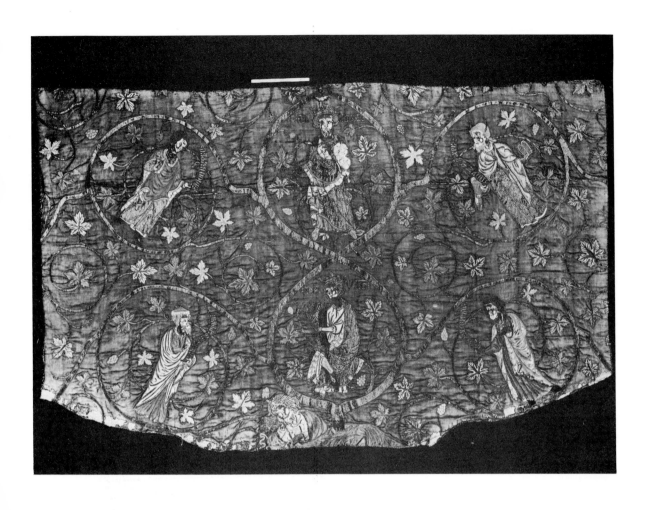

The 'Tree of Jesse' cope of c. 1340 used as a frontispiece by May Morris to her book Decorative Needlework, *published in 1893.*

'Belvoir' printed linen furnishing fabric designed by Frank Ormrod for Liberty's, c. 1933. The design is based on late 17th and early 18th-century crewelwork ('Jacobean' embroidery) and quilting.

Street's office in Oxford. This hanging, embroidered with flowering trees, birds, and his motto 'If I can', like his embroideries for Red House and those shown at the 1862 London International Exhibition, were conceived as substitutes for tapestries, and were all mediaeval in inspiration. Morris was to design for embroidery throughout his life, and embroidery remained one of the staple products of the firm. He also designed embroideries for the Royal School of Art Needlework, founded in 1872 under the Presidency of H R H Princess Christian of Schleswig-Holstein, with the two-fold aim 'of restoring Ornamental Needlework for secular purposes, to the high place it once held in decorative art, and to supply suitable employment for poor gentlewomen'. The School has always maintained close relations with the Museum. Its first premises were in Sloane Street, but in 1875 it moved to more spacious premises in Exhibition Road, where it remained until 1948.

In 1873 the committee of the Royal School of Art Needlework felt that 'an exhibition of ancient needlework, held under favourable auspices, would tend to promote the interests of art education and the employment of women'. Accordingly they approached the Committee of Council on Education who agreed that such an exhibition should be held at the South Kensington Museum. The exhibition, entitled *Special Loan Exhibition of Decorative Art Needlework made before 1800*, contained over 700 exhibits, divided into seventeen different classes, ranging from ecclesiastical embroidery, works with historical interest (including embroideries by Bess of Hardwick), crewelwork curtains, whitework and appliqué – in fact covering every possible type of historic embroidery, both English and foreign. The exhibition opened to the public in May 1873, and became the centre of study for the ladies of the Royal School of Art Needlework and for all those interested in the study of historic examples. It also served to focus attention on the value of the Museum's permanent collections, which continued to provide inspiration. Among the most favoured specimens were Italian Renaissance embroidered borders, considered suitable for chair-backs, table and tray cloths and mats, worked in red silk on linen, while formal Renaissance patterns with grotesque beasts and dolphins were considered suitable for mantlepiece borders, bell-pulls and screen panels. For larger items such as portières and coverlets, the English crewelwork

curtains of the late 17th century, the so-called 'Jacobean' designs with tree-of-life patterns and scrolling stems and leaves, were perhaps the most popular. For floral embroideries there was ample inspiration to be found in English 17th- and 18th-century embroideries, while the sprays of fruit (apple, pear, fig, apricots, cherries etc) which adorned tablecloths and doilies may well have been inspired by Philip Webb's gilt-ground painted panels in the Green Dining Room.

Today a link between the Royal School of Needlework (as it is now called) and the Museum is seen in the embroidery kits prepared by the School from Museum objects, one of which is the 'Flower Pot' firescreen or cushion panel designed by Morris about 1880.

In 1880 *The Magazine of Art* (vol III) in a series of articles on art needlework, pointed out that 'Our National Museum at South Kensington, in truth, furnishes us with a feast of various and rich materials of which, if we are so minded, we may feed, and teach ourselves, among other matters, the history of fine art needlework . . . The sight of 'old works' induces in thoughtful and willing people the desire to produce "new works".' The articles illustrated a number of embroideries from the Museum. In the latter part of the century numerous books were published on the subject of art needlework and virtually all of them stressed the value of the Museum's collections as a constant source of inspiration. Here it will suffice to quote one or two examples. Elizabeth Glaister's *Needlework*, published in the Macmillan 'Art at Home' series in 1880, stated: 'Dr Rock's Catalogue of textiles and embroideries at the South Kensington Museum is the best guide to that study of old needlework on which all modern production is founded'. Throughout the volume she mentions specific groups of embroidery as suitable models, among them the Cretan petticoat borders, with conventional pot-and-flower patterns, figures, birds and animals, a large group of which were acquired by the Museum in 1876, patterns which she regarded as 'traditional patterns of great antiquity'. She also picked out Italian and Spanish Renaissance embroideries, particularly those with conventional patterns worked in red silk on linen. Elizabeth Glaister also pointed out that not only the embroideries but many other objects in the Museum's collections furnished sources for designs – illuminated manuscripts, ceramics, metalwork, ironwork, damascene work on Indian water bowls, 'lotas' and Spanish braziers, borders on bells, monumental brasses, woodcuts in books, old herbals and paintings. Even the decoration of the Museum itself had its use. Writing about floral designs she stated that 'perhaps the best ornament will be found in some of the beautiful and varied Italian *Cinquecento* designs which may be made into a perfect study of colour, unfettered by reference to natural facts of the tints of leaf and flower. The colouring of Raphael's designs used for the decoration of the room at the South Kensington Museum where his cartoons are displayed will show what is meant.'[59]

May Morris (1862–1938), the younger daughter of William Morris, was herself a skilled embroideress and was put in charge of the embroidery section of the firm in 1885. In the introduction to the collected works of her father she recalls that the old South Kensington Art Schools were 'chosen for the training of some of us chiefly because of the Great

Museum next door' and that 'the South Kensington Museum was formed for the express purpose of helping the crafts'. In her book *Decorative Needlework* published in 1893, the first chapter is devoted to an 'historical glance'. 'One is glad' she writes 'to turn to a period of that art which repays all thought and search and fills one with joy, to the art of the Middle Ages, namely the 12th to the 14th centuries, where everything is instinct with life and originality in the handiwork of men . . . For anyone anxious to follow up this line of work in detail it can be done to a certain extent merely by walking through our South Kensington Museum, to go no further, carefully noting and comparing the true examples of early work displayed there. The great Syon cope is in itself a masterpiece of design and workmanship.' The frontispiece of the book is the almost as famous 'Tree of Jesse' cope of about 1340 acquired by the Museum in 1889 (175-1889). In 1897, when May Morris joined the staff of the Central School of Art, she regularly took her students to the Museum to study the historic embroideries.

Mrs Archibald Christie, perhaps the most skilled embroideress of her generation, who taught embroidery at the Royal College of Art, was equally enthusiastic in her advocacy of the Museum's collections as 'useful hunting grounds for the study of past work and inspiration for the future'. In her *Embroidery and Tapestry Weaving* (1906), one of the series of practical handbooks issued under the editorship of W. R. Lethaby, she thanks the authorities of the Museum for help in various ways and most of her illustrations are taken from the Museum collections. There is no doubt that she herself drew much of her unrivalled knowledge of technique and stitchery from them. This is clearly reflected in her influential book *Samplers and Stitches*, first published in 1921, for, as she stated in her preface, 'the study of old work forms the basis of the research which has made up this book'.

The Museum itself took a positive step in providing inspiration for those who were unable to see the actual objects for themselves by publishing a volume of fifteen large photographs compiled by Alan S. Cole, the second son of Sir Henry Cole, who became an assistant secretary in the Department of Science and Art and an expert on lace and other textiles. The book, entitled *Embroidery from the South Kensington Museum*, was published by R. Sutton & Company, London, in 1889 under the sanction of the Science and Art Department. In his introduction, Cole stated that 'embroidery may be described as ornamental enrichment by needlework of a material . . . the artistic interest is paramount in the present publication . . . and with this in view, the accompanying photographs have been made of specimens selected from a rich collection of embroideries of patterns from which suggestions of modern work may be derived'. The plates included a German 14th-century lectern cloth (8358-1863) and a German 15th-century linen altar cover, embroidered in white thread (4457-1858), Italian Renaissance and 17th-century borders, four of the Cretan petticoat borders acquired in 1876, and Spanish and Italian appliqué work.

Many writers advocated a study of Turkish and Persian embroideries in the Museum. The Persian textiles and embroideries were largely acquired through Major Murdoch Smith,

'The Magic Garden'. Fabric collage with embroidery in couched threads designed and worked by Rebecca Crompton, 1937.

who collected for the Museum from 1873 to 1885 when he was in Persia supervising the building of the telegraph line linking Europe with India.[60] In 1875 he acquired for the Museum the collection of the Frenchman Jules Richard, who had been tutor at the Shah's court, and the following year this was supplemented by an extensive gift from the Shah himself. The collection included 133 examples of embroidery and needlework, carpets and costumes, which provided inspiration for embroideries, both printed and woven textiles, and carpets, to many designers (including William Morris), particularly those adhering to the Arts and Crafts principles. The stylized motifs of plants and flowers, the flat patterns with no false three-dimensional effect, had an obvious appeal, an appeal that was enhanced by the fact that they derived from a living craft tradition, unspoilt by the commercialism of Western manufacture.

The Leek Embroidery Society and School of Embroidery founded in 1879 or 1880 by Elizabeth Wardle (1834–1902), the wife of Thomas Wardle (knighted in 1897), was to have a number of connections with the South Kensington Museum. The new interest in embroidery generated by the work of William Morris, the foundation of the Royal School of Needlework in 1872, and the exhibitions of historic embroidery at the South Kensington Museum, were to promote a number of organizations concerned both to improve the standard of art embroidery and to promote its sale. The Leek Embroidery Society had from its inception this two-fold purpose. Most of the designs were worked on tusser (or tussore) silk (printed at Wardle's works at Leek) in silk threads that were specially dyed there for the purpose.

Even before the establishment of the Society, a number of ladies, including Elizabeth Wardle, who married her cousin Thomas Wardle in 1857, had worked co-operatively on embroideries including an altar frontal for St Lukes Church, Leek, dated 1873. After an exhibition of the work of the Society, together with examples from the Royal School of Needlework, was held in 1881, Sir Philip Cunliffe Owen, Director of the South Kensington Museum, wrote to Thomas Wardle offering congratulations and encouragement. He wrote that 'considering the remarkable success which has attended the Leek School of Embroidery, it has proved itself worthy of being permanently established as an institution –

Banner of St. Matthew. Appliqué of fabric and leather with embroidery in fine split stitch and couched fillings. Designed and worked by Beryl Dean, 1956.

Mrs Wardle has shown powers of organisation in the interest she has communicated to other ladies in the very beautiful and artistic work she has produced'. He went on to state that 'to find a suitable home for it, to have a foundation for the maintenance of the same including the payment of a mistress, would be a great and good work. It would enable classes of females to attend schools of an evening, it would afford them the example of never having an idle moment and further would help to revive the silk trade, and one branch of it, embroidery, which would respond to the growing taste for the same amongst all classes of society . . . from Leek would go art teachers for the numerous schools of art needlework and embroidery which would spring up throughout the United Kingdom.'

The School obtained premises in St Edwards Street, next door to the Wardle family home, and produced embroideries for both church and domestic use. Many of them were worked on the Indian tussore silk or on velveteen printed at Leek from designs adopted from Indian sources by Thomas Wardle, or by his son Thomas Wardle junior, the architect J. D. Sedding, and William Morris, using the printed outlines as a guide for the embroidery in silk and gold thread. Some of the church embroideries were based on copies of mediaeval designs on East Anglian church screens made by George Wardle, Lady Wardle's brother, when he was manager of Morris & Company, the originals being preserved in the Museum. At least one of the Leek embroideries, a Chinese peony design, was copied from an embroidery in the South Kensington Museum.

The most ambitious work of the school however was probably a facsimile of the Bayeux tapestry. The idea of reproducing this famous embroidery appears to have occurred to Mrs Wardle when visiting the Museum some time in 1885 or 1886. Sir Philip Cunliffe Owen, the Director, drew her attention to the coloured photographic reproduction of the tapestry in the Museum which had been photographed in situ by E. Dossetter under the direction of Joseph Cundall, and was first publicly exhibited at the 1873 International Exhibition in the Albert Hall. It is probable that Mrs Wardle may have seen the original at Bayeux when she visited Normandy but the facsimile was worked from photographs lent to her by the Museum and traced by a Miss Lizzie Allen. It was a formidable task as the original frieze is 230ft 9in long by 20in wide. Thomas Wardle dyed the yarns to match the eight shades of the

original and thirty nine local ladies were employed in the project. The work was completed in the summer of 1886 and exhibited at the Nicholson Institute, Leek, in June or July of that year. This show was visited by 1,207 people, and the facsimile was then sent on tour to Tewksbury, Newcastle-on-Tyne, Stoke-on-Trent, Worcester and Chester, as well as to the United States and Germany. In 1887 it was shown for six months at the Saltaire Exhibition and in 1888 at the Royal Pavilion in Brighton. Following exhibitions in other cities, it was shown at the National Workmen's exhibition in London in 1893 where it was awarded a gold medal.

Although the Society received little financial reward from these shows, the embroidery contributed to the Society's fame, and eventually, after being on loan to Reading Corporation in 1895, it was bought for the Art Gallery by the then Mayor, Mr Owen Ridley, for the sum of £300. In 1927 the facsimile was cleaned and repaired and divided into 25 framed panels, since when it has again been lent to a number of other exhibitions, being cleaned and restored for the 900th Anniversary celebrations of the Battle of Hastings in 1966.[61] The fullest account of the facsimile and of the Leek Embroidery Society is given in a booklet published by the department of Adult Education, University of Keele, 1969, under the title of *The History of the Leek Embroidery Society*.

The South Kensington Museum's collections provided not only inspiration to individual needlewomen, but also an almost inexhaustible supply of designs for publishers of embroidery patterns. One typical booklet was that on *Jacobean Crewel Work*, published by 'Penelope' in 1934. The designs, almost all taken from Museum examples, were sold, traced on linen twill, by needlework shops throughout the country. The booklet included a popular history of English embroidery from Elizabeth to Queen Anne and reproduced examples of some of the best known crewel work curtains in the Museum. Some of the motifs from the famous Abigail Pett hangings (T.13 to I–1929) were adapted for a cushion cover under the title 'Castlemaine' and described as 'the jolliest of all the Jacobean patterns . . .' Three large 'Tree of Life' crewel work curtains were reproduced and some later floral examples, together with patterns adapted from them and suitable for working as portières, fire-screen panels, stool tops, chair seats, cushions etc. The so-called 'Jacobean' embroidery was perhaps the most popular type from the mid-1920s to the mid-1930s, for it went well with the oak 'Jacobean' furniture that graced everything from 'Stockbrokers' Tudor' to the half timbered suburban semi. The crewel work curtains in the Museum provided not only embroidery patterns, but designs for the innumerable 'Jacobean' printed linens and cretonnes sold by Liberty's and other firms in the 1920s and 1930s

In July 1932, an exhibition of modern embroidery and rugs, organized by the British Institute of Industrial Arts, was held in the North Court of the Museum and many of the items were purchased for the Museum's collections. In addition, mounted photographs of the exhibits were sent on loan to the art schools and training colleges throughout the country. The special 1933 Spring number of the *Studio*, under the title of *Modern Embroidery*,

X

'Angeli Laudantes', high-warp woollen tapestry designed by Burne-Jones, the background designed by J.H. Dearle. Woven at Merton Abbey, 1894.

The banners reading: "MOST BITTER WIND AND ARE SHORN the world without is waste and worn OUT HERE the guerdon WITHIN OUR ORCHARD CLOSE of our labour shows O VALIANT EARTH that works O HAPPY YEAR the MEAD of WINTER near AND HANGS ALOFT FROM HER TO HER the banners of the SPRING TO BE"

XI
'The Orchard',
high-warp
woollen tapestry,
the figures
adapted from
William
Morris's designs
for painted
decoration in the
nave of Jesus
College Chapel,
Cambridge, and
showing the
influence of
mediaeval figure
tapestries.
Woven at
Merton Abbey in
1890.

XII
'The Three
Fates', a Flemish
16th-century
tapestry acquired
by the Museum
in 1866 which
was particularly
admired by
William Morris
and which
provided
inspiration for
both Morris and
Burne-Jones.

was largely based on the exhibition. In the introduction Mary Hogarth, herself a skilled embroideress, pointed out that 'modern embroidery should be the invention of today in design and should express this age'. She felt that while a flourishing new school of embroidery design had grown up in Northern and Central Europe, England, possibly wisely, had been slow to adapt new ideas, although the 1932 exhibition showed that at last they had arrived here. She felt that pressures of modern life necessitated economy both in material and labour and advocated both appliqué and machine embroidery. But even here she stressed the importance of the Museum's historic embroideries: 'There is no limit to the variety of stitches and methods of work that can be adapted to the requirements of sewing machine embroidery and the study of the old embroideries from the Victoria and Albert Museum will enable the student of this new method to perceive its almost unlimited possibilities and bring the art of the ordinary household sewing machine into the world of decorative art, to an extent hitherto undreamed of.'

Perhaps the most influential embroideries bought from the exhibiton, together with later examples, were those by Rebecca Crompton, who was to provide inspiration for a whole generation of needlewomen. Her panel *The Creation of Flowers*, an experiment in textures, tones and colours, built up spontaneously without previous drawing, and other similar appliqué embroideries, brought about a new approach to embroidery design, enabling those who had neither the skill nor the time for elaborate stitchery to make original and attractive decorative pieces. The Circulation Department commissioned a series of samplers from Rebecca Crompton to demonstrate the effect of working the same design by different methods, or the use of materials such as braids or ribbons, combined with machine embroidery. The Department continued to buy contemporary embroidery throughout the 1930s and after the Second World War.

In 1952 the Circulation Department commissioned Iris Hills, of the Bromley School of Art, to design a series of panels demonstrating a method of teaching embroidery, initially for loan to art schools and training colleges. The demand, however, was so great that it was decided to reproduce the panels in full colour and issue them in book form.[62] The twenty plates were accompanied by technical notes and it was hoped that the ideas and methods would be of help to teachers in all types of schools, to bodies such as the Women's Institutes, and the individual needlewoman, who, without guidance, lacked the confidence or imagination to produce her own designs. When the Needlework Development Scheme, established by Coats in Glasgow, ceased operations in 1965, the bulk of the collections were transferred to the Circulation Department who used them to organize travelling exhibitions of modern embroidery to be sent to museums, art schools and teachers' training colleges throughout the country. The Department also maintained close relationships with the Embroiderers' Guild, particularly with the '62 Group, a section of the Embroiderers' Guild founded in 1962 to promote more experimental work, both in design and technique; a major exhibition of their work was held in the Museum in 1969. Since the establishment of the Craft Shop in the Museum in 1974, the work of individual embroiderers has been sold there and specimens acquired for the permanent collections. Embroideries of a more traditional nature feature in the do-it-yourself kits, prepared by the Royal School of Needlework from historic examples in the Museum's collections and on sale in the Museum shop.

Tribute to the inspirational value of the Museum's collections was also paid by Constance Howard, who was born in 1910 and trained at the Northampton School of Art and the Royal College of Art. She is universally recognized as a major figure in the field of embroidery, not only as a practitioner, but also as a teacher. Like William Morris and others before her, she acted as a catalyst in the merging of the fine arts with the crafts. As a lecturer at Goldsmiths College of Art from 1947 until she retired in 1975 as principal lecturer in charge of textiles and embroidery, she was able to ensure that embroidery was taught at a high level. In an interview with *Craft Magazine* (March/April 1982 p. 32 et seq) she stated: 'I believe in museum study as a means of understanding techniques of the past and as a social study. A great deal can be learnt that can be put to good use in today's work. Students should be given a background of appreciation and technical knowledge so that they can continue alone; inspired to continue with the craft when they find that it is too slow, difficult and often with boring preparation; made to realise that art is the basis of design, that many things are involved far from stitching!'

Until her retirement, Constance Howard, a distinctive figure with her hair dyed green, was to be seen regularly in the Museum with her students in tow, causing a whole generation to regard its galleries as a source of inspiration.

XV. FURNITURE AND WOODWORK

The influence of the furniture and woodwork collections of the Museum was felt in several ways. Firstly as a creative influence on individual designers and craftsmen who looked at the furniture of the past and interpreted it in their own way. Secondly, as a prime source of inspiration for manufacturers of reproduction furniture, and thirdly by setting fashions, or cementing trends that were already apparent, for different styles of period furniture. Thus the collections sometimes played a progressive role in promoting good modern design, sometimes a more reactionary role in reinforcing the public's tendency to feel 'safe' with genuine antique or reproduction furniture.

As in many other areas the earliest furniture acquisitions in the Museum reflected J. C. Robinson's preference for the Renaissance, which he described as 'probably as a whole more completely developed and more distinct as a style in furniture than in architecture'.[63] An analysis of the catalogue of *Ancient and Modern Furniture in the South Kensington Museum* by John Hungerford Pollen, published in 1874, reveals that between 1856 and 1874 no less than sixty Italian folding armchairs and elaborately carved Venetian chairs were purchased,

Cabinet of satinwood with marquetry of coloured woods, gilt mouldings and Wedgwood jasperware plaques. Made by Wright and Mansfield and purchased from the Paris Exhibition of 1867. An early and influential example of the 'Adams' revival.

'Free Renaissance' revival cabinet in rosewood with inlay of engraved ivory and mother-of-pearl. Made by Gillows of Lancaster about 1887.
Photograph: Sotheby's.

many from the Soulages collection, together with a number of carved and painted *cassoni*, or marriage coffers. The loan exhibition of furniture at Gore House, running from 27 May to 3 October 1853, had also contained many Renaissance pieces (although the outstanding 18th-century French pieces from the Royal Collection were of greater importance). Students were admitted free to the exhibition and permitted to make drawings and studies. Photographs of the furniture were made available and the *Art Journal* (1853, p.322) reported that 'the principal cabinet makers of Paris have obtained the series of Photographs which abound in information useful to manufacturers of furniture and metalwork'. The interest in the Renaissance generated by the Museum's collections persisted into the 1880s for expensive high quality furniture, especially for pieces made for successive international exhibitions from 1862 onwards. Details taken from Italian, French and Flemish Renaissance and Mannerist pieces of the 16th and 17th century were incorporated into sideboards, cabinets and buffets – details such as pilasters, pediments, sculptural figures, caryatids, grotesque masks and animal supports. Elaborate inlay in Renaissance style in coloured woods and ivory can be found in many high class pieces by firms such as Gillows of Lancaster, Jackson and Graham, and Collinson and Lock. The superb 'Juno' cabinet by Bruce Talbert, exhibited at the Paris Exhibition of 1878, recently acquired by the Museum, and the cabinet designed by Stephen Webb are fine examples.

The Italian folding armchairs, known at the time as Savonarola chairs, the carved Venetian chairs and *cassoni*, were much in favour with the artists of the period, and few of the artists' studios were without their examples, either as genuine antiques or as 19th-century copies.

The Elizabethan and Stuart furniture in the Museum collections also found favour with the manufacturers, particularly for halls and dining rooms. The so-called Jacobean style, which embraced elements taken from both early and late 17th-century furniture, was one of the most popular styles of the 1880s. It went particularly well with the oak-panelled or stamped-leather covered walls in the newly built terraces in the South Kensington and Gloucester Road area, whose wealthy inhabitants were no doubt frequent visitors to the

The 'Pet' sideboard. Oak with carved boxwood panels and metal hinges. Designed by Bruce J. Talbert and made by Gillows of Lancaster, 1873. Lent to the Museum by the Commissioners for the Great Exhibition of 1851.

A 'Chippendale' revival side cabinet in carved mahogany of about 1885. An identical example, stamped 'Edwards and Roberts' is in the Museum.
Photograph: Sotheby's.

nearby museum. Gillows of Lancaster produced fine pieces in this somewhat confused style which embraced bulbous-legged tables, court cupboards, panel-backed chairs, high-backed chairs with cane seats, as well as the modified 'Gothic' or 'Mediaeval' style introduced by Bruce Talbert, as exemplified by his 'Pet' sideboard of 1871, made by Gillows, which was purchased by the Museum. This was recognized at the time as a key piece, the corner stone of a style that was to filter down to lower levels of the trade, and was to be known alternatively as 'Early English'.

Another influential piece of the same period, bought from the London International Exhibiton of 1871, was an ebonised cabinet by the architect T. E. Collcutt, made by Collinson and Lock. John Hungerford Pollen described it as 'full of ingenious little drawers, shelves and receptacles reminding us in this respect of the quaint devices of Japanese cabinet-makers. The centre portion of the upper and lower stages is shut in by doors. These are panelled and the panels occupied by classical figures painted in white on vermillion and with birds all admirably drawn.' This cabinet was to be the prototype for the typical ebonised 'art furniture' of the aesthetic movement – cabinets, sideboards and overmantels, with shelves, inset mirrors and painted panels.

In 1871 two volumes of photographs of *Decorative Furniture*, one devoted to English, Italian, German and Flemish, the other to French pieces, were published by the Arundel Society 'under the sanction of the Science and Art Department, for the use of Schools of Art and Amateurs'. Most of the examples came from the Museum's own collections or from pieces in the Royal and private collections that had been included in the Gore House Exhibition of 1853. The Museum pieces, perhaps inevitably, showed a Renaissance bias, including an Italian 16th-century folding chair, two Venetian carved folding chairs, carved cabinets and *cassoni* with strapwork, masks and grotesques. One of the few 18th-century English pieces acquired by the Museum, a dressing table of *c.* 1780 (635–1870), was included, but the French 18th-century pieces were all from other collections. In the 1850s, when the Museum began to build up its furniture collection, 18th-century furniture was entirely out of fashion and it was not until the so-called 'Queen Anne' revival of the 1870s,

Cabinet of ebonised wood with painted panels. Designed by T.E. Collcutt and made by Collinson and Lock, 1871. Purchased for the Museum by the Commissioners for the Great Exhibition of 1851.

led by the architects Philip Webb, Eden Nesfield, and Richard Norman Shaw, that Georgian furniture came back into favour. In 1858 a fine Queen Anne walnut cabinet had been acquired (4619-1858) but this, apart from the two mirrors attributed to Chippendale (2387, 2388-1855), remained an isolated example until the late 1860s by which time some of the leading firms had already launched the 18th-century revivals. Wright and Mansfield had shown a bookcase and cabinet with 18th-century neo-classical detail at the 1862 Exhibiton and it is perhaps significant that the Museum should have bought their magnificent 'Adam Style' bookcase (545-1868) from the Paris Exhibition of 1867 – described by Yapp[64] 'as one of the chef d'oeuvres which are only produced at long intervals' – before they bought an original Adam piece. From 1869 onwards, however, the Museum began to buy English 18th-century pieces, by which time they were in competition with wealthy collectors. The new demand for 18th-century pieces with high prices and relative scarcity, meant that the Museum's specimens were eagerly copied by the manufacturers, and the last quarter of the 19th century was dominated by reproductions. In some cases more or less exact copies of the Museum's specimens were made, such as the satinwood dressing table by Hindley and Wilkinson based closely on that acquired by the Museum in 1870 as a genuine late 18th-century piece but now regarded as having been made in the 1860s and an early example of the Sheraton revival.[65]

Even Morris & Company reproduced 18th-century furniture styles in the 1890s and it is perhaps worth recalling that the firm's popular rush-seated Sussex chairs were a revival of 18th-century country furniture and that Rossetti had designed Sheraton-style furniture in the 1860s. French 18th-century styles had been revived in England since the 1840s but in an eclectic way as part of the historicism of the early 19th century. By the late 1860s, French late 18th-century styles, particularly Louis XVI, began to be interpreted and reproduced in a more scholarly way. The Museum played a considerable part in this revival, firstly by the display of the Wallace Collection at Bethnal Green Museum, and more importantly through the acquistion of the Jones Collection in 1882.

The *Handbook of the Jones Collection*, compiled by William Maskell, was published in 1883,

Cabinet and stand of macassar ebony inlaid with mother-of-pearl. Designed by Ernest Gimson and made in the Daneway Workshops about 1907. Now in the Leicester Museum and Art Gallery. Photograph: The Design Council.

Cabinet of walnut, elm, mulberry and bog oak with chased silver lock plate. Designed by Gordon Russell and made by Russell and Sons, 1927.

*Left:
A Spanish 'Vargueno' of the mid-16th century used as inspiration for the cabinets of Ashbee, Gimson, the Barnsleys and Gordon Russell.*

Cabinet of Italian walnut designed and carved by George Jack, 1892. Inscribed 'Hunting and slaying is my praying, my life is the dove's betraying. G.J. 1892'.

China cabinet of mahogany inlaid with satinwood. Designed by George Jack and made by Morris & Company, c. 1908. The cabinet shows the influence of Georgian furniture and the use of diagonal stringing first used by George Jack about 1887 and characteristic of 'Arts and Crafts' furniture.
Photograph: The Fine Art Society.

and from then on illustrations of pieces in the collection appeared in many books. No doubt many designers and cabinet-makers made sketches and drawings for themselves.

W. G. Paulson-Townsend produced a volume of *Measured Drawings of French Furniture from the Collection in the South Kensington Museum* (London, 1897–99) which included examples from the Jones Collection and also French 16th-century furniture from the Peyre Collection. Seven plates were devoted to the *éscritoire à toilette* (1043–1882), then attributed to Roentgen, and in his introduction the author states that 'my object . . . is to make a clear and practical work, which can only be accomplished by careful and patient measurements. I find there is so much of the refinement lost in making rough sketches from such pieces of furniture as these, where the greatest beauty lies in subtle proportion, in the curve of the legs for instance, it is impossible to get a correct facsimile without measured profile and front elevations. There are a great many lines in legs of this period of French furniture, from the strong and graceful to the slippery weak curve.' Unfortunately, in most of the commercial copies or adaptations of French 18th-century furniture it was the weaker curves that predominated. Reproductions of the various Louis styles have persisted to the present day, and the London and Provincial auction rooms bear testimony to the scale of such production from the late 19th century onwards. Many of these pieces owe their origin to the furniture in the Jones Collection, although they sadly lack the quality of the originals in both design and craftsmanship.

The late 1870s and 1880s also saw the publication of many books of designs and sketches of furniture in various revived styles such as G. T. Thompson's *Designs for Chimney Glasses, Girandoles, Cabinets and Cornices after the Style of Adam, Sheraton and Chippendale* (1878), and A. Jonquet's *Original Sketches for Art Furniture in the Jacobean, Queen Anne, Adams and Other Styles* (1879). By 1880 the *Artist and Journal of Home Culture* (November 1881) was to ask 'Are we to be forever looking backwards? Is there no power of primary design left among us, but only a faculty for the new combination of bits of our ancestors' work?'

As the century progressed the tendency towards reproduction increased and the Museum added considerably to the collection of English 18th-century furniture, particularly chairs.

Cabinet by Louis Majorelle shown at the Paris Exhibition of 1900 and acquired by the Museum through the Donaldson Gift.

An English inlaid mahogany cabinet showing the influence of French Art Nouveau furniture, about 1900.
Photograph: Sotheby's.

The final seal of approval was given by the *Special Loan Exhibition of English Furniture and Silks* held at Bethnal Green Museum from May to October 1896, organized by John Hungerford Pollen, and Casper Purdon Clarke, the Assistant Director of the Museum, who visited no less than seventy different collections, selecting the best examples. Bethnal Green was deliberately chosen as the venue for, as the catalogue stated, 'the manufacture of household furniture is largely carried on by the residents of that district of the metropolis and it is believed that a collection of fine examples of English furniture of the 17th and 18th century will be not only interesting but of considerable service to them.' Examples from the Museum's own collections were included in the exhibition but more significant was the fact that the exhibition gave the public and, above all, the trade, the chance to see some of the most important furniture from stately homes and other private sources and to reproduce it. While the furniture in the Jones Collection and the reproductions inspired by it received general approval, a major acquisition of French Art Nouveau furniture from the Paris Exhibition of 1900 was given a mixed reception. George Donaldson, vice-president of the Jury for furniture at the Paris Exhibition of 1900, was so inspired by the French Art Nouveau furniture, in which, he felt, 'superior ingenuity and taste are displayed than that shown in our own production', that he offered a gift of it, worth several thousand pounds, to the Victoria and Albert Museum. The gift consisted of some twenty major pieces by Majorelle, Gallé, Gaillard, Pérol Frères and others, together with some Hungarian and Norwegian pieces in their respective 'National Romantic' revival styles. Most of them were illustrated in the *Magazine of Art*[66] in an article contributed by George Donaldson himself. In accepting the gift and putting it on exhibition little did the Museum realize the furore it would cause. Four leading architects and designers, John Belcher, ARA, Reginald Blomfield (one of the founders of Kenton and Company), Mervyn Macartney (who designed 18th-century style furniture for Morris & Company), and Edward S. Prior wrote an indignant letter to *The Times*, published on 15 April

1901: 'It is to be much regretted that the authorities of South Kensington have introduced into the Museum specimens of the work styled "L'Art Nouveau". This work is neither right in principle nor does it evince a proper regard for the material employed. As cabinet-makers work it is badly executed. It represents a trick of design which, developed from debased forms, has prejudicially affected the design of furniture and buildings in neighbouring countries. In its present position it is in danger of being looked upon as a recognised model which has received the approval of the authorities for study by students and designers and the harm it may thus produce on our national art cannot easily be gauged.'

Similarly the *Journal of Decorative Art* (August 1901 p.196) stated: 'No greater disservice has been done to the cause of true art education for a long while past in this country than the acceptance by the authorities at South Kensington of the gift of George Donaldson ... The work was in its right place at the Paris Exhibition. It carried with it there no sanction beyond its own merit or audacity; but for a public educational authority like South Kensington to receive it and find it lodgement in their permanent collection, thus giving it the *imprimatur* of its environment, is a totally different and far graver matter.' The article went on to quote with approval the word of the *Builder* which described the furniture as 'bad and tawdry stuff . . . put there to be studied and copied, to the detriment of the taste of our own artisans; and (worse still) are, we are told, to be sent round to the provinces, so that the taste of the provincial art-workman may be alike corrupted. This is not what the South Kensington Museum was founded for; it was to be a storehouse of the best art, not a showroom for vagaries in design.'

An article in *The Furniture Record and the Furnisher* of 30 August 1901 (pages 165–8), entitled '*L'Art Nouveau What Is It?*' was much more restrained in its criticism. Describing Art Nouveau furniture as 'an aesthetic rendering of Louis Quinze', the article praised the marquetry as being magnificient but took exception to much of the carving. Referring to the French Art Nouveau furniture displayed at the Museum, in Paris, and in some of the leading London shops, the general conclusion was that it had little to commend it, save its foreignness, but 'it has many excellent features that we may study with profit and it will undoubtedly influence our fashions'. The *Studio* (1901, p.269) in a review of the Donaldson Gift, took a more balanced view, weighing up the pros and cons: 'Some of the furniture is faulty in constructive design, although certainly not more so than in many designs by Chippendale and other acknowledged masters. The ornamental details are in several cases decidedly weak, and show a lack of decorative knowledge on the part of the designers. The workmanship, however, is entirely satisfactory, and may be studied with advantage by many of our practical cabinet-makers.'

Such responses at least showed the extent of the Museum's influence. On 12 July 1901, realizing that showing the collection seemed to signify their approval, the Musuem authorities issued the following memorandum: 'Much of the modern continental furniture,

XIII
Cabinet of mahogany with carved marquetry decoration designed and made by Louis Majorelle (1859–1929) and exhibited in Paris in 1900. From the Donaldson Gift.

XIV
Dressing table of satinwood with marquetry and painted decoration acquired by the Museum in 1870 as a fine example of English furniture of about 1780.

XV
Dressing table of satinwood with painted decoration made by Hindley and Wilkinson of London about 1880 and copied from the similar piece acquired by the Museum in 1870. Photograph: Sotheby's

however, exhibits a style which is not consistent with the teaching of Art Schools of the United Kingdom. It is therefore necessary that students inspecting the examples in this collection should be guided, in forming an opinion as to their merits and obvious faults, by instructors who have given attention to such subjects as Historic Ornament, Principles of Ornament, and Architecture.'

In 1901 the collection (which also included pottery, glass, metalwork and jewellery in the 'new art' or Art Nouveau style) was lent to the Industrial Polytechnic Exhibition at the Bingley Hall, Birmingham, to the Museum of Science and Art in Edinburgh, and to the Science and Art Institution in Dublin, with, in each case, a note 'explaining the object of the collection and method recommended in studying the various objects'. It seems that the Museum, under the barrage of criticism, began to regard the collection as a warning rather than an inspiration. It probably came as no surprise to most of the art students, who were already familiar with the work of many of the designers represented through articles in the *Studio* and other periodicals. Indeed a glance through the competition pages of the *Studio* for the previous five years, or the retrospective review of students work published in 1897, shows that many British art students were already skilled practitioners of Art Nouveau – a style which most continental autorities considered to have its roots in England. The exhibition of the Donaldson Gift, however, popularized the style among the general public and had a considerable, although not altogether a beneficial, influence on the furniture trade. In the hands of outstanding designers such as Gallé and Majorelle, Art Nouveau produced some superb and elegant furniture, now universally admired, but when the style filtered down to the lower levels of the trade – in France as well as in England – the result was often merely eccentric. Somewhat spindly furniture, of somewhat curious form, in highly polished light rosewood had been produced since the 1890s, described as 'fanciful', 'quaint', or 'Anglo-French', and the exhibition of the Donaldson bequest gave a new emphasis to the style, characterized by asymmetry, strange projections and swirling floral and leaf motifs. A cartoon from *Punch* (1903) makes an amusing comment on the style. Undoubtedly the collection made an impact, but already Art Nouveau had passed its peak, although it lingered on in a debased form until the outbreak of the First World War. After its tour, the Donaldson Gift was banished to Bethnal Green, to come into its own again during the Art Nouveau revival of the 1960s, a revival in which the Museum was to play a considerable part.

Fortunately, while the Museum's collections were a convenient and impeccable source for the makers of 'reproduction' furniture, they also provided inspiration for original designers, particularly those working in the Arts and Crafts tradition. As well as producing Queen Anne and Georgian styles, Morris & Company marketed more original pieces, influenced by, but not copied from, 18th-century models, and designed by Mervyn Macartney, W. A. S. Benson, and George Jack (1855–1932) who had trained under Philip Webb. George Jack, taking his inspiration from late 17th-century and 18th-century English furniture, produced

Luke Fildes, R. A., in his studio in Melbury Road, sitting in a 'Savonarola' chair. Photograph: Sally Chappell.

'Savonarola' carved oak folding chair. Italian; about 1550. Acquired by the Museum in 1860.

outstanding pieces of inlaid furniture for Morris & Company in the 1880s and 1890s. He introduced the use of dark and light stringing, which was to become an outstanding feature of Arts and Crafts furniture, into a sideboard exhibited at the Manchester Jubilee Exhibition of 1887. This technique of stringing, usually in ebony and holly, in chequered or herringbone patterns, derived from English and Dutch 17th-century furniture, examples of which were found in the Museum's collections. George Jack was also a skilled woodcarver. His manual on *Wood-Carving and Workmanship*, published in 1903, with an introduction by W. R. Lethaby, illustrated a number of examples from the Museum. In it he stressed the advantage of having the handy reference of the Museum's specimens, although he was disturbed by the problem of architectural specimens wrenched from their proper setting. George Jack's own woodcarvings often show a Gothic inspiration and the influence of Webb in his treatment of birds and animals. A characteristic example is the chest he showed at the Arts and Crafts Exhibition of 1893.

In the last two decades of the 19th century, woodcarving was a popular pastime for both professionals and amateurs. In 1879 a School of Art-Woodcarving was established by the Society of Arts at Somerset Street, Portman Square, moving to rooms in the Albert Hall later that year. The school aimed at giving a thorough training to the professional carver but it was also open to amateurs. The extensive collections of the nearby South Kensington Museum provided a constant source of inspiration, particularly, according to the *Studio*, the Renaissance examples.[67] Handbooks were prepared by Miss Rowe, the manager and assistant teacher, and a series of photographs of the *Wood-carvings in the South Kensington Museum* was assembled for distribution throughout the country, as well as a series of lantern slides with accompanying notes 'for the further instruction of country classes who are unable to see the art treasures shut up in the various museums throughout the world'. The success of the school can be measured by the fact that the number of students increased steadily each year from 42 in 1881 to 375 in 1892.

Tribute to the lessons to be learned from the collections at the South Kensington Museum was paid also by the sculptor George Frampton (1860–1928) when he stated that 'half an hour [in the Museum] will be sufficient to convince us . . . that it was want of restraint on the part of the carver which led to that vulgar riot of unshapely form which marks the furniture of the most debased periods'.[68] He specifically mentioned (and illustrated) a French 14th-century carved pulpit, where the upper foliage panels 'were well nigh perfect examples of design applied to interior woodwork' but the whole was marred by the overworking of the lower portion. He also criticised some 17th-century chairs in the Museum, but praised some Chippendale examples: 'There is nothing to catch or destroy the dress; there is nothing to produce agonising sensations in the most sensitive portions of the spinal column which the chair back is designed to support. The genius of the material itself is not forgotten.' But he reserved his greatest praise for an Italian 14th-century carved wood coffer or *cassone* (80-1864) which he had 'for long regarded as one of these rare instances of artistic completeness which in their simple perfection produce the same sense of pure satisfaction as does the strain in some melody beloved in childhood! . . . The whole flat surface of the front is enriched by the cunning of the carver until it fairly palpitates with beauty.' Frampton himself trained at the Lambeth School of Art and the Royal Academy Schools from 1880–87 and worked at architectural carving in stone and woodwork while still a student, including a pulpit and choir stalls in a church at Bethnal Green. The qualities he admired in the woodcarvings at South Kensington and in the Florentine Renaissance relief carvings, were reflected in his own work, and he was to become one of the most influential sculptors of his time, and a leading member of the Arts and Crafts movements.

It was not Renaissance furniture but the Spanish and Portuguese 16th- and 17th-century *varguenos*, box-like cabinets equipped with numerous pigeon-hole drawers and cupboards, often with a fall front and set on an openwork stand of legs and stretcher, that provided inspiration for much of the 'Arts and Crafts' and 'Cotswold' furniture of the late 19th and early 20th century.

C. R. Ashbee(1863–1942), the founder of the Guild of Handicraft in 1888, used the *vargueno* form for much of his furniture, a cabinet of 1904–5 with tooled leather doors being a typical example, and also an inlaid cabinet of 1902.

The *varguenos* in the Museum's collections also provided inspiration for Ernest Gimson (1864–1919) as testified by the considerable quantities of Museum photographs formerly in his possession and now held by the Cheltenham Museum.[69] In 1886, Gimson, who was born in Leicester, entered the practice of John Dando Sedding, whose office premises were next door to Morris & Company's showrooms in Oxford Street, London. Ernest Barnsley (1863–1926) was a fellow student and through him Gimson got to know Sidney Barnsley and W. R. Lethaby. He also joined the Society for the Protection of Ancient Buildings, attended the meetings of the Art Workers Guild, and became friendly with both Morris and Webb. Gimson would certainly have been familiar with the Museum's collections. A number of his early pieces of furniture for Kenton & Company in the 1890s show the influence of the *varguenos* and late 17th- and early 18th-century English furniture in the Museum, influences that were to carry on to the 'Cotswold' period. The Museum photographs in his possession show that he also drew inspiration from the most unlikely sources. A German armchair of carved and turned ash with a rush seat, dated 1795 (1113-1904), shows the pegged construction and champfering that characterizes much of his work. Similarly a 17th-century Arabian bedstead, inlaid with ivory and ornamented with cut paper under glass (negative number 14259) has the head and footboards divided into panels, with borders round them, close in spirit to the innumerable drawers and cupboards on Gimson's cabinets. A large number of the Museum's photographs in Gimson's possession were of textiles and embroideries which seem to have provided a constant source of reference not only for Gimson's own embroideries but also for the floral decoration on his metalwork, inlaid furniture and plasterwork. Gimson clearly used the Museum's collections in an original, creative way, never for mere copying or pastiche. The same influence can be seen in the furniture of Ernest and Sidney Barnsley, Peter Waals, Gordon Russell and others working in the Arts and Crafts and Cotswold tradition.

In his autobiography[70] Gordon Russell (1892–1980), who was to become one of the most important English furniture designers of the 20th century, and in 1947 Director of the newly founded Council of Industrial Design, relates how he first became aware of the Museum's collections while a schoolboy at Chipping Camden Grammar School: 'Part of an old building which we used as the school woodwork shop was also taken over by Ashbee. In it were housed glass cases with plaster casts of all kinds of things from the Victoria and Albert Museum and I often dallied to look at them. It would have been an excellent thing if small parties of boys could have had the objects explained to them or have been taken to see the craftsmen at work.' While still at school, Gordon Russell made his first piece of furniture, a small set of bookshelves. He was to come into close contact with the V & A when in 1923 he was asked to exhibit in the B. I. I. A. Exhibition in the North Court; he was then beginning to produce furniture to his own designs, an enterprise that developed from the repair shop attached to the Lygon Arms and his father's antique business. His furniture at this time was very much in the Arts and Crafts style of Gimson and the Barnsleys, and Gordon Russell described the exhibit as 'not a bad little job, though a bit rustic and unfinished', and one which led to a commission for furnishing a complete room in Rochdale. From 1930 onwards, Gordon Russell's firm was to produce work comparable to that of the modern movement on the Continent, and he himself was to be the most important member of the committee for the production of Utility Furniture in the 1940s.

In April 1950, the Museum gave encouragement to rural furniture makers by housing the results of a competition for hand-made furniture organized by the Rural Industries Bureau; these pieces continued in the traditions of the 17th and 18th centuries, but, like the work of Gimson, Peter Waals and the Barnsleys, created new designs to suit the needs of their own time. The Museum also organized a travelling exhibition, including not only furniture but other crafts, to support the work of the Rural Industries Bureau.

The influence of the Museum's period rooms on interior decoration would require a book to itself and involve a detailed analysis of the changing fashions over the last century. The first complete room to be purchased by the Museum was that from the Hotel Serilly in Paris, a boudoir decorated by Rousseau de la Rottière in 1778–79, bought in 1869 for 60,000 francs. The first English rooms were added in the late 19th century, the Sizergh Castle room in 1891 and the early 17th century-room from Bromley-by-Bow in 1894. No 18th-century rooms were acquired until the 20th century, the room from Great George Street, Westminster, being acquired in 1910 and the Hatton Garden room in 1912. When they were installed, both rooms were stripped of their paint and were no doubt responsible for the vogue for stripped pine panelling in the 1920s and 1930s. The rooms have now been repainted as they would have been in the 18th century but to some extent the passion for stripping still persists. David Garrick's room from the Adelphi Terrace was acquired in 1936 and the Norfolk House music room in 1938, while the finest Adam interior, the grand drawing room from Northumberland House, was not acquired until 1955.

An amusing illustration of the influence of the period rooms occurs in an American publication, *Interior Decoration: its principles and practice* by Frank Alvah Parsons, BS, president of the New York School of Fine and Applied Art, published in New York in 1923. A photograph of the Hatton Garden Room (then in its stripped condition) is captioned: 'With extraordinary forethought the Albert and Victoria [sic] Museum has assembled, among others, this fine room by James Gibbs, done about 1730, as a background for the style of Queen Anne. It should appeal, particularly in America, for the country house.'

One of the most distinguished English interior decorators, John Fowler, CBE, who died in 1976, trained himself at the V & A which he regarded as his University. He joined Sybil Colefax in 1938 to form the firm of Colefax and Fowler, a firm which still exists, with premises in Brook Street, Mayfair. John Fowler had a vivid historical imagination and was as familiar with the 18th century as with the century in which he lived, but this imagination was combined with the approach of a serious historian and scholar. Everywhere he would search for the evidence, for scraps of wallpaper and fabric, carpets and layers of paint. This interest in historic furnishings led to frequent visits to the Museum to discuss datings and attributions. It was mutually beneficial, for, in return, John Fowler gave numerous pieces to the Museum – old silks and trimmings, pieces of carpet and wallpaper – saved from the historic houses whose decoration he was trying to conserve and restore. As an adviser to the National Trust on the redecoration of their properties, he used his taste and knowledge to recapture the original style of the rooms, a knowledge which owed a great deal to the collections and expertise of the V & A and its staff.

XVI. CERAMICS AND GLASS

The extensive ceramic collections of the Museum have continuously provided inspiration to both commercial manufacturers and individual potters. As Walter Smith stated in his 1863 report on the work of the French Schools of Design, 'the best possible view to take of the maiolica plates and Venetian glass, which are locked up in the glass cases at South Kensington, is a business view of their value as examples of study to the manufacturers of porcelain and glass in England, and not as objects of curiosity for the connoisseur and dilettante, or holiday sightseer of London'.

Many manufacturers did in fact see the collections in this light, notably Minton's of Stoke-on-Trent, who played a considerable part in the decoration of the Museum's buildings, including the Refreshment Rooms and the Ceramic Staircase and Gallery. The Ceramic Gallery itself, and its contents, are described in detail by Moncure Conway in the *Art Journal* of 30 October 1875 (p.226).

Henry Cole first met Herbert Minton (1793–1858) at a dinner party in November 1842 and the two soon became firm friends. After Herbert's death Cole kept up his connection with Minton's through the two nephews who ran the firm and a close association with the Museum was maintained. Apart from collaborating with Cole over the Summerly Art Manufactures, and supplying materials for the building, Herbert Minton was instrumental in the Museum acquiring the Soulages collection, which was particularly rich in Italian Renaissance maiolica, for it was on a joint visit to the Paris Exhibition of 1855 that Minton showed Cole photographs of the collection. It is difficult to assess precisely the influence which the Museum's collection had on the productions of the Minton factory, for the firm, as well as having its own collections, had access to several important private ones, including that of the Duke of Sutherland at Trentham Hall. However, there is little doubt that the 'historicism' of many of Minton's productions owed a good deal to the Museum's pieces, both as an inspiration and also in popularizing their wares among the general public, since many Minton pieces were acquired for the Museum at the time of production in the 1850s and 1860s.

In his lecture on 'Art Museums' published in the *Penn Monthly* in February 1877, Christopher Dresser stated that it was the South Kensington Museum's collection of maiolica that inspired Minton's to produce their 'Majolica Ware' and that the firm's success was largely due to this production.

The famous Minton majolica ware was introduced by Léon Arnoux (1816–1902) shortly after he joined the firm in 1849 as Art Director, and achieved an enormous success at the Great Exhibition of 1851. Majolica ware was soon adopted by other firms, including Wedgwood, Copeland, George Jones, and (somewhat unsuccessfully) by Sèvres, and a number of other continental factories. Few however approached the originality of design, skill in modelling and brilliance of the glazes of the Minton productions.

Throughout the 19th century, English as well as French ceramics were much influenced

A 16th-century ewer by Bernard Palissy copied by Minton and acquired by the Museum in 1860.

by the work of Bernard Palissy (1510-90) and his followers. By 1860 the Museum boasted a considerable collection, augmented in 1910 by that assembled by George Salting on the Museum's behalf over a number of years and on loan to the Museum from 1875. Minton copied not only the mannerist grotesques of Palissy's rustic style and his more formal French Renaissance styles, but the brilliant colour of his glazes – indeed this was clearly the inspiration of their majolica to which they gave the alternate name 'Palissy' ware. A Minton candlestick of 1858, based freely on a Palissy model, was acquired by the Museum in 1859 (5882-1859) and a ewer and stand, modelled by Hamlet Bourne after the Palissy originals in the Soulages collection displayed at Marlborough House in 1856, was also acquired by the Museum in that year (4730-1859).

Much of the Minton majolica, however, made use of animal and plant forms, continuing a tradition of 18th-century ceramic designs but reinforced by the Victorian passion for naturalism and ornament suggestive of the use of the object, such as was advocated by Henry Cole and his circle, and manifest in the 'Felix Summerly Art Manufactures'. The objects ranged from game pie dishes, decorated with pheasants, hares, pigeons, ducks, to teapots and purely ornamental pieces, including vast jardinières and garden seats in oriental and other styles.[71] A number of the zoomorphic designs were probably inspired by the publication of Darwin's *Origin of Species* in 1859.

From about 1855-65 a number of Minton's productions were inspired directly by Italian Renaissance maiolica, some based on examples in Marlborough House and in the South Kensington Museum (the Bernal and Soulages collections). These early Minton pieces, including the plaque of Queen Victoria, painted by Thomas Kirkby, and those designed by Alfred Stevens, were painted in enamels on an opaque glaze, rather than by using the coloured glazes of the majolica ware.

Painting in imitation of the 16th-century Limoges enamels, loosely based on models by Pierre Reymond and Jean de Court, was successfully carried out by Benjamin Lockett, Thomas Kirkby and Stephen Lawton. Again the Museum's

A Minton 'Maiolica' ewer modelled by Hamlet Bourne in 1858 after the original by Bernard Palissy and acquired by the Museum.

collection provided reference material, and a tazza and cover painted by Lawton seem to have been based closely on a Museum specimen. Such copies were also the speciality of Thomas Bott at Worcester.

Another outstanding example of Minton's historicism was the imitation of the 16th-century 'Henri Deux' or 'St Porchaire' ware (also known as Oiron ware). This was first produced by Leon Arnoux on 1858, using a combination of painted and inlaid decoration, but not based directly on extant examples.

In 1861 a book by C. Delange, *Recueil de toutes les pièces de la faience française dite Henri II*, was published in Paris, and Minton's were among the subscribers. At about the same time the South Kensington Museum issued a series of twenty photographs of 'Henri Deux' ware 'from the original works in the South Kensington Museum and private collections', and by 1875 the Museum possessed five outstanding pieces. Most of the Minton pieces were modelled by Charles Toft (1832–1909) in the 1870s, some of them copied exactly from the 16th-century examples illustrated in Delange, some from the specimens in the Museum, and others more freely adapted.

The Persian pottery in the Museum's collections also inspired a number of pieces. A drawing of a Persian bottle in the South Kensington Museum (now in the Minton archives) was used, with slight modification, for an earthenware bottle, printed in green, and painted in green and red, instead of the blue and red of the original. Similarly a bottle and stand, elaborately painted with coloured enamels and gilding in imitation of Islamic inlaid metalwork, was probably based on Museum's specimens.

The Japanese and Chinese influence apparent in the aesthetic movement of the 1870s was reflected in a number of wares, inspired by Chinese and Japanese cloisonné enamels, bronzes, ivories and jade, as well as actual Far Eastern ceramics. At least one Minton vase, with a rich turquoise glaze, seems to have been copied from a jade in the Museum's collection. A number of Minton cloisonné pieces were designed by Christopher Dresser (who was trained at the Government School of Design and lectured for the Department) and the Minton archives contain a number of signed drawings by him showing both Japanese and Egyptian influences. He may have been inspired by the cloisonné enamel of Barbidienne, an outstanding example having been purchased by the South Kensington Museum from the 1862 Exhibition, and Dresser himself singled out for praise many examples of French cloisonné work at the Paris Exhibition of 1867 in an article in the *Chromolithograph* of 1868.

A very direct connection between the Museum and Minton's was the establishment of the Minton Art Pottery Studios in 1871, which grew out of the work of the South Kensington Museum porcelain painting class where, between 1867 and 1870, the female students had painted the Minton tile blanks for the Dutch Kitchen. A site, between the Royal Albert Hall and the Horticultural Gardens, was leased from the Commissioners of the 1851 Exhibition and a studio and kilns erected. As an article in the *Art Journal* for 1872[72] stated, the site was

*A pair of Minton wall plaques,
with the date letter for 1873,
painted by Ellen Welby, who
participated regularly in the
Howell and James Annual
Exhibitions of painting on
porcelain.
Photograph: Sotheby's.*

155

ideal for 'the facilities at hand for studying floral forms in their richest manifestations, in the Royal Horticultural Gardens and its periodical flower shows, and also some of the finest examples of Keramic Art of the best periods, in the South Kensington Museum, together with the instruction obtainable in the Schools of Art . . . a combination of means to a given end which cannot well be over estimated.' Pottery in the biscuit state was sent down from Stoke and decorated and fired at Kensington, and W. S. Coleman (1829–1904), the designer and painter who specialized in depicting nude children, was put in charge of the studio. A group of professional male artists were brought down from Stoke, and a group of twenty to twenty five females, including Coleman's sister Rebecca, but mostly talented students from South Kensington, Queen's Square, and Lambeth, were employed in decorating a wide range of wares – tiles, plaques, plateaux, bottles, vases, pilgrim flasks etc.

The Studio became a popular show place and produced some of the most attractive art pottery of the 19th century but unfortunately the enterprise was shortlived. Coleman resigned in 1873 and was followed by a series of less talented managers, and in 1875 the studio was destroyed by fire.

Throughout the 19th century the influence on Minton of 18th-century Sèvres, both in shape and decoration, was considerable. Minton owned a number of original 18th-century Sèvres moulds and hand casts made from objects in the Sèvres Museum. The influence of Sèvres was strongest, however, between 1850 and 1880, and the most elaborate pieces seem to have been made after the South Kensington Museum set up the Circulating Museum in 1856, which included magnificent specimens of Sèvres, lent by Queen Victoria. The latter collection was sent to Hanley in the Potteries in its first year, when it was seen by over 20,000 people, and again in a re-arranged form in 1860 to Stoke-on-Trent itself. However it seems that the more spectacular Minton Sèvres copies, including the *Vaisseau à Mât* and the vases *à Têtes d'elephant* were copied from those in the collection of W. J. Goode, the eldest son of the founder of Thomas Goode & Company of South Audley Street, who

A French 16th-century 'Henry Deux' candlestick acquired by the Museum in 1864.

*Two plates from the 'Naturalist'
service designed by W.S. Coleman
for Mintons in 1869 and registered
by them in March 1870. Inspired
by the Braquemond service acquired
by the Museum from the Paris
Exhibition of 1867.
Private Collection.*

157

had a comprehensive collection of 18th-century porcelain, especially Sèvres. The firm had bought extensively from Minton since they set up business in 1827, and from 1840 Minton became their main supplier.

Most of the tablewares were of an essentially conservative nature but during the aesthetic period of the 1870s and 1880s more interesting, lively items were produced, designed by W. S. Coleman, H. Stacy Marks, John Moyr Smith and others, reflecting both the Japanese and 'mediaeval' influences. Outstanding was the 'Naturist' service, commissioned from Coleman in 1869, with randomly placed motifs of flowers, birds, fish and insects, inspired by the Felix Braquemond service (purchased from the Paris Exhibition of 1867 by the South Kensington Museum) which in turn took its motifs from the woodcuts of the celebrated Japanese artist Hokusai.

Godfrey Wedgwood, the senior partner in Josiah Wedgwood & Sons, in his evidence to the Royal Commission on Technical Instruction (1882), paid tribute to the value of the Museum's collection. Although he criticised the Art Schools for wasting too much time in finishing prize drawings, rather than training the eye for copying old designs or making new ones, he praised the way Mr Moody taught design at South Kensington 'setting the pupils to make designs in a given school and a given time, then lecturing on them in a manner to point out their merits and faults. But . . . [he added] this necessitates reference to a well arranged museum' – something they then did not have at Stoke. He went on to say: 'We are indebted to South Kensington for what they send down from time to time, for the best specimens we get . . . works of art, paintings and books, and works of industrial art, should be lent to a greater extent from South Kensington than is the case, sent down for study, and exchanged from time to time . . . no teaching of design can be attained without them. We suffer great loss from the drain of all our best students to London, caused by the facilities offered there which we want in all the provincial centres of industry.'

The influence of the Museum on Wedgwood, however, does not seem to be as strong as on Minton and the firm was generally less progressive, producing modifications of the 18th-century Jasper and other wares, although they followed Minton with majolica ware; they also marketed, during the aesthetic period, some interesting painted and transfer printed decorations designed by Emile Lessore (1805–76), Thomas Allen (1831–1915), who had previously worked for Minton's, Walter Crane and others. Even in the present century, new designs such as those by Keith Murray in the 1930s have tended to be influenced by the firm's own traditions, rather than by Museum's specimens.

In his lecture on *Art Museums* (already quoted), Christopher Dresser reported that the large and most interesting group of Japanese art objects in the South Kensington Museum 'has already resulted in the Royal Porcelain Works of Worcester having recently made great strides' and that 'their recent works have almost all resulted from the consideration of museum objects'. Among these productions may be cited two moon flasks, modelled by James Hadley and painted by James Callowhill with scenes in the style of Japanese lacquer,

*Salt-glazed stoneware jug
decorated by Arthur Barlow for
Doulton's of Lambeth in 1871.
The design shows the influence of
16th-century German stoneware.
Photograph: Sotheby's.*

which were shown at the London International Exhibition of 1871 and a number of porcelain dinner and tea services decorated with Japanese badges.

The firm of Doulton of Lambeth, founded in 1815, initially produced a range of utilitarian salt-glazed stoneware, with sanitary ware and architectural terracotta and garden ornaments added from the 1830s. The influence of the Museum's collections began in the late 1860s when John Sparkes, the principal of the Lambeth School of Art, persuaded Henry Doulton to employ a few of his students on an experimental basis. The students, limited to the standard clays, glazes and kilns, produced a series of pots with design and decoration based on well established historical styles. These early studio wares, some based on classical forms, were mostly inspired by German 16th- and 17th-century stoneware (specimens of which had been acquired by the Museum in the mid 1850s from the Bernal and other collections) and on Italian Renaissance designs. The success of these early studio wares at the Paris 1867 and London 1871 Exhibitions led to a dramatic increase in the number of students employed and by the 1880s the studio was employing over 250 men and girls, including the now famous names of George Tinworth, Hannah and Florence Barlow, Frank Butler, Mark Marshall and others. On 4 June 1878 Henry Cole wrote in his diary: 'Drove to Lambeth and went to his [Doulton's] works. Very large and seems struggling into a sort of untrained style, chiefly done by girls. Every piece passes through three or more hands who do what they like. No modelling except a little ornament. One turns and bends. Another scratches ornament, a third paints according to fancy. There was one man [George Tinworth] an untrained genius who could model.' In spite of this rather unenthusiastic report, the Museum had already by this time bought a number of specimens and continued to do so throughout the 19th century and after.

John Sparkes readily acknowledged the help and encouragement that Doulton's and the Lambeth School of Art got from George Wallis (1811–91), Keeper of the South Kensington Museum from 1858, a frequent contributor to the art periodicals of the time, and a prolific lecturer on design and kindred subjects. In his evidence to the Royal Commission on Technical Instruction in 1882, Sparkes described how, having first arranged with George Wallis that pots from all sections of the museum could be put together in one case, he could bring a class of some eight to ten throwers and say to them: 'Here are certain objects offering you typical instances of difficulty of manufacture or beauty of form'. He stressed that nowhere in the provinces, or indeed in France, was there anything comparable to the resources of the South Kensington Museum: 'When I find a man at Lambeth is repeating himself, and wants to do a new thing, I tell him to go to Kensington for a few days and look at certain sections. If he does come here [the Museum] the firm will pay for half his time; if he shows them that he has done his work here, and not simply taken a holiday elsewhere, they give him half his pay. They do so to encourage a constant reference to this Museum.'

These Doulton artists of the 1870s are often seen as the precursors of the studio potters in England, but this distinction must really rest with the Martin brothers, Robert Wallace

*...e God of Love and Alcestis': stained glass window designed by Edward Burne-Jones and made by Morris,
...rshall, Faulkner & Company. Bought by the Museum in 1864.*

XVIII
Panel of 16th-century Damascus tiles acquired by the Museum in 1886.

XVII
Six-tile panel in 'Persian' colours by William De Morgan showing the influence of Damascus tiles. Fulham period, 1888–97.

(1843–1923), Walter (1859–1912), Edwin (1860–1915), and Charles (1846–1910), who mostly took charge of the business arrangements.[73]

Robert Wallace Martin began his career carving Gothic detail at the House of Parliament, before becoming an assistant to the Pre-Raphaelite sculptor, Alexander Munro. Later in the 1860s he began attending classes at the Lambeth School of Art, where his closest friend was probably George Tinworth, with the aim of becoming an independent sculptor. Like Tinworth, he began to work extensively in terracotta. Both Walter and Edwin were employed for a while by Doulton's. In 1873 Wallace negotiated an arrangement with C. J. C. Bailey to have his own stoneware fired in the saltglaze kiln at Fulham and Walter began experiments on his own, in his mother's kitchen, while Edwin coloured the pieces his brother made. Four years later the brothers built their own studio and kiln at Southall. Some of their earliest pieces showed a strong affinity with the Doulton stoneware, with the same colouring of buff, brown and blue, but they were more Gothic in character, with angular decoration inspired by the designs of Christopher Dresser. A vase which Wallace made in 1873 has a design close to Dresser's sketch representing 'power, energy, force and vigour . . . such lines as we see in the bursting buds of spring', published in his *Principles of Decorative Design* (1873), and later Wallace explained to his friend and patron Sydney Greenslade that this was the idea he was trying to express. Various historic styles appear in their work at this period, with Celtic, Persian and even Classical motifs.

In the late 1880s or early 1890s (but probably earlier), according to the late Sir Ernest Marsh,[74] representatives of the V & A visited the shop to select some pieces for an exhibition. Charles Martin related how 'he could not get them interested in the pieces he wanted them to have, and said they would have those he thought were the worst with one exception: a square shaped bottle with a lizard as the handle, and decorated with very primitive fish, one of the earliest of this type of decoration'. The Museum officials then advised Charles that they 'should not try out new ideas in shapes and decoration but should conform to the old traditional forms based on the Greek vases'. Ernest Marsh considered that 'this was a most fatal and futile policy and the effect was reflected for a time on much of their subsequent work. Much better advice was given by Greenslade and others and they sought by study and experiment to strive for something better.' Whether the Museum's advice was misguided or not can be a matter of opinion, but certainly from the mid 1880s they seem to have produced a large number of pots of conventional form, decorated with Classical and Renaissance-inspired motifs, while Wallace Martin continued to produce a superb series of 'grotesques'. The Japanese influence was also strong, with designs of fish, dragons, flowers and grasses, and their final period, towards the turn of the century, was dominated by vegetable forms, with surface textures often imitating the skins of lizards and snakes.

William De Morgan (1893–1917), one of the most distinguished artist potters of the 19th century, drew much of his inspiration from the Museum. Trained at the Royal Academy

Salt-glazed stoneware vase by the Martin Brothers dated 12–1892 showing the influence of Italian 17th-century Calabrian pottery. Photograph: Sotheby's.

Salt-glazed stoneware vase by the Martin Brothers dated 6–1894. Both the shape and decoration show the classical inspiration advocated by the Museum authorities.

Schools, he made the acquaintance of Morris, Burne-Jones and Rossetti in the early 1860s; under their influence he turned to design and worked for Morris for a period before experimenting with ceramics on his own in about 1869. According to his own account, in the early 1870s he 'rediscovered the lost art of Moorish or Gubbio lustres' of which there were superb examples in the Museum's collections, and many of the themes in De Morgan's designs can be linked to the Museum objects, although none are exact copies. The superb Hispano-Moresque bowl (486–1864) seems to have been the inspiration for the numerous galleon designs, with fish swimming in the waves below, which De Morgan executed in both lustre and his Persian colours. Many other pieces have designs inspired by details on Deruta and Gubbio Renaissance majolica. The so-called 'Persian' style of De Morgan was based largely on Isnik, Syrian and Damascus tiles and pottery of the 15th to the 17th century and again many motifs in both his tiles and vessels can be linked to Museum specimens. De Morgan sought inspiration not only in ceramics; a covered jar by him, purchased by the Metropolitan Museum of Art, New York, from Morris & Company in 1923, is based on a 14th-century Lucca silk brocade in the Museum collection. The debt that he owed to the Museum is shown by the fact that on his death in 1917 he bequeathed a vast quantity of his original designs to the Museum; two years later his wife Evelyn bequeathed 'the finest specimens of her husband's lustre ware of which she died possessed' to the V & A.[75]

Another pottery closely connected with the Arts and Crafts Movement was the Della Robbia Pottery of Birkenhead[76] founded late in 1893 with the aim of applying artistic quality to objects of everyday use, under the direction of Harold Rathbone (1858–1929) a pupil of Ford Madox Brown. The initial inspiration came from the 15th-century della Robbia ware. Harold's father, Philip Rathbone, owned an original della Robbia plaque and Harold would certainly have known the superb collection of della Robbias in the South Kensington Museum during his student days at Heatherley's and the Slade in the late 1870s. The majority of Rathbone's

Della Robbia ware was made from reddish or buff-toned clay coated with opaque white and decorated with lead glazes mainly in shades of green, turquoise and yellow, with incised decoration. Celtic and floral motifs were used, but the Italian Renaissance influence predominated, particularly the incised earthenware of Tuscany. Just after the Pottery had got going, in February 1894, the South Kensington Museum sent on loan to nearby Liverpool a number of examples of della Robbia maiolica and other Italian wares, and there is little doubt that this provided invaluable source material for the newly founded Pottery across the river.

In an article in *Pottery and Glass* in November 1950[77] John Adams (1882-1953) (of Carter, Stabler and Adams, Poole-now Poole Pottery) described his student days in London at the Royal College of Art in the early 20th century, and pointed out how 'it was an advantage to a potter to be able to study the unrivalled collections in the Victoria and Albert Museum. The Museum and the RCA had similar origins in mid Victorian days – they may be said to have grown up together – and the Museum has always played an important part in the designer's training. There he can find examples of almost every known ceramic decorative process done by master hands. The young potter can match himself against these old masters and find books and priceless historic manuscripts in the Museum library that give details of the various techniques. Bernard Rackham was Keeper of Ceramics when I studied in the Museum galleries and I have grateful memories of his unfailing courtesy of taking a specimen out of the glass case to examine its material, or discuss the qualities of workmanship and for want of a better words, its surface "texture". In those respects the English student was, and still is on velvet.' Another designer at the Poole Pottery, who also trained at the Royal College, was Reginald Till (1895-1978). He was particularly inspired by the della Robbia roundels in the Museum's collections, as shown by his advertising plaque for Osman Towels of 1923.[78]

In the late 19th and in the 20th centuries many of the studio potters both in England and on the Continent experimented with high-temperature, flambé and crackled glazes, and crystalline effects. The oriental ceramics in the V & A, particularly those in the Salting collection, and later in the Eumorfopulous collection, provided constant inspiration, but since comparable collections were available in the British Museum and elsewhere, it is difficult to assess the influence of individual museums.

The glass collection of the V & A is probably the most comprehensive in the world. In the 19th century the most influential items were specimens of Venetian glass, both ancient and modern. The interest in old Venetian glass was already apparent by 1850 when specimens were included in an exhibition of the Royal Society of Arts, mostly lent by Felix Slade (whose collection was bequeathed to the British Museum on his death in 1868) and in subsequent shows, including the loan exhibition at the South Kensington Museum in 1862.

In 1853 the Museum of Ornamental Art acquired some thirty pieces of old Venetian glass and further outstanding items were purchased from the Bernal collection in 1855 and the Soulages collection in 1859. The interest in old Venetian glass by both museums and

A della Robbia roundel acquired by the Museum in 1859 showing the inspiration for Reginald Till's 'Osman' panel (see pl. VIII).

private collectors coincided with a revival of the glass industry in Venice and Murano,[79] and in 1860 the South Kensington Museum acquired its first specimens of contemporary Venetian glass, a group of *calcedonio* glasses by Lorenzo Radi. The leading figure in the revival was undoubtedly Dr Antonio Salviati whose glass was first shown in London at the 1862 International Exhibition, and the Museum made its first purchases from him in 1863. In 1866, with encouragement and financial support from Sir Austen Henry Layard and other prominent Englishmen, Salviati set up in London as Salviati & Company, supplying both table glass and mosaics, including mosaics for the new buildings for the South Kensington Museum.

The first English glass manufacturer to take a serious interest in Venetian glass was Apsley Pellatt, who had shown his Anglo-Venetian glass at the Great Exhibition of 1851, but the most successful of the Venetian style glasses were those by James Powell of Whitefriars, which were undoubtedly inspired by the Museum's collections. The superb chandelier, with rope twists, hanging bells and furnace-wrought twisted leaves in clear, pink and turquoise glass was acquired from Powell's by the Museum in 1866 (235-1866), followed by many other pieces in 1877.

In 1863 the Society of Arts had instituted a series of annual art-workmanship prizes, including carving, chasing, enamel painting, and the following year the subjects were expanded to include glass blowing and engraving. The examples selected for copying were mostly objects in the South Kensington Museum, reproductions of them in the form of lithographs or casts being available as models. These competitions continued until 1870, and in 1867 the prize for glass blowing was awarded to Joseph Leicester, a glass blower at Powell's, for a copy of an original Venetian goblet in the Museum. The competition also allowed for original works by the competing workmen and in 1869 Joseph Leicester again won a prize for a goblet of blue-green glass, striped with white, and covered with trailing, of his own design, but inspired by the Venetian models (105-1870).

Not only the English glassblowers but even the Venetians,

Two Isnik tiles acquired by the Museum in 1871 showing motifs used by William De Morgan.

Panel of De Morgan tiles painted in 'Persian' colours at Merton Abbey, 1882–88. Photograph: Sotheby's.

Three Venetian wine glasses of the 16th or 17th-century acquired by the Museum in 1859.

Three Venetian style glasses made by James Powell and Sons, Whitefriars in 1876 and purchased by the Museum.

themselves were inspired by the Museum's collections. In 1870 Angelo Fuga, a Venetian glassblower who had come to London with two fellow glass workers, Seguso and Barovier, for the Workmen's International Exhibition, wrote in *La Voce di Murano*: 'We do not omit visits to the principal museums of London, above all the South Kensington Museum and the British Museum, in both of which we found numerous examples of antique glass, some of which I naturally copied.'

The enamelled glass designed by Philip Webb for William Morris's use at Red House, the designs for which are now in the V & A, shows the influence of both the late 15th-and early 16th-century Venetian glass and German drinking glasses of the 16th and 17th century, all of which could be found among the Museum's collections at the time when Webb was known to frequent its galleries.

Both Venetian glass and its English derivations were to be much favoured not only by Ruskin and Morris, who both declared cut glass to be 'barbarous', but by all the devotees of the Aesthetic and Arts and Crafts Movements. Venetian glass was also much praised by Eastlake in his influential *Hints on Household Taste* published in 1868. The architect William Burges in a series of lectures published under the title *Art Applied to Industry* in 1865, asked; 'Would it be asking too much of our modern manufacturers to look carefully at old Roman and the mediaeval Venetian glass, and give us greater variety in our choice than they do at present . . . I believe it would really do an immense deal of good if anyone were to order, regardless of expense, a dessert service either like the early Venetian glass, or still better, like the Roman glass; in the latter case we should see new forms applied to the old material and colour and perhaps hit upon something new.'[80]

This something new did come about, no doubt through the influence of the Roman and Islamic glass in the South Kensington Museum, when in the 1880s James Couper & Sons of Glasgow commissioned a range of glassware from Christopher Dresser (1834–1904) who held the same views on glass as Morris and Ruskin. The glass known as 'Clutha' was deliberately bubbled and streaked, and many forms were derived from ancient Roman and Islamic glass. Although the glass was made in Glasgow, Dresser himself was living in

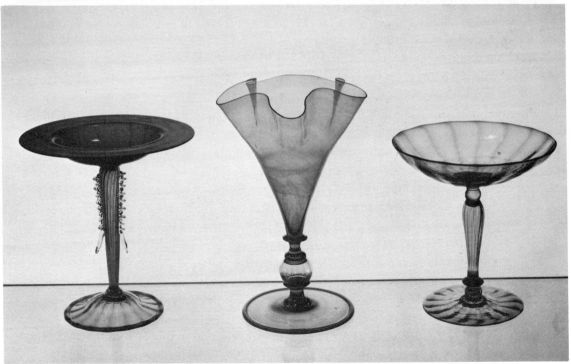

Overlay glass bowl with rustic and pincered decoration in clear glass designed by John Northwood and registered by Stevens and Williams under the title of 'Matsu-no-kee' in 1884.
Private Collection.

A Chinese rock crystal vase acquired by the Museum in 1882. The decoration on this, or a similar vase, probably inspired the 'Matsu-no-kee' glass of John Northwood, registered in 1884.

London and would almost certainly have drawn his inspiration from the glass at the South Kensington Museum: one vase at least is copied from a Persian rosewater sprinkler in the collection. Drawings of both Roman and Islamic glass appear in his *Principles of Decorative Design* (1873) as shapes to be emulated. The 'Clutha' glass of Christopher Dresser (and that designed at a later stage by the Glasgow architect, George Walton) was extensively sold by Liberty's who affixed to it their 'Lotus' registered trade mark.

Later in the century Harry Powell of James Powell & Sons produced a number of highly original glasses in an Art Nouveau style and copied specimens in the V & A and elsewhere, as well as the glasses depicted in Old Master paintings. Both the Venetian and German enamelled glass in the Museum provided models for Nelia Casella, a prominent member of the Arts and Crafts Movement, who also specialized in leatherwork inspired by Museum examples of *cuir bouilli*.

In the South Kensington Museum Art Handbook on *Glass*, Alexander Nesbitt (who had written the descriptive catalogue in 1878) pointed out that 'Chinese glass deserves attentive examination, particularly from those who are interested in the manufacture of glass, for the colours are in many instances singularly fine and harmonious, and a good collection would probably be of great use in an industrial point of view'. One of those who did take a great interest in Chinese glass was the great French artist, Emile Gallé (1845–1904). He was sent by his father to take charge of the Gallé exhibit of St Clement faience and glass at the London International Exhibition of 1871, held in the Albert Hall and specially built pavilions in the gardens of the Horticultural Society.[81] Much of his time was spent studying in the South Kensington Museum, and it was the carved Chinese snuff bottles and glass he saw there that caused him to embark on cameo glass. Soon after he went to Paris, where, according to Fourcaud,[82] he saw copies of Arab mosque lamps by Brocard. The inspiration for Gallé's copies, which are more imaginative, was more likely to come from the original 14th-century pieces acquired by the South Kensington Museum in 1860 and 1869.

'Latticinio' Venetian glass goblet of the 16th-century acquired by the Museum in 1855.

In the latter part of the 19th and first decades of the 20th century, most of the English and Scottish glasshouses remained staunchly conservative, continuing to produce more or less traditional shapes and patterns of cut glass, apart from some items of fancy glass which continued to reflect Venetian influence. In the 1930s Stevens & Williams (now Royal Brierley Crystal) commissioned good modern designs from Keith Murray and Stuart's commissioned designs for both cut and engraved glass from leading artists including Paul Nash, Eric Ravilious and Graham Sutherland. From the 1930s onwards Scandinavian glass has provided an important stimulus and the Museum has assembled a good and representative collection.

Generally speaking, however, the Museum's glass collections have provided more inspiration for the individual artist-craftsman, glass engraver and studio glass worker. The Museum has encouraged the development of studio glass in this country by building up an extensive collection of both British and foreign modern studio glass and by arranging a series of shows: the first, in 1969-71, was a travelling exhibition, 'Design in Glass', showing student work from three British art colleges, Edinburgh College of Art, Stourbridge College of Art and the Royal College of Art. Major exhibitions devoted to the subject include the Flöckinger/Herman Exhibition in 1971, which brought Sam Herman's glass vessels and sculptures to the notice of a wide public; the Dominick Labino exhibition in 1974 and the recent exhibition of New Glass, organized by the Corning Museum of Glass, and presented at the Museum by the Pilkington Group in co-operation with the V & A in 1981.

The latter half of the 19th century saw a revival of stained glass in Great Britain, an art that had been in decline since the Middle Ages. The Museum played an important part in the revival, not only by collecting and exhibiting ancient stained glass, but by mounting in 1864 an exhibition of contemporary stained glass designed and executed by British artists. As the introduction to the catalogue (written by T. Gambier Parry and Richard Burchett) stated, the object was to 'encourage the art of glass painting as a fine art, to raise it,

Goblet of blue-green glass striped with white and covered with trailing. Made by Joseph Leicester and awarded a Society of Arts Prize for 1869-70.

'Clutha' glass vase of yellowish green glass streaked with red, white and silver. Designed by Christopher Dresser and made by James Couper and Sons, Glasgow about 1890. Photograph: Sotheby's.

as is much required, to that standard; and also to elevate the public taste in the appreciation of it'.[83] Most of the leading firms participated in the exhibition, some producing works specially for it.[84] Some of the windows, notably those by John Hardman & Sons of Birmingham, designed by Pugin's chief assistant, John Hardman Powell, were closely modelled on mediaeval lines. The predominant influence was however Pre-Raphaelite with nineteen examples by Morris, Marshall, Faulkner & Company (who had won a Gold Medal for their glass at the 1862 Exhibition), six of which were bought by the Museum for the permanent collections. Another outstanding purchase from the exhibition was 'The Advent of Beatrice' window designed by N. H. J. Westlake for Lavers and Barraud of Bloomsbury. These windows, together with examples designed by Henry Holiday (1839-1937) for James Powell & Sons of Whitefriars, were to set the pattern for the 'aesthetic' glass of the 1870s and the glass of the Arts and Crafts Movement. Not only did the Museum buy examples for the collections but also further encouraged the art by commissioning it for the new buildings, including an outstanding series of windows by William Bell Scott for the Ceramic Gallery and the glass in the three refreshment rooms.

The exhibition also included a section devoted to mosaics and mural decoration. Mosaics, both in glass and ceramic, were extensively used throughout the Museum buildings, the most impressive being in the so-called 'Valhalla' in the South Court, with its fullsize mosaic figures of famous artists and sculptors ranging from Apelles to Sir Joshua Reynolds, with a bias towards the Italian Renaissance. The production of these mosaics continued from 1862 to 1871 and to help in their execution Cole set up a special mosaic class of female students from the School of Art, including his daughters Letitia, Florence and Mary. Harland and Fisher of 33 Southampton Street, Strand, contributed five examples to the 1864 exhibition, and James Powell & Sons showed specimens of their opaque glass mosaic, which was later to become their speciality in an Arts and Crafts style. N. H. J. Westlake showed a panel of the Annunciation executed in 'wax vehicle', while the firm of Jesse Rust & Company of the Lambeth Glass Works included designs based on the mosaics at Monreale as well as designs by Matthew Digby Wyatt and 'a lady amateur'. The Science and Art Department staged their own exhibit, including a panel by Salviati, priced at £200, and designs showing the proposed use of mosaics on the outside of the 1862 Exhibition Building (which presumably had not been used). There is little doubt that this exhibition and the extensive use of mosaics, both by Salviati and English firms, in the Museum buildings in the 1860s and 1870s, did much to promote the art of mosaics both in ecclesiastical and secular buildings, particularly by members of the Arts and Crafts Movement. Numerous examples could be cited, among them Anning Bell's mosaic at the Horniman Museum, built by Harrison Townsend between 1898 and 1901, the mosaics by Gaetano Meo at Debenham House (now the Richmond Fellowship) built by Halsey Ricardo in 1905-07, the mosaics at St Bartholomew's, Brighton (1899-1908), and the earlier Walter Crane's mosaic frieze at Leighton House begun in 1877.

'The Vision of Beatrice'. Stained glass panel designed by N.H.J. Westlake for Lavers and Barraud and exhibited at the Museum in 1864. The dense colouring and strong leading was to be characteristic of the glass of the Arts and Crafts movement.

The mural section included a specimen of wall painting, exhibited by Frederick Preedy, executed in spirit fresco, the medium introduced by Gambier Parry, one of the organizers, and used for some of the murals at the Houses of Parliament. Preedy also showed a specimen of opaque glass painting for wall decoration, with the colours burnt in and therefore permanent. A similar type of ceramic mosaic, patented by Minton's, with fired-on painted decoration, was used on the ceramic staircase at the Museum, and the 1870s saw an increasing use of mural decoration in both churches and municipal buildings. One such commission was for a mural of 'King John and the Barons' at the Rochdale Town Hall, given to Henry Holiday in 1871. In his memoirs[85] Holiday describes his researches for the costumes and arms and armour, and relates that 'there was no difficulty in getting all I wanted for the Bishops from brasses and from actual vestments at the South Kensington Museum'. The Museum itself had earlier given encouragement to the art by commissioning the two great frescoes 'The Industrial Arts as Applied to War' and 'The Industrial Arts as Applied to Peace' from Lord Leighton in 1871. The frescoes, largely executed by students of the South Kensington Schools under Lord Leighton's direct supervision, occupied him from 1873 to 1879 and from 1883 to 1885.

In more recent years, an exhibition of *Mural Art Today* organized at the Museum by the Society of Mural Painters in 1960, sought to suggest to architects new possibilities of both external and internal wall decoration for the numerous new buildings that were springing up in London and the Provinces. The exhibits included tile murals, the John Hutton panels for the Great West Screen of Coventry Cathedral, enamel colours fired on a metal base by Stephen Knapp (recalling the ceiling in the Gamble Room), cartoons and stained glass by John Piper, tapestries and designs for sgraffito and mosaic. The show also contained a series of specially commissioned standard size panels which were designed to form a travelling exhibition to be sent on tour by the Circulation Department after the London showing.

Stained glass window from the Church of St. Lawrence, Brondesbury, by L. Walker, dated 1913.

Cup and cover of wood with silver mounts and enamel. Designed by William Burges, 1878. Photograph: The Fine Art Society.

XVII. JEWELLERY AND METALWORK

Most of the English jewellery shown at the great Exhibition of 1851 was in the style of imitative naturalism, soundly condemned by Henry Cole and his colleagues, who advocated a return to Classical and Renaissance styles, or Eastern models. The Museum's early purchases of jewellery reflected this trend and Cole himself had lent a collection of Chinese and Indian jewellery to Marlborough House.

Examples of the Renaissance-style work of the French jeweller François Froment-Meurice (1802–55) were purchased from the 1851 Exhibition and the Paris Exhibition of 1855. Medieval ring brooches were acquired with the Bernal collection; Greek, Etruscan and Roman jewellery was added in 1863 and 1971, with further examples from the Castellani collection in 1884. Although a number of Spanish 16th-and early 17th-century pendants were acquired in 1870, the early collections did not contain many original Renaissance pieces, probably because they were too expensive; however, a number of modern pieces in the Renaissance style were included.

The Museum began to buy peasant jewellery in the 1860s, including a collection of Italian jewellery shown by Castellani at the Paris Exhibition of 1867. By 1873, the *Art Journal*, while generally approving the Museum's acquisition policy, felt that there was excess in 'adding a considerable quantity of useless specimens of Indian jewellery, and also peasant jewellery of the various European states . . . which is not of an art-character to make it in any way suggestive to the designer or producer of jewellery'. While such specimens may not have provided inspiration for the commercial jewellery trade, they found favour with the devotees of the Aesthetic and Arts and Crafts Movements.

In his influential book *Hints on Household Taste*, first published in 1869, Charles Lock Eastlake complained of the current taste 'for rare and expensive gems, and a ceaseless demand for showy designs'. He greatly admired the jewellery of Castellani (examples of which were acquired by the Museum in 1884) and even approved of the moderately priced examples copied or imitated from his designs, which were derived from antique models; 'but

if we wish to find specimens of really artistic jewellery', he wrote, 'we must seek them in the Museums . . . At South Kensington alone there are countless treasures from which, if they were properly studied, might be formed a standard of taste far higher than that of their own day. It is not only from the much prized *Cinquecento* work of France and Italy – beautiful as most of it is – that we may learn a lesson. Even the rudely made peasant trinkets of Russia, the unskilled manufactures of Central India, the quaint and early devices of Rhenish Byzantine artists, are all infinitely superior to what we have made or invented during our boasted 19th century.' He mentioned specifically the oriental jewellery lent by Sir R.N. Hamilton, mostly Bhopal and Indore, which was exhibited at the Museum, as being 'remarkable not only for extreme simplicity, but for an elegance and appropriateness of design which our jewellers would do well to imitate'.

The same point was made by Lewis F. Day in an article on *Decorative Art, its Importance and its Omnipresence – Taste, Novelty and Fashion, Dress, Jewellery etc.* published in 1880. When quoting Dr Birdwood, he described how 'the Indian jeweller thinks nothing of the intrinsic value of the precious stones he employs. He is an artist, and to him the value is their colour and effect; he cares as much for them as a painter cares for his pigments, and no more. They are simply a means to a decorative end. The consequence is he is able to use rich emeralds and rubies as lavishly as if they were enamel, and whenever he wants a point of light, bits of diamond are at hand, commercially of no value, but artistically valuable as though they were priceless.'

In 1862 the Museum held a loan exhibition of *Ancient and Modern Jewellery and Personal Ornaments*, 'for purposes of public instruction', ranging from classical to modern times and including peasant and oriental jewellery. R. Soden Smith in his introduction, like Eastlake, stressed the value of peasant jewellery which, he said, 'has of late years attracted some of the attention it merits, partly on account of good design and occasional beauty of some of the specimens, and partly for the sake of the light which these traditional ornaments, unchanged through many generations, throw on the history of the goldsmith's work'.

It was quite understandably the jewellery in which the emphasis was on design, rather than the intrinsic value of the stones, which was to make an impact on the Arts and Crafts jewellers of the late 19th century and they sought their inspiration in the peasant and Indian jewellery in the Museum's collections, as well as in the splendid Renaissance pieces.

The Arts and Crafts jewellery, both by individual artists, craftsmen, small workshops and from shops such as Liberty's, was not on the whole particularly well made, for Arts and Crafts principles were opposed to the specialization in separate skills which was the practice in the high class jewellery trade. Silver was preferred to gold, the latter being used only for its decorative qualities, and semi-precious stones such as garnets, amethysts, turquoise, peridots and opals in particular were used together with misshappen baroque or river pearls, or long houndstooth pearls for drops on pendants.

This attitude is reflected most clearly in the Guild of Handicraft jewellery designed by

C.R. Ashbee. An important article in the *Studio*, (*A visit to Essex House*, the Guild Headquarters) in 1898, emphasised that the characteristic feature was the insistence upon the aesthetic as opposed to the commercial value of the precious stones, and that colour was a quality always held in view. Ashbee was undoubtedly influenced by some of the pieces in the Museum's collections, notably the rock crystal ship pendant of 1600 (295-1854) and some of the peasant jewellery, while his peacock pendant and brooches have an affinity with Indian models.

One of the finest and most influential of the Arts and Crafts jewellers was Henry Wilson (1864-1934) who, after studying at the Kidderminster School of Art, trained as an architect, taking over J.D. Sedding's practice in 1891. At about that time he became more and more absorbed in metalwork and jewellery, joining the Art Workers Guild in 1892. He taught metalwork at the Central School of Arts and Crafts from 1896 to about 1901 when he joined Lethaby at the Royal College of Art.

In his introduction to *Silverwork and Jewellery* by Henry Wilson [86], first published in 1903 and still a standard text book, W. R. Lethaby advised that 'the best complement to workshop practice is to study the old work stored in our museums, without intention to copy specific types, but to gather ideas generally applicable. From this point of view all ancient art is a vast encyclopaedia of methods and experience. The London student should frequent the Gold Room and Medieval Department of the British Museum, the general collections at the South Kensington, and the marvels of the Indian Museum.'

Henry Wilson drew much of his inspiration from the Museum's pieces, an influence which is reflected in the collection of some five hundred designs, mainly for jewellery, given to the Museum by his daughter in 1955. Writing on design in *Silverwork and Jewellery* Wilson stated: 'My method of design is to make each jewel enshrine some story or symbol. I try to make the ornament allusive to the gem, to its legendary history, to its qualities, or to the ideas suggested by it. For example, you take an aquamarine; the name itself, no less than the colour, at once suggests things of the sea.' For his illustrations he selected many examples from the Museum's collections – Roman earrings, 16th-century Spanish pendants in silver gilt, enamel and pearls, and a French 13th-century gold brooch showing the use of leaves with settings made from simple cones of sheet metal wrapped around the stones and at the back a border of niello – 'every student should see this brooch and study it for himself'. He also illustrated a Norwegian peasant bridal crown to show the possibilities of work in thin sheet metal. The larger objects included an Italian 14th-century staff and copper gilt ciborium to show the use of the enamelling.

Many of the Arts and Crafts jewellers, such as John Paul Cooper (1869-1933), were greatly influenced by Wilson's work and would also have studied the Museum's collections. For example, his Madonna and Child pendant of 1910 (now in the Birmingham City Museum) seems to have been inspired by some of the Spanish examples.

The interwar years were not an inspired period for jewellery design but from the 1950s

Silver-gilt cup and cover with London hall-mark for 1660/1.

Tazza and vase of silver, embossed and chased with flowers in the manner of 17th-century English silver. Made by Gilbert Marks with London hall-marks for 1897 and 1901.

Desk set of silver, chased and repoussé in the style of English 17th-century silver. Designed by C.R. Ashbee and made by the Guild of Handicraft, 1904.
Photograph: Sotheby's.

onwards, the Museum, working in co-operation with the Goldsmiths' Company and the Craft Advisory Council, has done much to promote good modern jewellery design. In 1961 a major *International Exhibition of Modern Jewellery* organized by Carol Hogben of the Circulation Department, was held at Goldsmiths Hall, including a collection of jewellery modelled by painters and sculptors from which a number of purchases were made.

The first of a series of artist/craftsmen exhibitions organized by the Circulation Department, was devoted to the jewellery of Gerda Flöckinger and the glass of Sam Herman. Since the demise of the Circulation Department, the Department of Metalwork has continued to buy modern jewellery, and include it in changing displays in the jewellery gallery.

The late 19th and early 20th century saw a marked revival in the art of enamelling, a revival that was to a considerable extent due to the South Kensington Museum. Testimony to this is provided in an article by Edward Strange[87] where he writes that much of the credit for the revival of the art of enamelling lay with William Morris and the first members of the Arts and Crafts Society, but that 'no slight assistance has been afforded by the collection and exhibition of much of the best old work in the Victoria and Albert Museum'.

The Museum already had a considerable permanent collection of enamels, when, in 1874, a special loan exhibiton of over one thousand examples, drawn from all countries and all ages, was mounted in the South Court. The arrangement of the exhibition was in the reverse, the starting point being the most recent examples, including pieces presented to the museum in 1869 by the Paris enameller and jeweller, Alexis Falize (1811–98), to show the processes of making *cloisonné* enamel, together with jewellery by him in the Japanese taste. Other Spanish, French and Italian enamelled jewellery was included in the exhibition together with a superb *Cinquecento* necklace attributed to Benvenuto Cellini and lent by the Countess of Montcharles. The fine collection of Limoges enamels already in the Museum was supplemented by a few important loans, and painted enamels were also represented by Bilston and Battersea examples, together with French and German watches, boxes and trinkets. The oriental section comprised mainly Japanese and Chinese *cloisonné* enamels and a few Indian examples.

The impact made by this exhibition was further enhanced when, in 1885, under the auspices of Thomas Armstrong, the Director of the Art Division of the Museum, a series of demonstrations and lectures on the art of enamelling were given by the Sèvres artist L. Delpayrat. The first two lectures were enough to inspire Alexander Fisher (1864–1936), then a student at South Kensington, to experiment on his own account, so that he was to become not only the most skilled enameller himself, but was to teach the art to many others. Fisher was awarded a scholarship to study in Paris where he experimented with layered effects in translucent enamels, sometimes with metal or foil inclusions.

As well as teaching, Alexander Fisher wrote extensively on enamelling in the *Studio* and other periodicals, illustrating his articles with specimens from the Museum's collections, as well as his own work, in which their influence could be traced.

The revival of enamelling by the Arts and Crafts metalworkers and jewellers was reflected in a number of books devoted to the subject, all of which drew heavily on the Museum's collections for their illustrations. Edith Dawson, whose work, together with that of her husband, Nelson Dawson, was ranked second to that of Alexander Fisher, published a book on *Enamels*,[88] with the aim of describing 'some of the principal methods and all of the best known examples, which can be seen in public collections from either the Victoria and Albert Museum or the British Museum.' The Victoria and Albert Museum examples predominated, as did those in *European Enamels* by Henry H. Cunynghame, published by Methuen in the same year, 1906.

The Museum's collections no doubt had an influence on the enamelled jewellery of the firm Child & Child, first established in 1880 at Seville Street, London. In 1891 they moved to South Kensington, making up some designs for Burne-Jones and also producing high quality enamelled work until their closure about 1915.

In recent years the difficult technique of *plique à jour* enamelling has been revived in the delicate jewellery of Georgina Follet (b.1949) who trained at the Central School of Art and Design and at the R.C.A., and now teaches at the John Cass School of Art. This technique has been rarely used in this century and Georgina Follett was undoubtedly inspired by the the Art Nouveau examples by Lalique and Feuillâtre, and the Norwegian pieces in the Museum's collections.

When Ashbee moved the Guild headquarters and workshops to Chipping Camden in 1902, he realized the importance of source material for the guildsmen, and the museum and the library went with them. Realizing they would no longer have access to the V & A or the Bethnal Green Museum, shortly before the move Ashbee negotiated a substantial loan of objects from the Circulation Department, representing all the crafts to be practised at Chipping Camden (fine examples of lettering and printing, metalwork, inlay, damascening, niello etc) with the intention that they should go on show in the local grammar school and inspire the boys and the local population as well as the guildsmen.

The importance that Ashbee attached to the V & A, is also shown by his treatment of

Philippe Mairet (1884–1975) whom he recruited in London as a draughtsman in 1906. Before he joined the architectural office at Camden, Ashbee insisted that he spent a number of weeks making drawings of objects in th V & A to get him trained for the job, which was to involve making detailed drawings from Ashbee's sketches and providing working drawings for the Guild craftsmen. The 200 superb line drawings in Ashbee's *Modern English Silverwork* (1909, reprinted 1974) were from his hand. Philippe Mairet was an enthusiastic member of the Guild, taking part in all its activities, particularly acting, and he was later to marry the distinguished handweaver Ethel Coomaraswamy (nèe Partridge, the sister of the artist Frank Partridge).

C.R. Ashbee (1863–1942), who founded the Guild and School of Handicraft at Toynbee Hall in the East End of London in 1888, was undoubtedly one of the most original designers of silver associated with the Arts and Crafts Movement[89]. Although critical of the South Kensington system which, he said, 'turns out a number of skilled workmen and gives them no field wherein to employ their power',[90] he recognized the value of the Museum for the boys attending the School, as well as drawing inspiration for himself.

His steeple-cups, such as the Painter-Stainers cup of 1900 (M 106 and A–1966), show a subtle re-interpretation of 17th-century silver design, and the embossed floral motifs on many of his pieces show the influence of English and Dutch 17th-century silver, while his ecclesiastical pieces are more influenced by medieval examples.

The Arts and Crafts silversmiths were generally more inspired by the early silver and metalwork in the Museum, pieces ranging from the Byzantine period to the 17th century, rather than by 18th-century examples.

The Arts and Crafts influence, particularly that of Henry Wilson, continued in the period between the two World Wars but most of the craftsmen's pieces were reworkings of earlier ideas. The trade, ever conservative in its approach, continued to reproduce the established Georgian styles of 'Queen Anne', 'Rococo', and 'Adam', with some angular 'art deco' designs. Since the end of the Second World War, largely as a result of the efforts of the Goldsmiths Company, a much more original approach to silver design has emerged, a trend that has been encouraged by the Museum in commissioning pieces from leading silversmiths to add to the permanent collections.

An exhibition of 19th- and 20th-century French and British posters held in the North Court of the Museum in 1931.

'English pottery old and new'. An exhibition organized jointly by the Museum and the Council for Art and Industry held in the North Court in 1935.

XVIII. THE INTER-WAR YEARS: THE V & A AND THE DESIGN ORGANIZATIONS

By the late 1870s, the building programme of the South Kensington Museum had petered out, and, in spite of the continued pressure by the Director, Philip Cunliffe Owen, it was not until 1890 that the Treasury and the Office of Works sanctioned the completion of the work. The foundation stone of the new building, by Aston Webb, was not laid until May 1899 and construction took ten years to complete, the official Royal Opening being held on 26 June 1909.

Inevitably the last decade of the 19th century saw a considerable amount of criticism of the South Kensington Museum being voiced particularly in the art periodicals of the day, some of it probably justified, much of it niggling and petty. However, even the sternest critics had to admit the beneficial influence of the Museum's collections. At the National Association for the Advancement of Arts Congress held at Birmingham in 1890, a number of speakers made reference to the Museum. Philip Rathbone, in his presidential address, stated: 'We have every reason to be proud of the South Kensington Museum in spite of all the defects which are constantly being discovered in it. Men and bodies who have done nothing for art in England worth speaking of, think they prove their knowledge of it by indiscriminate abuse of that institution. Any fool can discover faults, but it requires a wise man to appreciate merits.' At the same Congress, George Simonds also referred to the Museum, where 'are collected together such vast treasures of all that is rare and beautiful, as to stagger even the most ambitious designer with the vision of what long since had been done in every branch of art industry. I have nothing but praise and wonder for this institution, it is marvellously organised and its influence can hardly be overrated.' George Simonds however, felt that perhaps it had become 'a mere forcing-house for the production of professional artists', rather than an inspiration for the humbler handicrafts. The same point was made by Ralph Nevill who felt that the Museum catered more for the taste of the virtuoso and the connoisseur, rather than that of the practicing craftsman or artisan. 'Common sense would say that Museums should begin with the humbler and simpler objects and work up to the finer examples . . . Elaborate and ornate examples are provided which too often puzzle and pervert the workman who has not yet formed a sound taste in the humbler matters.' He urged the acquisition of simple vernacular examples of Jacobean furniture, Georgian doorways and mantlepieces, and English metalwork. In fact most of the criticism concerned the tendency of the Museum to collect foreign work at the expense of English work, which it was felt would be of use and help the everyday practice of art. Ralph Nevill felt that an architect should be able to say: 'I want carving of such and such a sort, go and look at examples, numbers so-and-so, at the Museum', or say to the manufacturer: 'I want brass and ironwork of such a character as in the Museum'.

Similar criticism of the lack of English material, the expenditure of vast sums of money on expensive foreign objects, the overcrowding of the galleries, lack of labelling and so on, occur throughout the 1890s, but no one could deny the value of the Museum in fulfilling its function as a museum for study and education. An enthusiastic defence of the Museum, and a plea for its completion by the planned new building, was made by M. Charles Yriate, the French Inspector General of Fine Arts in a letter published in *The Times* in 1897. The letter commences with a brief resumé of the history of the Museum and the fact that England had overtaken France in the matter of art applied to industry. This was largely due to the influence of the South Kensington Museum, 'the most fruitful source, the most colossal depôt of *objets d'art* of all sorts, the most varied and complete types and examples, capable of favouring the development of artistic taste from its simplest forms, as seen in the artisan who overcomes common material, transforming it into a precious object, to the creators, the architects, painters and sculptors, who embody their dreams and fancies, giving them form, colour and life, and awakening thought in us while making a sanctuary of the home where we live. Today for all of us foreigners, South Kensington is a Mecca. England there possesses the entire art of Europe and the East, their spiritual manifestations under all forms and Europe has been swept into the stream in imitation of England. Berlin, Budapest, Vienna, Nuremberg, Basle, Madrid, St Petersburg, Moscow, the large towns of America itself have now their South Kensingtons.' Mr Yriate concluded his letter with a plea for a new building, as 'the inconceivable treasures are becoming so much heaped up as to be a veritable obstacle to study'.

The last few years of the 19th century and the first two decades of the 20th were not the most progressive period for the decorative arts in Britain. The Arts and Crafts movement had lost its initial impetus, and although fine work continued to be produced, there was little innovation. This was clearly reflected in the Exhibition of Decorative Art of Great Britain and Ireland, held in the Pavilion de Marsan in Paris in 1914, which relied largely on a retrospective section for its impact. The French art critic, Gabriel Mourey, in his essay *Essai sur l'Art Decorative Française Moderne*[91] remarked that the revival started by Morris had reached stagnation point, that English decorative art was increasingly going back to the methods of the past, and that manufacturers and industrialists limited themselves to copying ancient styles: Sheraton, Chippendale, Hepplewhite and Adam. He went on to remark that modern English decorative art, instead of going forward, retrogressed. In the London shops, formerly so charming, so lively, one now saw only furniture and furnishing fabrics or knick-knacks 'of Style'.

Such criticism was justified, for at a commercial level there were on the one hand innumerable bastardized versions of period styles, or debased, clapped out lingerings of Art Nouveau, with the Museum collections often used as the basis of straight reproduction or copies rather than as an inspiration to produce something new and vital.

Fortunately there were a number of architects and designers who realized that something was wrong and set about putting it right; the Victoria and Albert Museum was to become closely involved with the attempts to improve British design.

The first organization founded for the improvement of design in British industry was the Design and Industries Association, inaugurated in May 1915, the inspiration for which was the Deutsche Werkbund, created in 1907. The first council included Sir James Morton (of Morton Sundour Fabrics), H.H. Peach (founder of Dryad Handicrafts which made cane furniture under German and Austrian influence), Sir Frank Warner (head of the textile firm), from commerce and industry; and Cecil Brewer (of the architects, Smith and Brewer), Sir Ambrose Heal (of Heals, Tottenham Court Road), W.R. Lethaby (Professor of Design at the Royal College of Art), and Harold Stabler (metalworker and designer), representing architecture and the arts.

Sir Cecil Harcourt Smith, Director of the Museum, was present at the inaugural meeting and it was reported in the minutes that 'he came as a representative of the Board of Trade, not to make an official announcement, but to take cognisance of this excellent movement and to give it on behalf of the Board of Education a welcome. In the last few years they had been brought more closely into co-operation with the Board of Trade, and he held that the Victoria and Albert Museum would not properly fulfil its functions unless, with the best models of form and design, it took cognisance of the modern commercial spirit. In co-operation with the Board of Trade they were doing that, he hoped. They had been able to render some slight assistance in the series of exhibitions organised by the Board of Trade in Brussels, Turin, Paris, Ghent and last but not least in the exhibition now being held at Islington. The principle of the Association had the approval of the Board of Education and they had every reason to wish hearty success to the Association.'

The Design and Industries Association organized exhibitions, ran a journal, and published a series of pamphlets, in which they set forth a set of principles echoing those of the Museum's early days at Malborough House: 'No simulations, substitutions or fakes of texture, eg linoleum should not be grained to represent parquet, a mantlepiece should be frankly painted, not "marbled", celluloid should not pretend to be ivory or tortoiseshell.' In 1917 one member, Miss Ernestine Mills, suggested that the ladies of the Association should get together a Chamber of Horrors, a proposition that was not carried. A good account of the DIA's activities was given by Nikolaus Pevsner in the DIA yearbook for 1964-65.[92]

Even before the DIA was founded, the Government had realized the necessity for some organized effort to improve the state of industrial design and in 1914 the Board of Trade and Board of Education planned to found a quasi-official institute to promote the collaboration of designers and craftsmen, manufacturers, retailers and the general public. The outbreak of the First World War prevented the implementation of these plans and it was not until February 1920 that the British Institute of Industrial Art was incorporated under the chairmanship of Sir Hubert Llewellyn Smith, President of the Board of Trade. From the beginning the Victoria and Albert Museum was closely involved. In an article in the *Furnishing Trades Organiser* of August 1920, Sir Cecil Harcourt Smith, Director of the

Museum, welcomed the new organization and pointed out that the Museum had been founded 'to aid the improvement of such manufactures and crafts as are associated with decorative design'. He went on to state that 'the Victoria and Albert Museum, which should logically be a storehouse of the best products, not only of the past but also of the present, had been prevented from fulfilling its full purpose as regards modern production by two principal difficulties. In the first place, there has never been an organised exhibition, performing for modern industrial art what the Royal Academy does for painting and sculpture, so that it has been difficult to get in touch with the outstanding examples. Furthermore, it is difficult even for the most catholic taste, to decide among contemporary productions which things will be of permanent value or interest; and even if space would allow, it is undesirable to spend public funds on things which may afterwards have to be relegated to obscurity. The result has been that, except in one or two directions, the Museum has accentuated the gap between past and present, and . . . has suffered through its inability to acquire outstanding examples of recent years until those have become unattainable by reason either of their variety or expense.'

Sir Cecil Harcourt Smith became the Vice-chairman of the BIIA and Major A.A. Longden, DSO, the Director. At first the BIIA had its own gallery in Knightsbridge, but owing to the postwar slump, which was already severe by 1921, the Government grant was not renewed and thereafter the annual exhibitions were held in the North Court of the V & A, and in various towns in the provinces. A review of the 1923 Exhibition in the *Pottery Gazette and Glass Trades Review* of 1 October 1923 opened with the words: 'The application of art to industry is a popular present day topic; with some it is a hobby and others a business. The Underground Railway endeavours to educate public taste with its posters, which may be termed art[93] . . . and even members of parliament develop enthusiasm on the question of art combined with street architecture.' The review, quite naturally, was confined mainly to the ceramic exhibits which they felt lived up to the organization's slogan of 'Fitness for Purpose' and utility combined with art, but felt that those in the art pottery section were too expensive and ranked only as collector's pieces. The need to improve the artistic quality of inexpensive goods was recognized by the BIIA when in 1929 they held in the North Court of the V & A an exhibition under the title of 'Industrial Art for the Slender Purse'. The Institute also carried out research and published a number of pamphlets and, perhaps most importantly, built up a permanent collection of what were considered the best products in each annual exhibition. When the BIIA was disbanded in 1934 the collection was given to the Museum, providing a valuable nucleus of a 20th-century British collection spanning the years 1919 to 1934. By this time another important organization, the Council for Art and Industry, had come into being and the V & A was to be even more closely involved.

In 1931 the Board of Trade appointed a committee on Art and Industry under the chairmanship of Lord Gorell. Sir Eric Maclagan, Director of the V & A, was a member of the committee together with Roger Fry, the art critic and founder of the Omega workshops in 1913, Sir Hubert Llewellyn Smith, chairman of the BIIA, Professor E.W. Tristram of the Royal College of Art, the architect Clough Williams Ellis, Harry Trethowan, the pottery designer, and others. The committee supported the idea of a permanent exhibition of industrial art in London, separate from but under the auspices of the V & A, and travelling exhibitions in the provinces. A direct result of the Gorell report was the establishment of a Council for Art and Industry under the chairmanship of Frank Pick, at that time the President of the DIA. The Council began its work in 1934, and although a permanent industrial art centre was not set up, a series of exhibitions was mounted at the Museum, examples from which were acquired for the permanent collections.

The first exhibition, held in 1934, was one of ancient and modern silverwork with historic examples drawn from the Museum's collections to show how they could be used as an inspiration for good modern design. A number of the modern objects were acquired.

The second exhibiton, *English Pottery Old and New*, followed on the same lines. It was organized jointly by W.B. Honey and Bernard Rackham of the Museum's Ceramic Department, the potter W.B. Dalton, and Harry Trethowan, a buyer from Heals; its aim was 'to show some of the best work done in English pottery, old and new, and at the same time to illustrate the living tradition maintained in the art from medieval times to the present day'. The greater part of the exhibition was devoted to table services and wares for domestic use and the majority of the modern exhibits chosen were 'produced for sale at low prices well within the reach of buyers of moderate means'. Wedgwood was well represented with items designed by Keith Murray and Victor Skellern, with historic pieces to show the continuing tradition. The painted pottery of Carter, Stabler & Adams of Poole was shown with the 17th-century Lambeth 'Delft' chargers, while the earthenware jugs of C.H. Brannum and T.G. Green & Company, related more closely to English country pottery. An important section of the exhibition was devoted to the work of contemporary English studio potters, including Bernard Leach and William Staite Murray, which was shown alongside pieces of Chinese, Korean and Japanese stoneware, the source of their inspiration. Some purely decorative pieces, such as figures and vases, were also included. Chelsea porcelain was 'chosen to represent the highest level of luxury as well as taste and accomplishment', but it was recognized that modern economic conditions and the altered standing of porcelain painters ruled out such productions, and examples of the more modest, New Hall type of Staffordshire porcelain were included as being 'more suitable models for the present day'. The historic examples were selected from those already in the Museum's collections and many of the contemporary pieces were bought by the Circulation Department.

The third exhibition in the series arranged by the Council for Art and Industry in collaboration with the Museum was devoted to English domestic metalwork: it was intended to show the historical and artistic development of base-metal implements connected with the home and fire-side, objects relating to cooking, lighting, heating, smoking and writing, and also some door and window fittings.

Antique pieces were juxtaposed with modern examples, the most conspicuous exhibit being a model of an open hearth, complete with adjustable cranes, fire-dogs, spit and spit-jack and all the old-time cooking apparatus, contrasted with modern gas and electric cookers, showing how all the old paraphernalia had become obsolete. An elegant toasting fork of 1728 was contrasted with a modern electric toaster, and the smoker's tongs were shown to be superseded by the modern petrol lighter. It was hoped that the exhibition, in addition to drawing attention to fine traditional work that had become obsolete (but nevertheless could provide lessons for the designer) would also illustrate the change in fashions and lifestyle brought about by modern inventions and labour-saving devices.

Yet another joint exhibition covered *Tiles and Tilework*; it was held at the Museum in 1939, and, like the previous ones, juxtaposed the old with the new.

In 1939, the Council for Art and Industry, in co-operation with the leading textile manufacturers of the country, mounted in the Museum an exhibition aimed mainly at students of textile design, to show 'the technical processes involved in the commercial production of woven and printed furnishing fabrics'. The exhibition included everything from the original design to the finished product, with the print papers and cards used with the jacquard loom, and sections on hand-woven velvets and silks. The principal methods of textile printing (hand-block, screen-printing, surface-printing and copper roller or machine-printing) were illustrated with examples of the equipment used as well as the fabric. For the first five weeks of the exhibition representatives of the various firms were available on two afternoons a week to explain the technical details to visiting students and members of the public. Once again many of the exhibits were acquired for the permanent collections.

An unpublished report by the Council for Art and Industry dated 3 December 1937 and entitled *Proposals for an Industrial Art Centre*, recommended that as one of the objects of the Victoria and Albert Museum was to influence and display current production, the Museum's collections should be extended to form an exhibition of contemporary design.[94] The Council suggested that this extension, which they preferred to call an 'Industrial Art Centre' rather than a museum, should have separate accommodation of its own, so that 'industry and craftsmen may realise that the institution has a character distinct from the Victoria and Albert Museum itself'. The Council also recommended that a limited number of more distinguished examples of industrial art should be added to the Museum's permanent collections. These recommendations were not put into effect, although the Boilerhouse project, set up by the Conran Foundation in 1981, was intended to fulfil much the same function. The Boilerhouse project, although housed in the basement of the V & A, is entirely independent. The five-year lease expires in 1986, and a series of temporary exhibitions have done nothing to augment the Museum's collections of contemporary industrial art.

At the outbreak of the Second World War in 1939, the Council for Art and Industry was replaced by the Central Institute of Art and Design under the Chairmanship of Charles

XIX
Pendant-brooch in enamelled gold and silver set with rubies and an emerald, designed by Henry Wilson and probably made in his Kent workshop around 1906.

XX
Ship pendant (the 'Craft of the Guild'). Enamelled gold set with opal and diamond sparks and hung with three tourmalines. Designed by C.R. Ashbee and made by the Guild of Handicraft about 1903.

XXI
Pendant in the form of a three-masted ship acquired by the Museum in 1893 as 16th-century Venetian, but now thought to be Greek Islands work of the 18th-century.

Tennyson with T.A. Fennemore as the Director. Among its activities, it organized two-week courses to refresh the minds of designers already working in industry. From 1942 the Institute published a monthly bulletin, *Art and Design*, and maintained a national register of industrial designers, but it was a short-lived organization and was dissolved in 1948, largely because its work was superseded by the Council of Industrial Design, established in 1944. The V & A maintained close links with the Council and in 1952 Sir Leigh Ashton, then Director of the V & A, was a member of the Board of Governors.

Apart from co-operating with other bodies in the inter-war years the V & A often took the initiative in promoting good modern design, an initiative that was perhaps expressed more in temporary exhibitions than in acquistitions for the permanent collections, the latter function being fulfilled largely by the Circulation Department. In 1931 an important exhibition of posters was held in the North Court: it included a historical section as well as a selection of distinguished modern examples, both British and foreign. As Martin Hardie pointed out in his introduction to the catalogue, the Museum 'was concerned less with the economic aspect, the publicity value of the poster, than with its technical method and the artistic impulse whcih finds expression in the special means employed'. It aimed to show that there was more to poster art than the reproduction of a finished oil painting such as Millais's *Bubbles* to advertise Pears Soap – a type favoured by many – and such posters were contrasted with more abstract images. Martin Hardie singled out the work of Edward McKnight Kauffer whose posters for London Transport, and later for Shell, pioneered abstract designs (he was to have a one-man exhibition at the Museum in 1955 and again in 1973). Among the early British posters was Fred Walker's silhouette design for the *Woman in White*, staged as a play in 1871, posters by Aubrey Beardsley, the Beggarstaff Brothers and wartime posters by Frank Brangwyn. British railway and travel posters were claimed to give a 'lead to the whole world'. An important section of the exhibition consisted of 'a reconstruction of what might have been the aspect and variegated colour of a Paris hoarding of 1895' – the work of Cheret, Toulouse-Lautrec, Forain, Steinlen, Willette, Grasset, Mucha and the rest. It is a strange irony that these latter posters, now commanding thousands of pounds apiece, were then regarded as mere ephemera and were not officially registered as museum objects until the 1960s.

Another graphic exhibition was one of Modern Commercial Typography held in the V & A Library gallery during 1936 and early 1937, including the work of 'constructivists, surrealists, cubists, and just common or garden printers'. Reviewing the exhibition in the *Studio* (Vol. 21, 1936 p. 241–246) Robert Harling described it as 'one of the most stimulating we have had in London for a long time', but he regretted that it was too small – only one hundred examples. Even so he reckoned that 'Master Printers should be escorted over the exhibition to see what was being done first by a handful of printers in their own country; second, by rather more French, German, Swiss and American printers'. As the press handout stated, modern commercial typography reflected the developments that had taken place in the other arts, particularly architecture, during the past thirty years, and the graphic element both in style and technique had been directly influenced by abstract movements in painting, beginning with the emergence of Cubism in Paris about 1910. The influence of Russian Constructivism was evident in the typographical layout in combination with many innovations in the use of photography and photomontage. Avant-garde typography was found not only in the foreign examples but also in the work of the Baynard and Shenval presses, designed by Serge Chermayeff, Ceri Richards and others. The impact of such an exhibition was soon to bear fruit and provide a contrast to the careless typography of the jobbing printer and the studied preciousness of the private presses, still conservatively holding on to the Arts and Crafts tradition.

The Post-War Period

XIX. 'BRITAIN CAN MAKE IT'

The Victoria and Albert Museum involvement with modern design after the Second World War began with the *Britain Can Make It* exhibition held at the Museum from September to November 1946, and organized by the Council of Industrial Design. As Sir Stafford Cripps, President of the Board of Trade, stated the exhibition was seen as 'the citizen's opportunity to examine the profit and loss accounts of industrial design in the period 1939-46'. The exhibition was a great success and was praised by British and foreign critics alike. Walter Bernays, editor of the Anglo-Swiss-American Commercial Review, Basle, remarked '*Britain Can Make It* is definitely comparable to any of the best European and international shows I have ever seen, both in its purpose and direction and in its display and organisation'.

The Council of Industrial Design had been set up in December 1944, with aims that echoed those of Sir Henry Cole, almost a century before, and 'the mandate of improving by any means possible the design of British consumer goods'. The *Britain Can Make It* was the Council's first exhibition which aimed 'to show in concrete terms – that is by means of the goods themselves – that good design, whatever else it is, is a good business operation'.

The 'Principles of Design' of the Museum of Ornamental Art were echoed in what was regarded as perhaps the most important section of the exhibition from the point of view of educating the public on the fundamentals of design. The designer Misha Black, OBE, FSIA, was in charge of this section: he illustrated the theme in the terms of 'The Birth of an Egg Cup', presenting this as a typical problem facing a designer – fitness for purpose, materials, methods of manufacture etc – all very much on the lines of Richard Redgrave or Christopher Dresser, a real 'South Kensington' exercise. This was followed by a display of a section on 'Great British Designers', ranging from William Kent, Chippendale and Sheraton, to Gimson and Barnsley, Josiah Wedgwood, the Adam Brothers and Charles Rennie Mackintosh, with a typographical section including the work of Eric Gill. A small section was devoted to the 1851 Exhibition and the catalogue pointed out the 'the building in which the Britain Can Make It Exhibition is being held was provided from funds supplied from the profits of the 1851 Exhibition'. It paid tribute also to other organizations concerned with promoting good design – the Royal Society of Arts, the Art Workers Guild, the Design and Industries Association, the Society of Industrial Artists and the Central Institute of Art and Design.

The greater part of the exhibition covered the whole range of consumer goods, including dress, all items of household and garden furnishing and equipment, and articles of sport and leisure, some arranged in room settings. The aim was to show the best of British contemporary design, design that in many cases was to anticipate the styles that were to feature at the Festival of Britain South Bank Exhibition in 1951. Some designs, such as an incredible air-conditioned bed, were included in a section of 'Designs of the Future'. The exhibition attracted nearly one and a half million visitors, including 43,000 trade buyers from Britain, and over 7,000 from overseas. Lectures on the principal industries and different aspects of the exhibition, organized by the Design and Industries Association, were given daily at 3 pm and 7 pm in the lecture theatre, and there is little doubt that the exhibition did a great deal to sell good modern design to the British public. It also marked the beginning of close co-operation between the Museum and the Council of Industrial Design, and some of the items shown found their way into the permanent collections of the V & A. From 1957 onwards, the Circulation Department of the V & A acquired all the objects that received the Council of Industrial Design Annual Awards, as a basis for a collection of good British industrial design: items ranging from plastic tableware and furnishing textiles to room heaters and refrigerators, in fact a whole range of consumer goods. Where the Award was given to an object which was too large to be accommodated in the Museum's collections, such as a street standard lamp or a piece of heavy machinery, a model or photographs or drawings would be acquired as a substitute for the actual object. These objects, supplemented by direct purchases or gifts from manufacturers, have formed the basis of the Museum's post-Second World War British collections.

Throughout the 1950s, 1960s and 1970s, the Circulation Department continued to buy examples of good modern design, both British and foreign, initially for specific exhibitions, the objects then becoming part of the permanent collections.

XX. THE INFLUENCE OF TEMPORARY EXHIBITIONS: THE SCANDINAVIAN INFLUENCE AND THE VICTORIAN REVIVAL

The British Arts and Crafts Movement had a profound influence on Scandinavian design, and in turn, by 1930, Scandinavian design began to have a marked influence in Britain. Alvar Aalto's laminated plywood furniture began to be imported about 1929 inspiring native examples, and the pottery and the glass shown in the Swedish Exhibition in London in 1931 made an immediate impact with its clean, uncluttered lines and restrained decoration. The Circulation Department of the Museum acquired a representative collection of Swedish

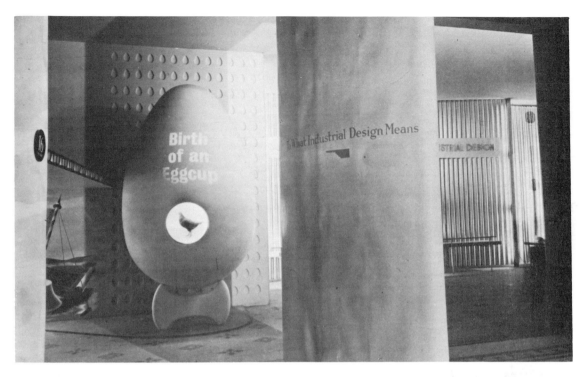

What industrial design means: the birth of an egg-cup. Didactic display by Misha Black, in the 'Britain Can Make It' exhibition held at the Museum in 1946. Photograph: The Design Council.

The birth of an egg-cup in the 'Britain Can Make It' exhibition at the Museum in 1946. Photograph: The Design Council

Cups and saucers from the Tuscan 'Caravelle' service designed by Richard Brockman for R.H. and S.L. Plant Ltd, 1958, showing the influence of Scandinavian design. Photograph: The Design Council.

The 'Finlandia' exhibition of modern Finnish design held at the Museum in 1961. The display was designed by Timo Sarpaneva.

Part of the 'Beardsley' collection produced by Poole Pottery Ltd in 1977. The Beardsley drawings were adapted by Ros Summerfelt, a young designer working at Poole. Photograph: Poole Pottery Ltd.

glass in the 1930s, and a number of tapestry rugs by the Swedish weaver Mårta Måås Fjetterström.

The Scandinavian influence on British design was even stronger after the Second World War; here the V & A played a considerable part through a series of temporary exhibitions, beginning with one of *Danish Art Treasures* in 1948, which included a small contemporary section. More significant was *Two Centuries of Danish Design*, held twenty years later, in 1968, which included furniture designed by Arne Jacobsen, Finn Juhl and Kaare Klint, silver by George Jensen, and simple elegant glass from the Kastrup and Holmegaard glassworks.

An exhibition of Finnish 18th- and 19th-century hand-woven rya rugs had been held at the Museum in 1930, but in a second show, held in 1958, the emphasis was on contemporary examples. As the Director Sir Trenchard Cox wrote in his introduction to the catalogue, 'Two years ago [1956] the Circulation Department . . . acquired an attractive Finnish rug. Our delight in this acquisition was matched by that of visitors to the Museum who began to make interested inquiries about it as soon as it was shown in a public gallery.' This interest was reinforced by the exhibition and the glowing, vibrant colours and abstract designs of the long-piled rugs made an immediate impact on British hand-weavers and also inspired commercially produced copies.

One of the most important Scandinavian exhibitions was *Finlandia*, a show of modern Finnish design in a setting by Timo Sarpaneva, held at the Museum from November 1961 to January 1962. Sir Trenchard Cox stated, in his introduction to the book produced for the occasion: 'The modern handicrafts and industrial arts of Finland . . . are among the most distinctive and original pieces of our age'. The items showed a remarkable unity of style, with a successful merging of the crafts and industrial design. The Finnish glass in particular, which exploited to the full the essential qualities of the material, influenced British manufacture: blown in wooden moulds to produce a textured surface, it was soon imitated by James Powell & Sons of Whitefriars, who also produced a bright, orange-coloured glass, first seen in Finland. The cylindrical shapes of much of the Finnish items were echoed in the simple elegant forms of the glass of Dartington and Caithness, which was entirely

'Kilta' table service designed by Kaj Franck for Wärtsila-Arabia, Finland. Included in a Circulation Department travelling exhibition in 1957 and in the 'Finlandia' exhibition in 1961. Photograph: The Design Council

'Grosvenor House' hotel tableware designed by R.D. Russell and Partners for R.H. and S.L. Plant Ltd. The design shows a Scandinavian influence and the hot water jugs and teapots have interchangeable lids and the same diameter making for easy stacking. Photograph: The Design Council.

contemporary in feeling and far removed from the traditional cut glass of most of the Midland glasshouses. Kaj Franck's classic 'Kilta' service and the 'Ruska' service by Ulla Procope, both produced by Arabia, were to bring a new simplicity and sturdiness to British tableware, seen in the work both of old established firms, such as Wedgwood and Denby, and of newer firms such as the Hornsea Pottery, and Govancroft in Scotland. Similarly the cast-iron casseroles of Rosenlew & Company, designed by Timo Sarpaneva, no doubt inspired Robin Welch to produce his own range of cast-iron ware in 1965. Later the Scandinavian influence was also felt in two-dimensional design. Two exhibitions of Scandinavian textiles and wallpapers were organized by the Circulation Department and held in the Museum in 1956; they reinforced the trend for well drawn floral designs, influenced by Danish examples, and geometric patterns with clear bright colours, inspired by textiles and wallpapers from Sweden. Although throughout the 1950s and 1960s Scandinavian design could be found in a number of the leading stores (particularly Heals, Woollands, and Liberty's) and in smaller, more specialist shops, the Museum's exhibitions gave an enhanced status to the productions and set the seal of approval on the Scandinavian influence.

While the Scandinavian exhibitions looked to the design of the future, the exhibition of Victorian decorative arts, held in the Museum in 1952, brought more than a touch of nostalgia to British design. The first half of the 20th century had, perhaps quite naturally, rejected Victorian design, for there is nothing so unfashionable as the styles of one's immediate forbears, although, with a faster pace of living, the second half of the century has already seen revivals of the 1940s and 1950s styles and fashions. Papier-mâché, Staffordshire figures and china dogs, wax and shell flower groups and other decorative items appealed to certain tastes and could be found in smart antique shops, or obtained through interior decorators, but the furnishings of the Victorian period were not to be taken seriously. The exhibition of *Victorian and Edwardian Decorative Arts* was the result of many months of research into the period by Peter Floud and his staff in the

Circulation Department: rescuing objects, and their designers, from obscurity, applying the same scholarly approach that had hitherto been reserved for earlier periods of the decorative arts. A new collecting trend began, not only for 'Victoriana', but also for the work of designers such as Christopher Dresser, Bruce Talbert, C.F.A. Voysey, C.R. Mackintosh and a host of others, attracting serious collectors such as Charles and Lavinia Handley Read who were to state that it was the exhibition that fired their enthusiasm. Hitherto unsaleable items began to fetch huge prices in the salerooms and antique shops.

Firms such as Coles of Mortimer Street began resurrecting their old wallpaper patterns and reprinting them, and the flat diaper patterns of Owen Jones became fashionable particularly for halls and dining rooms. Sanderson's began reissuing the Morris wallpapers, and also using the designs for fabrics which have remained best sellers into the 1980s. 'Victorian' became the 'in' style for restaurants and public houses, many of which had had their original Victorian or Edwardian interiors stripped, to be once again fitted with engraved glass, flock wallpapers, plush upholstery and oil lamps connected to electricity.

This interest in the decorative arts of the Victorian period was reinforced by the opening of the Victorian Primary Galleries in October 1964. Even the *Sun*, that organ of the popular press, was then aware of the changed public attitude: 'Have you noticed that we are having less of that denunciation "Victorian Monstrosity" these days? You may have acted ascetic-as-ever-was five years ago, walking on Finnish carpets and sprawling in Danish chairs, but you are likely to be hanging around the bric-a-brac shops this autumn. We have all been nobbled.'

The *Sun* felt that the new buying generation liked Victorian things because they could not remember the fusty Victoriana of their parents' or grandparents' childhood homes, and were tired of plain Scandinavian styles. Sidney Foot, then Education Officer at the Design centre, was quoted as thinking it was the result of a reaction against post-war austerity, while 'John Betjeman and his Victorian Society (founded in 1958) are eagerly awaiting for signs that the craftsmanship and fantasy common among Victorian artists are catching on among our young industrial designers'.

The proto-Art Nouveau (so designated by Nikolaus Pevsner) designs of the early 1880s by Mackmurdo and his fellow artists in the Century Guild and the works of Charles Rennie Mackintosh and the Glasgow School, which were first brought to the public eye in the 1952 exhibition, showed that Art Nouveau was not purely a continental movement, but something that had its origins in the British late 19th-century revival of the decorative arts. A good deal of the credit for the initial post-war revival of Art Nouveau should perhaps be given to Bill Poole of Liberty's who, having seen a small Art Nouveau exhibition in Paris, and hearing that there was to be a larger one in New York in June 1960, raked through the Liberty archives for turn-of-the-century designs, and reproduced them as the 'Lotus' collection of dress fabrics. It is unlikely, however, that this would have come about if attention had not been drawn to the original fabrics by the *Victorian and Edwardian Decorative Arts* exhibition of 1952 and the *English Chintz* exhibition of 1956, both of which featured textiles by C.F.A. Voysey, Lindsay Butterfield, and Arthur Silver and Harry Napper of the Silver Studio, many of them produced by Liberty's in the 1890s – designs which were reprinted in the 1960 'Lotus' series.

Two other Museum exhibitions, *Art Nouveau and Alphonse Mucha* in 1963 and *Aubrey Beardsley* in 1966, set the seal on the Art Nouveau revival and were largely responsible for its popularization. Posters, graphics and advertisement, wallpapers, textiles and jewellery, both reproductions of the originals and pastiches, proliferated in the Art Nouveau style, while the original articles became highly sought after – and expensive – collector's items.

XXI. THE CRAFTS REVIVAL

Since the Second World War the Victoria and Albert Museum has forged ever closer links with the crafts by means of special exhibitions, seminars and demonstrations by craftsmen in the Museum, as well as the acquisition of objects by contemporary craftsmen, the establishment of the crafts shop in August 1974, and a continuing and expanding link with the Crafts Council.

J. Noel White (the European Vice-president of the World Crafts Council) pointed out in a letter to the *Daily Telegraph* on 17 November 1983 that 'in circumstances of social and economic interest the work of the artist craftsman has moved into the mainstream of British cultural life', and that, against the background of a technological revolution, the confusion between crafts and industrial design began to wane.

The Crafts Centre of Great Britain was set up under John Farleigh just after the War and the crafts gradually began to gain ground; in 1973 the Crafts Advisory Committee was founded, later becoming the Crafts Council.

The inauguration of the Crafts Advisory Committee was celebrated by a major exhibition, *The Craftsman's Art*, at the V & A, an exhibition which surveyed the work of the British artist craftsmen and women of the 1970s, and showed a craft tradition enriched by new ideas and new techniques. The exhibition did much to prove that the crafts were not necessarily backward looking and an alternative to industrial production, but a supplementary independent stream which, with new, imaginative designs and techniques, could bring a healthy influence on industry. The introduction to the catalogue pointed out that 'the V & A has brought considerable influence to bear on the enhancement of the artist craftsman in recent years in inaugurating a series of exhibitions of the work of individual artist craftsmen'. As Hugh Wakefield wrote in his introduction to the catalogue of the Collingwood/Coper exhibition in 1969, 'It has long been clear that artist craftsmen in Britain are suffering from both the indifference of commercial galleries to their relatively low priced wares and from the absence of exhibition facilities in larger museums'. This exhibition, devoted to the wall-hangings and rugs of Peter Collingwood and the studio pottery of Hans Coper, was an attempt to redress this deficiency, and was followed by an

Stoneware vase by Hans Coper, 1958 from the Collingwood/Coper Exhibition in January, 1969.

equally successful exhibition in 1971 of jewellery by Gerda Flöckinger and glass by Sam Herman, one of the first exhibitions in this country to draw attention to the growth of the studio glass movement that had begun in the United States.

An important boost to the crafts was given by two exhibitions, organized by Madeleine Maidstone, Keeper of the Education Department, in association with the Crafts Advisory Council. The first, entitled *The Makers*, held from 19 December 1975 to 3 January 1976, involved thirteen craftsmen working in museum galleries appropriate to their individual crafts: embroidery, silversmithing, jewellery and gem-cutting, calligraphy and illumination, wood-engraving, book-binding, ceramics, tapestry-weaving, and lacemaking. The public were thus able to see the work of the contemporary craftsmen in the context of historic specimens, to understand the techniques involved, and discuss them with the craftsmen and women themselves. A souvenir booklet with poems by Edward Lucie-Smith was produced in a limited edition, together with a more popular mass-produced version. Such was the success of the demonstrations that the idea was repeated the following year when thirteen craftsmen demonstrated their crafts, again in the appropriate galleries, from 1 December 1976 to 30 January 1977, under the title *Man Made*.

The Circulation Department also mounted many craft exhibitions, shown first at the Museum, and then sent on tour. One major show, *International Ceramics*, was held in Room 45, the main exhibition room, in 1972. The show, organized in association with the Geneva based International Academy of Ceramics, was drawn from 39 countries, including those of Eastern Europe, and brought the work of many distinguished overseas potters, much of it of an experimental nature far removed from the English studio pottery tradition, to the notice of public and potters alike. Some 25 of the most important pieces in the exhibition were acquired for the Museum's permanent collections and assembled into a travelling exhibition.

The work of the distinguished Belgian potter, Pierre Culot, was exhibited in June and July 1974, and a travelling exhibition of six British studio potters, accompanied by tape recordings of the artists explaining their work, was organized in 1976. A major retrospective exhibition of the work of Bernard Leach was arranged by Carol Hogben of the Circulation

Department to celebrate Leach's 90th birthday in 1977, an exhibition which was attended by 35,000 people. Later, in 1982, the work of one of the most celebrated living potters, Lucie Rie, was shown in a major retrospective exhibition, which included her most recent work. Such shows have proved an inspiration to younger potters, and helped to establish studio pottery as a major art form and an area of international collecting, a fact that is supported by the high prices that studio pottery now commands at public auction. They influenced professionals and amateurs alike, and the amateurs were given their share of exhibition space. The Arts and Crafts Exhibition Society held its 1950 and 1957 shows in the Museum, including work by professionals and also by those who treat the crafts as a hobby and as a rewarding antidote to the lack of job satisfaction in their day-to-day life. The same was true of the Women's Institute Exhibition of Handicrafts in 1952 and 1960, and the Townswomen's Guild National Arts and Crafts Exhibition in 1964, all held at the Museum.

Exhibitions such as that of *Modern American Wallhangings* in 1962 gave the practising craftsmen and the public the opportunity of seeing new concepts of weaving, unhampered by the limitations imposed by representational designs. The artists showed a new approach to the use of textile decoration, extemporising with combinations of colour, textures and new materials which showed that they were truly creative in the same sense as sculptors and painters. These events, together with exhibitions of the work of the avant-garde Polish weavers at Whitechapel and elsewhere, gave a new impetus to British hand-weaving.

The Museum also played an important part in a campaign to revitalize the craft of the artist-blacksmith in this country. The Museum possesses an unrivalled collection of wrought iron-work, but with the industrial revolution, in the Victorian period, wrought iron-work was largely replaced by cast iron which in the hands of designers such as Christopher Dresser produced original and striking pieces. There was somewhat of a revival of wrought iron in the 20th century but the design was deliberately traditional and derivative. The Rural

Two glass vases by Sam Herman from the Flöckinger/Herman exhibition in 1971. Photographs: James Mortimer.

A tapestry weaving demonstration by Eva Louise Svensson at 'The Makers' exhibition at the Museum from 29 December 1975 to 3 January 1976.

Industries Bureau and more recently the Crafts Council, have striven to rehabilitate the craft of the artist-blacksmith and free it from the popular image of 'old-world' scroll work and suburban garden gates. With this aim in view, in 1982 the Metalwork Department of the Museum mounted an important Loan Exhibition of contemporary ironwork, *Towards a New Iron Age*, drawn from collections and individual artists from Europe, Japan and the USA. Each Sunday afternoon during the course of the exhibition, craftsmen demonstrated the techniques of forging by hand and with the power hammer in the garden court of the Museum. The wide variety of objects ranged from fire-grates, screens, weather-vanes and candle-sticks to necklaces – no doubt inspired by the Berlin ironwork jewellery of the early 19th century. One of the organizers of the exhibition was Richard Quinnell, who runs a large firm of architectural metalworkers and blacksmiths at Rowhurst Forge, near Leatherhead in Surrey, with an adjacent gallery exhibiting work of designer-blacksmiths from all over the country. His work was illustrated in an article in the *Daily Telegraph* of 30 August 1983, entitled 'The Dawning of a Bright New Iron Age'. The writer pointed out that, following the V & A exhibition, architects have been quick to recognize the powerful strength of work by the new generation of designer blacksmiths, and instanced James Horrobin's gates for the Ironwork Gallery at the Museum as demonstrating that metalwork can be vastly more interesting than a collection of traditional scrolls.

XXII Stoneware jug with 'tenmoku' glaze made by Mick Casson in 1974.

XXIII
*Detail of
hand-knitted
waistcoat by
Kaffe Fassett,
1982.
Photograph:
Kaffe Fassett*

XXIV
*Two millefiori
Roman glass
bowls acquired
by the Museum
in 1868; they
provided the
inspiration for
hand-knitted
garments by
Kaffe Fassett.*

XXII. COMMERCE AND INDUSTRY AS PATRONS OF THE ARTS

As we have seen, in the earliest days of the Museum its first director, Sir Henry Cole, maintained close contacts with industry and with the leading figures in the trade and commerce of his day. In 1976 Sir Roy Strong launched a charitable body, the Associates of the V & A, in a new venture to strengthen the links between the Museum and business and industry. The main aim was to encourage annual subscriptions from major commercial concerns and thus build up a corpus of benefactors who would sponsor specific items connected with the whole range of the Museum's activities. These included temporary exhibitions, display of the permanent collections, lectures, concerts, scholarships and help with publishing. Among the first activities are the guides to several galleries sponsored by Mobil, the Heinz Travelling Fellowship enabling curatorial staff to study in the United States, and the Drapers Company Scholarship for research into textile conservation. More recently, a major exhibition in 1984, *Rococo: Art and Design in Hogarth's England*, was sponsored by Trust House Forte.

By this enterprise it was hoped that not only would the Museum benefit financially but in turn industry would be more aware of the value of the Museum's collections as a source of design. One specific instance of this was a range of bed linen, produced by Marks & Spencers (one of the first firms to become an Associate) and based on 18th-century printed textiles in the Museum's collections.

Whereas in the 1970s the emphasis was on the craft tradition, in the 1980s more attention is being given to industrial design, particularly that of our own time, reflecting the technological age in which we live, and to some extent echoing the alliance of art and science in the early days of the Museum. As Carol Hogben rightly pointed out in his introduction to *British Art and Design 1900–1960* (Victoria and Albert Museum, 1983), 'the function of conveying the very latest consumer technology goes on in Earls Court, Olympia, Birmingham, or, come to that, Harrods. But only museums can set present-day creations in an unbroken line of comparisons with the past, or lay out what our people admire most against the best of the world ... For a tradition is not a sum of everything we were used to having in our own homes ... It is a sum of those things which as a people we admire in public places; take pleasure in; seem to express some feelings we have had ourselves on what could make the world a better place in time to come.'

That is the true message of the Museum; it is not merely a repository of the past but a pointer to the future, and an inspiration for generations still to come.

*Dining table and chairs in English oak with leather
upholstery. Designed by John Makepeace and made in his
workshops at Parnham House, Beominster, Dorset, by Derek
Christison, 1983.*
Photograph: John Makepeace.

*Jug in silver and black enamel, with a carved ivory handle,
made by Gerald Benney, commissioned by the Museum in
1979.*
Photograph: Professor Gerald Benney.

XXIII. POSTSCRIPT: 'WHAT THE V & A HAS MEANT TO ME'. SOME LEADING DESIGNERS AND CRAFTSMEN GIVE THEIR VIEWS

The influence of the Museum collections on designers and craftsmen is probably as strong today as at any period during the Museum's existence. In this section a number of distinguished contemporary designers and craftsmen pay tribute to the impact of the Museum's collections on their work. It must be emphasized that the selection is fairly arbitrary and necessarily influenced by the personal contacts of the author, although the designers represent a number of different crafts.

JOHN MAKEPEACE, FSIAD FRSA; *Furniture designer and manufacturer*

The influence of the Victoria and Albert Museum's collections upon my work is a fascinating question.

Foremost in my mind are those many occasions when, almost unexpectedly, I have discovered some deep affinity with a particular object, a feeling so strong that one has sensed a discovery of the greatest personal significance. This has not been limited to the objects in a single collection, or to a particular period of my life. Most commonly it has occurred when an object has achieved the kind of integrity for which I have been looking, and, by its existence, challenges me to renew the search.

For example, at an early stage, the directness and clarity of 'joined' furniture, particularly the hutch; the drama of Pugin's architectural forms wrestled with the excitement of Godwin's sideboard. The fluid forms of *papier mâché* spoke to me more convincingly than their injection moulded successors. The Chinese tables have never ceased to thrill me with their noble proportions, colour and delightful details.

A visit to the Museum is a stimulating but exhausting experience. I have had to learn to get more from less – to reserve my responses for one or two items on each occasion. The stimulus comes for me not so much from an academic or a technical knowledge of the objects, but from the feelings they convey, the rich vocabulary they reinforce and the scope they engender for the future.

PROFESSOR GERALD BENNEY, RDI FRCA; *Goldsmith and silversmith*

The overwhelming quality of all the pieces on show at the V & A has drawn me time and time again to regard it as a sort of reference library of uses for materials . . . ivory, glass, enamel, gold, silk, wood etc.

I remember attending drawing sessions there during my days as a student at the Royal College of Art and really got hooked at that time. I also remember one term when I left my research into cutlery so late that there was only one afternoon left to do the whole thesis and all the drawings! That afternoon was such a revelation, though, that I can still feel the incredulity that was my reaction when I first looked at such pieces.

Please don't think I am overdoing this! I have my original drawings from that day hanging in my study at home right now.

DAVID PEACE, MBE FSA; *Glass engraver*

Even the building itself, so familiar yet seldom examined, is an influence on this designer: here is the work of a highly inventive mind, a work of cheerful authority, rooted in history. The Museum and the things it enshrines are saying, 'Come in and observe, see what history has to say, and then go away and be a creative designer'; a new aspect of the old motto 'Love God and do what you like'.

In my own fields of lettering, heraldry and three-dimensional design in engraved glass, the V & A has for years been a source of inspiration – a source which does not dry up. One goes there to breathe ('inspirare' is to breathe), to be inspired by the great 'animateur', to see what the finest standards were assumed to be in the past, and to emulate them – not to copy the objects at all – in one's own sphere of action.

Where else in the field of lettering, within a few paces, could I study for example the Trajan column inscription in Roman capitals (with all it teaches about form and spacing), 11th-century Runic treated in an architectural way, a flamboyant Norwegian doorway in stone-like interweaving calligraphy and low relief lettering on a medieval tomb? To see things in the round and subject to light and shade, teaches so much better than photographs.

Again, within a few paces, and indeed throughout the V & A, I can study the early heraldry and learn with what freedom – yet perfect control and response to materials – one should be able to design today.

Obviously the large study collection of glass is a regular source of education; but it is not there that the most important influence is brought to bear. And this is for a reason seldom recognized – that the most penetrating lessons are learned, not by direct teaching, but by the law of *indirectness*. In this method of teaching by indirect example, the V & A is supreme.

For me, the greatest influence of these miles of galleries consists in the opportunity to absorb from media other than my own. At any moment some unexpected work of art appears, irrelevant yet surprisingly relevant by analogy; a design problem has been recognized and solved. The designer *knew* he had got it right. And I am challenged to move from abstract theorizing to a clearer state of knowing, having received again and again a little more training of the eye.

Sanctuary lamp of clear glass engraved by David Peace in 1962.

MICK CASSON; *Studio potter*

I have certainly been influenced by pots and other artefacts shown in V & A collections, but by the very nature of 'influence' rather than 'copy' the relevance is often far from obvious. The early Greek pots shown in the V & A and in particular bronze age clay vessels from Cyprus of about 1000 BC have influenced my work. For example, forms and colours have been adapted from these pots, even though techniques of manufacture and particularly firing have changed radically. Although the V & A collection showed pots which were low fired earthenware and I fire to 1300° C and over, it was their freedom and vigour of design that inspired me.

JACK LENOR LARSEN; *American weaver, designer and writer on textiles, founder of Jack Lenor Larsen Inc.*

The Victoria and Albert Museum is perhaps most important in that it exists and probably will for a long time. This fact in itself proves the continuing importance of decorative art.

It is of course a remarkable depository and provides so much inspiration to all designers. I particularly enjoyed using its facilities to research our Crystal Palace collection (1979). It seems extraordinary that we can find not only wallpaper of that period but the actual examples that were shown in that Great Exhibition.

BERNARD NEVILL; *Freelance textile designer and Professor at the Royal College of Art*

The V & A represents an important educational and cultural landmark in my life from the days when I was a student at St Martin's and later at the Royal College of Art; I always remember the slightly 'holy' cathedral hush and smell, and feeling the blanket of cosy warmth which descended on me as I entered and passed through the various galleries, laden with my portfolio en route to the marvellous library. I would unpack my drawing-board and case containing designer's colours, poster colours, inks, brushes, pastels, a baking tin for a palette and a jam jar for the water (all carefully spread out on a large sheet of *The Times* so as to protect the black leather desk tops), irritating some of the regular scholars, but interesting others who would find any excuse to look over my shoulder and see what I was drawing. I recollect the thrill of researching in the catalogues and wading through dozens of volumes one had ordered to find one gem of an illustration or drawing. Being able to research among the old archives in the Circulation Department was also a constant source of inspiration. I spent many blissful years occupied thus; it was a sad moment when I realized, in wandering round the galleries, that a lifetime was never going to be long enough to draw and study all the beautiful and fascinating objects one's eyes longingly embraced.

Later, when I was teaching theatre design and book illustration at the Central School of Art, fashion design and drawing, and history of costume at St Martin's and textile design and fashion at the RCA, I led my students not only to the V & A Library teaching them how to research but also behind the scenes of the Textile and Costume Departments to draw from the marvellous collections there. Among the students I introduced to and who came under the spell of the V & A were Ossie Clark, Bill Gibb, Tuffin and Foale and many others who formed the nucleus of the great English design talent of the '60s.

ANN LYNCH; *Chief designer for G.P. & J. Baker Ltd.*

One of the great pleasures for a textile designer visiting the Victoria and Albert Museum is the surprise in discovering an idea for a design in a gallery where one would least expect it. 'Chinese Waterlily' and 'Chao' originated from the interior of a colossal Chinese vase of the Ch'ien Lung Dynasty 1739-95. I came upon this vase while taking a short cut with some friends to the main entrance of the Museum.

From the outside it is just an ordinary Chinese vase whereas inside it is quite magnificent with a giant carp circling the base, lotus flowers, leaves, smaller fish and weeds trailing up the sides, and around the rim various geometric designs.

The lotus flowers and leaves I developed into a furnishing design for upholstery using one of the geometric designs as a background to it. This geometric, which incidentally was not at all geometric in a mathematical sense, I then used on its own as fabric, wallpaper and a carpet, and it has proved a great success for the company I design for.

Designers in England are extremely fortunate in having the Victoria and Albert Museum at their disposal for reference in many subjects whether on display or in the cellars. The staff are always so willing to help one or find another reference which is similar, regardless of the amount of cross referencing they may have to do to obtain it.

KAFFE FASSETT; *Painter and knitter*

Kaffe Fassett, who was born in California and trained as a painter, taught himself to knit after a visit to Scotland in 1964, where he was amazed and inspired by the range and subtlety of the available yarns. He works his designs out on the needles and tends to let the colours and patterns grow with the work. His garments heralded the revival of knitting as a creative art, initially by individual artist craftsmen, a movement that has now spread to amateur knitters. Later Kaffe Fassett became interested in needlework 'tapestry' and since about 1975 has produced a range of designs for chair seats and cushions, published by Ehrman; many of them are inspired by objects in the V & A, including the 'Carpet Garden', produced as a kit in 1983, and based on an Indian Mughal carpet of about 1640 (I.M. 188-1929). When a study day was held at the Museum in October 1982 entitled 'Colour in

'Chinese water-lily' screen-printed cotton furnishing fabric designed by Ann Lynch for G.P. and J. Baker, c. 1976.
Photograph: John R. Freeman & Co.

A Chinese bowl of the Ch'ien Lung Dynasty (1739–95) in the Museum which provided the inspiration for Ann Lynch's 'Chinese Water-Lily'. The design of the rim was used for the background and for a co-ordinating diaper pattern called 'Chao'.
Photograph: John R. Freeman & Co.

Knitting – Knitting in Colour', Kaffe Fassett talked about his work, his research and the continuing inspiration of the V & A collections, particulary of the colour and texture of objects. A guide prepared by him enabled those attending the study day to see for themselves the objects which he found inspiring, many of which he had shown during the course of his talk together with the garments that related to them. A fluent and engaging speaker, Kaffe Fassett felt unable to produce a written statement but authorised me to enumerate some of the many objects which had fired his imagination, objects which were incredibly wide ranging and in some cases surprising, being far removed from the textile arts. Among them were fragments and bowls of Roman *millefiori* glass, together with glass paperweights 'filled with wonderful little patterns, in iridescent colours, reflected in hand-knitted cardigans and waistcoats'. The colours and dot patterns of Chinese 18th- and 19th-century snuff bottles were another source; the 'high' pastels of a pair of *Famille rose* candlesticks and Canton enamels; the shells on Worcester porcelain or the iridescent splashes on Loetz 'Papillon' glass, together with the more likely sources of Chinese and Japanese robes, Norwegian tapestries, Spanish and Persian carpets – never copying but using each object as a starting point for colour or design.

Notes

1   It is also not possible here to go into the detailed history of the Schools of Design and the National Art Training Schools with all the ups and downs and criticism that attended their development. The story is set out in full in the *History and Philosophy of Art Education* by Stuart MacDonald (University of London Press, 1970) and in *The Schools of Design* by Quentin Bell (Routledge & Kegan Paul, London 1963)

2   *Fifty Years of Public Work of Sir Henry Cole, KCB*, London 1884, and Elizabeth Bonython *King Cole*, Victoria and Albert Museum, London 1982

3   Pseudonym of John Leighton, 1822–1912; published by D. Bogue, 86 Fleet Street, London, about 1850

4   *Art Journal*, 1852, p. 227. School of Ornamental Art, Department of Practical Art, Marlborough House

5   For details see Anna Somers - Cocks *The Victoria and Albert Museum. The making of the collection*, Windward, London 1980

6   Quoted in the *Modern Language Review*, XLVIII, 1953, 'Charles Dickens and the Department of Practical Art'

7   Owen Jones, *Grammar of Ornament*, 1856

8   Macmillan's Magazine, April 1870 p. 551–556

9   1858 p. 20

10 *Fine Art. A Sketch of its History, Theory, Practice and Application to Industry*, London and New York, 1870

11 The piecemeal construction of the Museum building during the 1860s and 1870s is described in detail in John Physick's admirable account of *The Victoria and Albert Museum. The History of the Building*. London 1982

12 W.R. Lethaby, *Philip Webb and his Work*, Oxford University Press, 1935

13 *Thomas Armstrong C.B. A memoir 1832–1911*, London 1912

14 *The Treasury of Ornamental Art. Illustrations of objects of Art and Vertu Photographed from the originals and drawn on stone*, F. Bedford, London 1857.

15 *The Industrial Arts. Historical sketches with numerous illustrations*. SKM Art Handbook. Chapman & Hall, London 1876 (new edition 1885)

16 Michael Darby, *The Islamic Perspective*, London, 1983, p.118

17 See John Physick, *Photography & the South Kensington Museum*, London 1975

18 A detailed account of the growth of the collection is given in Malcolm Baker's leaflet on the *Cast Courts* published in 1982

19 'The Department of Science and Art: what it has done, is doing, and may do', *Art Journal*, August 1860, p. 225–88

20 'On National Art Collections, Provincial Art Museums'. *The Nineteenth Century*, June 1880

21 'Trajan Revived' in *Alphabet*. Vol. 1, 1964 p. 17 et seq.

22 Eric Gill, *Essay on Typography*, 2nd ed. 1936

23 See Susan Beattie, *The New Sculpture*, the Paul Mellon Centre for Studies in British Art, Yale University Press, New Haven and London 1983

24 See Judith Collins, 'Eric Gill's Stations of the Cross in Westminster Cathedral', in *The Journal of the Decorative Art Society*, November 1982

25 Sir Sidney Colvin (1845-1927), critic of art and literature, Slade Professor of Fine Art, Cambridge 1873-85; Director, Fitzwilliam Museum 1876-83; Keeper of Prints and Drawings, British Museum 1883-1912, knighted 1912

26 See *The Magazine of Art*, Vol. I, 1878

27 H. Schwabe: *Die Forderung der Kunst - Industrie in England und der Stand dieser Frage in Deutschland*, Berlin 1866

28 For the development of the Hamburg Museum from 1900 see Heinz Spielmann: *The Jugendstil Collection at the Museum für Kunst und Gewerbe, Hamburg*, in the journal of the Decorative Arts Society 1890-1940, November 6th, p. 37 et seq.

29 See Gottfried Semper; *Der Stil in den Technischen und Tektonischen Kunsten oder Praktische Esthetik*, Munich 1860-63

30 *An Artist's Reminiscences*, Methuen, London 1907, p. 1467

31 From the volume published by the Zagreb Museum to celebrate the 90th anniversary in 1970

32 *Travels in South Kensington*, London 1882

33 *Report on the works of pupils in the French Schools of Design recently exhibited in the Palais de l'Industrie, with a comparison of the French and English Systems of Art Education* By Walter Smith; London, Simpkin Marshall & Co.

34 Published by Lockward, Brooks & Co., Boston 1877 for the Pennsylvania Museum and School of Industrial Art

35 The teaching included designing for paper-hangings, calico prints, iron work, woven textiles, carpets, wood engraving and

lithography. Later china decorating was added.

36 p. 165

37 *Travels in South Kensington*, p. 25

38 Vol. LlI, no. 321, new series December 1892, p. 813-14

39 Walter Crane, *An Artist's Reminiscences*, London 1907

40 Vol. XXIl, 1897-8

41 William de Belleroche, *Brangwyn Talks*, London 1944

42 *Potters, Their Arts and Crafts*, London 1897

43 See Barbara Morris, *William Morris and the South Kensington Museum* in *Victorian Poetry*, West Virginia University, Vol.13 number 3 & 4 Fall - Winter 1975

44 *Philip Webb and his Work*, OUP 1935, pp. 39-40

45 Fifth Day, Friday 17 March 1882, p. 155

46 ibid p.150

47 See Peter Floud, 'Dating Morris Patterns' in *Architectural Review*, July 1959

48 See Linda Parry, *William Morris Textiles*, London 1983

49 Morris & Co. circular issued in May 1880

50 W.R. Lethaby, *Philip Webb and his Work* (revised edition with introduction by Godfrey Rubens), London 1979

51 op. cit.

52 Mary Lago, *Burne-Jones talking*, London 1982

53 Published in London 1854

54 *Gazette des Beaux Arts*, Vol. 13, 1862, p. 224

55 Quoted by Moncure Conway in *Travels in South Kensington*, 1882

56 In the 1870s and 1880s both Christopher Dresser and Bruce Talbert produced many designs for Wards of Halifax who also wove some fabrics for Morris & Company.

57 *A London Design Studio 1880 - 1963. The Silver Studio Collection.*

58 For a more detailed account see Barbara Morris, *Victorian Embroidery*, Herbert Jenkins, London 1962

59 This decoration no longer exists

60 A catalogue of the Persian collection by Major Murdoch Smith was published by Chapman and Hall as one of the *South Kensington Art Handbooks* in 1876

61 Page 2; illustrated in an article on *The Leek School of Embroidery and its Work* by Walter Shaw Sparrow in the *Magazine of Art*, Vol. XXVI, 1901-02, pp. 550-54

62 *An Introduction to Practical Embroidery: A New Approach to Embroidery Design.* Commissioned by the Circulation Department of the Victoria and Albert Museum and designed and carried out by Iris M Hills, ARCA; HMSO, London 1953

63 In a lecture given in 1853 on the occasion of the Gore House Exhibition of Furniture

64 W.G. Yapp, *Specimens of Art Industry, Furniture and Metalwork*, London 1877 (2 vols)

65 See Clive Wainwright, 'The Dark Ages of art revived' in *Connoisseur* Vol. 198, June 1978, p. 95 et seq.

66 Vol. XXV, 1900-1901, p. 446-71

67 'The School of Art Woodcarving, South Kensington', *Studio*, Vol. 1, 1893, p.56-60

68 *The Art of Wodcarving*, in the *Studio*, Vol. XII, 1897

69 See Mary Comino, *Gimson and the Barnsleys*, Evans Brothers, London 1980

70 Sir Gordon Russell, *Designer's Trade*, Allen and Unwin, London 1968

71 For illustration see Victoria Cecil, *Minton Majolica*, Jeremy Cooper Ltd, London 1982

72 'Improvements in Minor British Industries, Minton's Art-Pottery Studio, South Kensington', *Art Journal*, 1892, p. 100-102

73 Malcolm Haslam, *The Martin Brothers, Potters*, Richard Dennis, London 1878

74 *Reminiscences of the Martin Brothers of London and Southall, Middlesex*, by Ernest Marsh, 'written from memory' October 1937. Revised in November 1939

75 See A.M.W. Stirling, *William De Morgan and his wife*, London 1922

76 For a detailed account see *The Birkenhead Della Robbia Pottery 1893 to 1906*, Jeremy Cooper Ltd, London 1980

77 Number 18 in the series *Potters Parade*

78 See Jennifer Hawkins, *The Poole Potteries*, London 1980

79 See *Vetri di Murano dell'800*, Alfieri, Venice 1978

80 In the same volume Burges remarked that 'The Kensington Museum has been formed with reference to the special object of instructing the workman and designer, and the consequence is there is no rubbish in it' and that 'it will always remain the "Mecca" of designers and sightseers'.

81 See Gabriella Gros-Gallinir, 'A French Connection', in *Connoisseur*, September 1979, p. 50-55

82 Louis de Fourcaud, *Emile Gallé*, Paris 1903

83 *A Catalogue of the Exhibition of Stained Glass, Mosaics, etc Designed and Executed by British Artists*, London,1864

84 See also Martin Harrison, *Victorian Stained Glass* in *Connoisseur* April, 1973, p. 251-54

85 Henry Holiday, *Reminiscences of my Life*, London 1914

86 One of the *Artistic Craft Series of Technical Handbooks* edited by W.R. Lethaby; John Hogg,

London 1903

87 The *Studio*, 1900, p.169

88 In the series of Methuen Little Books on Art, 1st edition, 1906

89 See Shirley Bury, *An Arts and Crafts experiment; the silver work of C.R. Ashbee*, V & A Bulletin Vol. III no. 1, 1967, pp. 18-25

90 *Proposal for the Establishment of a Technical and Art School for East London*, C.R. Ashbee, Toynbee Hall

91 4th edition, 1921

92 Reprinted in his *Studies in Art, Architecture and design: Victorian and After*, London 1968

93 Frank Pick had presented 43 London Underground posters to the V & A in 1911, the first of many acquisitions.

94 See Michael Farr, *Design in British Industry*, Cambridge 1955, p. 204-5

Index